Loonis!

Celebrating a Lyrical Life

Jerry Shinn *with* Loonis McGlohon

East Carolina University Foundation   Greenville, North Carolina

Sources:

The lyrics of "Nobody Home," "I Like It Here," "It's A Quiet Town," "Songbird," and "Good Old Friends," all written by Loonis McGlohon, and of "North Carolina Is My Home," by Charles Kuralt, are copyright © by Melody Trails, Inc.

Thinking in Jazz: The Infinite Art of Improvisation, by Paul F. Berliner, is published by The University of Chicago Press and copyright © 1994 by The University of Chicago.

Swing to Bop, by Ira Gitler, is published and copyright © 1985 by Oxford University Press, Inc.

Alec Wilder In Spite of Himself, by Desmond Stone, is published by Oxford University Press, Inc. and copyright © 1996 by Desmond Stone.

The song "While We're Young," by Mortimer Palitz, William Engvick, and Alec Wilder, is copyright © 1943 (renewed 1971) and 1944 (renewed 1972) by Ludlow Music, Inc.

Jazz, by John Fordham, is published by Dorling Kindersley, Inc., text copyright © 1993 by John Fordham.

Listen: Gerry Mulligan, by Jerome Klinkowitz, is published and copyright © 1991 by Schirmer Books, a division of Macmillan, Inc.

Lost Revolutions: The South in the 1950s, by Pete Daniel, is published by the University of North Carolina Press for the Smithsonian National Museum of American History, and copyright © 2000 by the Smithsonian Institution.

Material quoted from periodicals and newspapers is attributed in the text and is copyright © by the publishers of those periodicals and newspapers.

Except where noted otherwise, all photographs are courtesy of the McGlohon family.

Design and production by Julie Allred, BW&A Books, Inc.

Typeset in Monotype Bulmer

Printed in the United States of America by Worzalla

Library of Congress Control Number: 2004113194

ISBN 0-9758874-0-8 cloth

ISBN 0-9758874-1-6 paperback

5   4   3   2   1

For Anne

Contents

Introduction I, *by Jerry Shinn*, *ix*

Introduction II, *by Loonis McGlohon*, *xv*

Prelude: December 19, 2001, *xvii*

I : Pastorale

1 : Ayden, *3*

2 : Music, *15*

3 : On the Road, *25*

4 : Cousin Ralph's Punch, *31*

5 : Legends and Discoveries, *35*

6 : Nan, *43*

II : Making a Life

7 : The Wild Blue Yonder, *55*

8 : Bebop, *63*

9 : Charlotte, *69*

10 : Making the Scene, *77*

11 : WBT/WBTV, *83*

12 : Rock, *97*

13 : Home Base, *103*

14 : Good Deeds, *115*

III : Songs and Singers

15 : Alec, *123*

16 : McGlohon on Wilder, *143*

17 : Eileen, *155*

18 : McGlohon on Farrell, *161*

19 : Other Voices, *169*

20 : Songbirds, *175*

IV : A State of Grace

21 : Fruition, *197*

22 : North Carolina Is My Home, *207*

23 : Friends and Heroes, *215*

V : Elegy and Ode to Joy

24 : The Real Blues, *241*

25 : Bonus Tracks, *245*

26 : Obbligatos, *257*

27 : Coda: Sacred Music, *261*

Thanks, *263*

List of Patrons, *265*

Index, *267*

Introduction I

One day in January of 1996, I telephoned my friend Loonis McGlohon to ask how he was doing, and to ask if I could come to his house that evening and interview him. Loonis had been diagnosed with lymphoma two years earlier. He was weak and sick from chemotherapy. Despite the aggressive treatment, he knew his prognosis was not hopeful, and he was depressed. He told me he felt terrible. He wanted to know why I wanted to interview him, what I wanted him to talk about. I told him I wanted him to talk about his life, and about music, and to tell some of his funny stories. I said he needed to get all that on tape, and I wanted to help him. *Before I die,* he must have thought. Finally he said he didn't really feel up to it, but to come on.

After dinner I drove to the house Loonis and his wife, Nan, had built almost forty years earlier, a modest three-bedroom brick ranch on a narrow, shady, suburban street. As I walked down the gravel driveway and into the carport to the side door that everyone but strangers always used, it occurred to me that this was a house where no one ever had felt unwelcome. It was a place where visitors quickly felt at home, wherever their real homes might have been, whatever the circumstances of their lives.

Over the years the attractive but unimposing house had welcomed neighbors, friends from church, colleagues from the broadcasting industry, journalists writing about Loonis, local musicians, celebrities from the entertainment capitals of the world, and the McGlohon children's schoolmates. It had been a "bed and breakfast" for touring performers such as the venerable trumpeter Joe Wilder and the erstwhile Hollywood leading man and crooner Dick Haymes. It had been a sweet southern home away from home for the great opera and concert soprano turned pop singer Eileen Farrell, and for the eccentric, acerbic New Yorker and legendary composer Alec Wilder.

It was a cozy, comfortably furnished home, but there was more to it than that. It had a warmth that embraced anyone who entered. It was the warmth of a loving family and loving friends, of the unfailingly generous, hospitable, and good-humored people who had lived there—who, in the best sense of the term, had lived very well there—for so many years.

Nan McGlohon greeted me with a hug and her soft smile. She appeared tired, as I knew she must be. Loonis's normally ruddy redhead's complexion was a tallowy gray. He was a man who laughed a lot and who'd kept a heartfelt smile on his face for most of his seventy-four years, but that evening he could barely muster a weak grin. I felt guilty intruding on his misery, but I could tell Nan was very glad to have someone keep him company for a while. And I felt the need to get him on tape—to get, in his own words, the story of one of the most remarkable lives I had ever encountered, and stories told by one of the most talented raconteurs I had ever known. I wanted to get it all preserved while he was still able to talk to me— while he was still alive, which at the time I feared might be only a few more weeks or months. About that, thank God, I was wrong.

I had brought a small recorder and a fresh cassette, with a label already affixed and inscribed: *Loonis McGlohon 1/30/96.* We sat on a sofa in the small den, and I put the recorder between us and pushed the button. I asked him about his childhood, about the small, rural community where he grew up, about how he first encountered music. As he began to reminisce, he seemed to enjoy it. Nan would call me later to say she hoped I would do it again because it seemed to lift his spirits. I came back a couple of weeks later, and again, and again, continuing into April. Eventually I had about six hours of conversation on tape, and would have had more if Loonis hadn't started inquiring about my motives.

One evening in the early spring, after we had been talking for a while, he asked, "What are you going to do with all this?"

I said I didn't really know, but that maybe I'd write a book.

He said he didn't want me to write a book about him. He would help me write a book about his "heroes," he said, about some people he had known and admired. But he would not cooperate in any book about himself. I tried to persuade him to let me continue, but he was adamant. As I argued with him, he became edgy and maybe even a bit angry. I decided I would rather be his friend than his biographer, so I dropped the subject, and that was my last taped interview with him.

Months later, when he was feeling better, performing, recording, traveling, I occasionally encouraged him to start writing down his stories, and I told him I'd be glad to be his editor.

In the late summer of 2001, my wife, Anne, and I happened to be vacationing at Beech Mountain while the McGlohons were staying at their vacation home there.

We invited Loonis and Nan to come by for a drink and then go out to dinner. When they arrived in the late afternoon, Loonis was carrying a large manila envelope and asked if he could talk with me privately. We stepped into a bedroom and he handed me the envelope.

"You and my children have been telling me I should write down my stories, so I've finally done it," he said. "See what you think."

The envelope contained a little over one hundred pages of computer-printed manuscript—stories about famous people and not-so-famous people, funny stories, touching stories, all entertaining and readable, for Loonis was, as I said, a great raconteur, and a fine writer. A few days later, after I had read it all, I called him and said I thought what he had written was very good and that he ought to try to get it published. I suggested that it needed a little smoothing out and tightening up, which I would be glad to do, and that it would be even more interesting, and more likely to appeal to a publisher, if he would put the stories in the context of his own story. Plenty had already been written about some of these people, I told him. What made these stories so interesting was the unique perspective Loonis brought to them. So the reader would need to know about Loonis, too. No, he said, he didn't want to do a book about himself. He would have no part of that.

So I told him I would get the manuscript into my computer (as was his infuriating habit, he deleted it from his computer as soon as he had printed it). I would begin editing it, and we would talk more about it later. Surely, I thought, we could reach some compromise within which we could work together on a book about Loonis McGlohon and his friends—his story, and his stories, all humorous, touching, inspiring, extraordinary.

A few weeks later the cancer had returned with a vengeance. He was soon in bed at home, and the family called hospice to help care for him. He made one more significant trip out of town, and he went into a recording studio to play one more time.

The trip was to New York to receive an honor from the North Carolina Society of New York City. His physician, oncologist Jim Boyd, insisted that he go and went with him, to be standing by with the care and medication he might need to get through the event and make it back home.

The recording date was at the request of his old friend and fellow pianist Jim Stack, who had played vibraphone on many of Loonis's recordings and concert dates. Jim had booked a recording studio and invited Loonis to join him. Nan reminded Loonis that he wasn't even supposed to be up and around, but Loonis dragged himself out of bed and went to the studio. Even that late in the debilitating progress of the disease, he was buoyed and energized by the opportunity to play music.

After Loonis died early the next year, I asked for and got the approval of the McGlohon family to write the book Loonis always said he didn't want me to write. Forgive me, Loonis, for proceeding against your wishes. You were right about so many things, but you were wrong about this, and I think you probably know that now. Your family and close friends certainly don't need this book to remember you, but they would like to have it, and they deserve it. But you deserve to be remembered and honored beyond those inner circles of loved ones and colleagues. You deserve to be remembered for as long as people hum tunes, or fall in love to the accompaniment of a song, or find joy, comfort, romance, and inspiration in music.

Fame is fleeting, and more so every day in this age of instant celebrity, rapid obsolescence, and ever shorter attention spans. Ours is fast becoming a disposable culture. But you were part of something that has endured and will continue to endure, and this book will serve to remind people of that.

With every passing year it becomes clearer and more certain that what has become known as the American popular songbook, both on its own and as the predominant repertoire in the development of modern jazz, represents the most lasting and significant American musical achievement of the twentieth century. The innovators who created that music—Jerome Kern, George Gershwin, Irving Berlin, Richard Rodgers, Cole Porter, Harold Arlen, Hoagy Carmichael, and others—took the melodic and harmonic conventions of European classical and romantic music and distilled them into pure song. And the melodies were matched perfectly to the poetry of Ira Gershwin, Lorenz Hart, Oscar Hammerstein, Dorothy Fields, and Johnny Mercer, to name a few. Jazz musicians then infused and enriched that music with the spirit of indigenous African American blues. With due respect to contemporary American "serious" composers, those songs and the jazz interpretations they inspired constitute America's true "classical" music.

But in the second half of the century, a less urbane, less sophisticated branch of the evolution of the blues, known as rock and roll, became America's most popular and most economically significant musical genre, and America's most influential cultural export. With its raw energy, heavy visceral rhythms, and almost primitive simplicity, it came to dominate the radio and recording industries, crowding out the older forms of popular music as well as much of the potential for anything new and experimental.

Through all those changes, through all the dumbing down of the entertainment media and popular culture, you continued to cultivate, nurture, promote, and make your own contributions to the Great American Songbook. As your treasured friend and collaborator, Alec Wilder, said of himself, you were part of the "derrière-garde." It is an honorable designation. It represents fidelity to certain traditional values in an age when more and more of American popular culture is defined by the exploitation of the lowest common denominator of popular taste, and often by the blatant manipulation and titillation of our basest instincts and emotions.

Against this tide of trash you stood fast, asserting civility over boorishness, understated intelligence over aggressive ignorance, elegance over vulgarity, romance over lust. To the relatively small but significant group of people who share those values, you were an important ally and an authentic hero. You should also be a hero to those, now very young or yet unborn, who will carry on that tradition but will never have an opportunity to know you.

Loonis, if you still do not want me to write this book, I am sorry. For someone who loved to perform, who loved the spotlight, who loved applause, your modesty was ironic but very real. It was bred into you, and I think it was, paradoxically, essential to your sense of who you were. Yet you had a lot less than most people to be modest about, and you no longer have a vote about this book. It is not for you, but for everyone else.

I do, however, hope you like it.

Jerry Shinn
January 2003

Introduction II

Nan and our children have been on my case for several years now about setting down some experiences I have had in my long life. I have given this family request some thought. In eighty years one is pretty certain to meet some interesting people. It is those interesting people I have met and been privileged to know that I would like to talk about. Some of them are famous, some should be famous, and others you would not have heard about. All these folks have made a distinct impression on my life, and you might like to hear about a few of them.

After an eight-year battle with lymphoma, I have learned that relationships are the most important thing we have in life. Work can be rewarding, but it does not last long. After twenty-five or thirty years, most employers want you out of there. They give you a rhodium-plated watch (whatever happened to gold watches?), a strange gift when you consider you're running out of time. But relationships can last if you work at them. And there are great rewards. You may bond with some people in a short time—days, perhaps. Others may take longer. But it can be worth the trouble.

I am not a writer, but I do have a kind of photographic memory, so I can run the film through the projector and recall where we were, what we were doing, the world around us. I have trouble remembering dates. I can remember very well one day when Nan and I dozed in Kensington Gardens in London. It was spring, and the chestnuts were in full bloom. We were sitting beneath a huge, red-flowering chestnut. We could hear children playing near the bandstand, and occasionally the brakes squealing on one of the red double-deckers would rouse us for a count of three, at most four. I know the sky was one of those rare blue skies in London, and the sun was warm enough to make us sleepy. But I could not tell you what year that was, not even the month, much less the day.

So I may not be able to tell you the exact date when I first met Alec Wilder or Mitch Miller or Eileen Farrell or Stanly Hicks (you never heard of him?), but I do remember where we were, what we talked about, what we laughed about. In my memory book, that's good enough for me. If you get bored, just turn the pages faster.

Loonis McGlohon
March 2001

Prelude: December 19, 2001

Loonis McGlohon wasn't supposed to leave home that day, or maybe ever again. He was spending most of his time in bed, and nobody thought he was physically able to do much of anything else. The illness he had battled so bravely for almost eight years had finally won. The medicine he was taking was no longer for healing —just for pain. The doctor had said there was nothing else anyone could do but try to keep Loonis comfortable. As it turned out, he had only a few more weeks to live.

But on December 19, he got up, dressed, and, over his wife's objections, got into his car and drove to a recording studio called the Acoustic Barn.

A day or so earlier he had received a card from his old friend Jim Stack, a jazz pianist and vibraphone player who had often worked with Loonis in concerts and on recording dates. Stack had booked the Acoustic Barn for December 19 to record a compact disc. It would be the first recording he had ever made under his own name, or as leader. It would be produced by John Snyder, a Charlotte native who had left home and over the past twenty-five years had produced recordings for some of the country's best-known jazz artists, including Dizzy Gillespie, Dave Brubeck, George Shearing, and the Count Basie Orchestra. Snyder had been lured back to Charlotte for this occasion by his cousin, Murray Whisnant, a Charlotte architect and friend and fan of Jim Stack.

The card from Stack invited Loonis to participate in the recording—if he felt up to it. From what Stack had heard, that seemed unlikely, but he wanted to make sure Loonis knew about the session and knew he would be more than welcome.

When the time came, Stack, Snyder, bassist Tom Hildreth, drummer Jim Lackey, saxophone and clarinet player Doug Henry, and engineer Rick Dior arrived at the studio and began getting ready to record. In the liner notes he wrote for the CD they recorded that day, Snyder tells what happened next:

> As we were about to start, we were surprised when the great Loonis Mc-Glohon came through the front door. "What the hell is going on here?" he said in mock gruffness. "Who are these people?"
>
> . . . It had been forty years since I'd seen him. When I was twelve he had organized a bunch of us "musical" kids into a group he called the "Newcomers," as part of his responsibilities as musical director for WBTV. . . . Loonis was my earliest musical influence. He was always so encouraging to us kids—a bigger than life, redheaded man who smiled constantly and always had a twinkle in his eye. . . .
>
> "Don't think I've forgotten about you," he said to me, thumping his finger on my chest. "I've been keeping up with you. You're one of my successes. It's nice to see you, John."

Everyone there knew about Loonis's condition, and even if they hadn't, it would have been obvious when they saw him that he was seriously ill. But, as Snyder wrote: "Everyone acted as if it were just another day, even Loonis. Loonis was obviously struggling. He was obviously suffering, but after some stories and small talk, he sat down at the piano and started playing, as if he were suddenly immune to his condition. Jim moved to the vibes and suggested that they record some of Loonis's songs."

Loonis started playing "Blackberry Winter," perhaps the best-known of the many songs he wrote with Alec Wilder. To people familiar with McGlohon's music, or Wilder's, those first five notes are instantly recognizable—as recognizable as, say, the first three notes of Erroll Garner's "Misty." Loonis kept the rest of his statement of the song quite simple, cutting a few melodic corners, maybe giving his fingers time to warm up. He played one spare, almost hesitant solo chorus and then Doug Henry's throaty tenor saxophone took over the melody. Loonis spent the rest of the piece comping comfortably behind Henry's sax and Stack's vibes solo.

Then Loonis played his own "Songbird." There was some talk of making a full quintet version, but his piano solo stood beautifully on its own, so they decided to leave it at that. Loonis said goodbye and left. The two selections he had played would be his last recordings. The remaining musicians recorded the other nine songs that would be on Jim Stack's CD.

On most of his recorded performances over the years, Loonis's playing often has been close to flawless. This time it was not. Jim Stack said there were times when you could tell it took a heroic effort for Loonis to get his fingers where he wanted them to be.

On most of his recorded performances, Loonis's playing is often rather conservative. He usually was accompanying singers, which was what he most liked to do, and he was always careful to keep the focus on the vocal, not the piano. This time, there was no singer. On "Songbird" there was just the piano, and suddenly there was a surge of energy, of intensity, an edge almost of reckless bravado. Perhaps it was the performance of a man and an artist determined to play every note as if it might be his last. In his notes, John Snyder wrote,

> Listen to the last chord. It seems to go on forever, like he didn't want to let it go, he didn't want it to end.

Pastorale : I

Loonis Reeves McGlohon, age 12 years, a pupil in the seventh grade of Ayden Public Schools, made an unusual record in the achievement tests given the seventh grade pupils of the state this year. The average score necessary for promotion to the eighth grade is 7.5. Loonis Reeves made an average of 10.8. This score is above the average necessary for promotion to the 11th grade. His total average score was 107.8. So far as is known, this is the highest record made by any pupil of the seventh grades of the state, or elsewhere.

Loonis Reeves has broadcast from WPTF, WEED and WLVA in Lynchburg, Va. He broadcasts once each week from Greenville, having been doing this since last summer. He has also taken prizes each time he has taken part in the amateur contest at the Princess Theater. He has a wonderful ear and is talented for music.

Loonis Reeves, who is the son of Mr. and Mrs. Max McGlohon, is pianist at the Sunday School of the Christian Church.

—The *Ayden Tribune,* circa 1933

The swing hangs empty on the front porch now,
But I can close my eyes and see
Mama sittin' there shelling butterbeans,
Waitin' for Papa, waitin' for me.
—From "Nobody Home," words
and music by Loonis McGlohon

Ayden : 1

From Greenville, North Carolina, you drive south about nine miles down Highway 11 through flat fields, some fallow, some stubbled, some bright green with tobacco leaves, stretching from the roadside to distant borders of dark pine forest. You pass occasional dusty lanes that lead to modest farmhouses, ennobled by age and weather and by the stature of the old trees that shade them, and beyond the houses are the weathered outbuildings—sheds, barns, garages, a sloping rusted roof on four posts sheltering a tractor. In contrast and much newer are the occasional manufactured houses, some solitary, some in clusters, all the same shoebox shape on treeless lots, unadorned, graceless, functional but vulnerable—fragile reminders of the ambiguity of progress. Then you come to a few commercial buildings along the highway: convenience stores, gasoline pumps—harbingers of a town. You turn left at the sign that says Ayden.

It is an uncrowded, unhurried town of about 5,000 people. It is the home of the annual Collard Festival. It is the home of the inexplicably named Skylight Inn, also known as Pete's, which has no skylight and is not an inn but a venerable barbecue joint. (At lunchtime, follow the deep, sweet aroma of wood smoke and roasting pork until you come to a plain cinderblock building with an incongruous faux cupola on top, a rutted, potholed parking lot full of cars, and a waiting line of hungry people stretching from the order counter inside, through the screened door, and outside toward the street.)

Ayden was also home, once—and perhaps, in some sense, always—to a jazz pianist, composer, television producer, hymn writer, church choir director, and raconteur named Loonis McGlohon. The town was the first and a very significant piece of the collage of paradoxes that was his life—a life that was long but all too short, creative, generous, gracious and benevolent, finally legendary, and all the more remarkable because it began here, in Ayden.

His formative environment, his interests and tastes, his talents, his beliefs, biases, and passions, would represent deeply contradictory elements. That was enough to make him a complex and interesting man, but hardly unique. What perhaps was unique, and certainly exceptional, was the synthesis of those contradictions in the Loonis McGlohon we knew, a persona greater than the sum of its parts.

He was, for example, hip. That is an adjective for which no dictionary has an adequate definition. As Louis Armstrong reportedly said when asked for a definition of jazz: If you have to ask, you'll never understand. In part it means that he was very much of his time and place, culturally and socially aware and attuned almost to the point of prescience; worldly, generally unflappable, and culturally shock-proof, to a point. Yet his values and virtues were all but antithetical to some of the commonly assumed connotations of what it means to be hip. His personal tastes and standards were all but immune to many of the changes in mores, manners, and expectations that transformed American society and culture—mostly not for the better, he would say—in his lifetime. He was so naturally, intuitively sensitive to contemporary cultural vibrations that he had no need to try to be hip—to embrace the latest pop music fad, for example, or the latest anything else, unless he recognized something of value there.

He had an almost foolproof trash detector, and he never felt the need to pretend to like something that he considered tasteless or meaningless, whether it was young black performers dumbing down their own rich African American musical heritage, or certain "avant-garde" piano players. He knew the difference between raw emotional honesty and gratuitous vulgarity, between creative dissonance and pretentious noise.

He never made any effort, seemed never to have had any inclination, to pull up or disavow his rural, small town roots. Yet he was as much at home in the great cities of the world, in the most civilized and sophisticated milieus, as he was in the place where he was born, or in Charlotte, the culturally and socially conservative southern city where he spent almost all of his adult life. Maybe it was because he was so secure in who he was, so unabashedly comfortable with his hometown and his adopted city, that he was immediately and always secure and comfortable at Carnegie Hall or Lincoln Center, in Harlem or Greenwich Village, in London, Paris, Rome, or somewhere on a washed-out country road in China.

His rural heritage included an enduring appreciation of the rhythms and smells and flavors of country life and the patterns of rural southern speech, and an inveterate sensitivity to the changing seasons, to the colors and textures of earth and water and sky. All of that seasoned and enriched his music, but it was never a parochial influence. It never limited his aesthetic vision or his melodic or harmonic imagination, which in fact were largely inspired by the most urban of all American musical genres.

He grew up in a racially segregated society, in a part of the country where what today would be rightly condemned as racism in any corner of America was, among white people, a standard and largely unchallenged way of thinking about, and relating to, African Americans. (One-on-one personal relationships between the races were often affectionate and mutually respectful. But that involved reaching, individually, across the social and legal barriers, while taking great care not to tear them down.) Yet three of his favorite playmates as a boy were black, and the style of music to which he was attracted at an early age, and to which he would devote much of his career, had some of its roots in Africa and grew largely out of the black experience in the American South. Many of his early musical heroes were black. And many of his most treasured friends and musical collaborators would be black. (One of them—the great blues singer Joe Williams—once said to him: "It ain't easy being white, is it, Loonis?")

While segregation and discrimination were a way of life in the South through the first half of the twentieth century and beyond, the substantial black population in the South made a certain amount of cultural cross-pollination inevitable. Perhaps nowhere was it more obvious than in popular music. It was a phenomenon observable in the late 1940s and early 1950s, when rhythm and blues recordings by black musicians and singers became the most popular dance music among white teenagers across the Carolinas, particularly at summer beach resorts; it reached its apogee in the music and persona of a southern white boy named Elvis Presley.

Loonis grew up in the rural Protestant church and apparently never seriously questioned its teachings or rebelled against its behavioral restrictions—although as an adult he did drink alcoholic beverages and occasionally used profanity. But his musical ambition took him, even before he was out of his teens, into bars and night clubs, places considered sinful and perhaps even off-limits by many southern Christian church people of his parents' generation. As an adult he maintained a loyal and active church affiliation, directed his church choir, and wrote church music, even as he moved easily in and out of a musical and cultural environment notorious for illegal drug use, alcohol abuse, and little regard for the sexual morality he learned as a boy and apparently practiced for the rest of his life. The sacred music he wrote, as well as his personality and behavior, suggested that he remained forever buoyed by the simple faith he learned as a child. But his faith, as the Apostle Paul said of charity, was "not puffed up." And he apparently found no conflict between his personal beliefs and his tolerance of those who believed or behaved differently. (When the great pop singer Margaret Whiting married a star of hard-core pornographic movies, Loonis was not particularly happy about it and declined to offer sincere congratulations, but he remained her loyal friend.)

His tolerance ended abruptly, however, when it encountered hatred, bigotry, meanness, or dishonesty.

Those and other contradictory threads woven through his life and experiences produced a durable, consistent artistic and personal integrity, a resilient confidence and optimism, a resplendent creativity. He was a joy and an inspiration to behold, to encounter, to engage, to befriend. And this is where it began, in Ayden, in Pitt County, North Carolina.

The McGlohon family tree, its branches bearing the descendants of a native of Scotland named John McGlohon, is deeply rooted here. In 1819 a son of John McGlohon, Jeremiah, whose last name was spelled McGlawhorn in the Pitt County deed book, gave his son Jonathan, then about twenty-one years old, some land on the east side of Little Contentnea Creek. Jonathan became a wealthy farmer and at the beginning of the Civil War owned twenty-three slaves.

Some of Jonathan's land was inherited by one of his sons, Benjamin Franklin McGlohon. Benjamin and his wife, Lois, had seven children, among them Caleb Joseph McGlohon. Caleb and his wife, Winifred Eugenia, known as Minnie, had nine children. The fourth was Max Cromwell McGlohon, born in 1891.

Max McGlohon married Bertha Andrews on May 4, 1919. Their first child, Joseph Allen McGlohon, was born May 22, 1920, and died November 2 of that same year. The second child, born September 29, 1921, was Loonis Reeves McGlohon. A third, Raymond Berkley McGlohon, was born in 1923.

Some friends and admirers of Loonis have speculated over the years that his first name, with its almost echoing double vowels—particularly euphonious with the last name McGlohon—was an old family name, perhaps traceable back to Scotland. In fact, Max McGlohon had an army buddy named Loonis, and liked the name well enough to christen his second son with it.

Bertha Andrews McGlohon, circa 1920.

Loonis once described the house where he grew up as "a modest, two-story L-shaped house . . . built in the early 1900s," and he said, "Ayden had forty or fifty houses that looked just like ours on West Third Street." West Third Street stretches along a leafy corridor through a historic district of old homes—some modest, some more imposing, but none grand; some proud and well-kept, some shabby and flaking, on weedy lots—and into the old downtown business district. The first house where Loonis lived was and is at 480 West Third Street. It has a spacious porch wrapped around one end, and at the other end is a second-floor apartment that was home to Max and Bertha McGlohon and their sons. Max worked as an automobile mechanic at a garage just a short walk away.

As Loonis was learning to walk and talk in Ayden and on his grandparents' nearby farm, urban America—the Northeast, the old port cities along the southern coast, New Orleans, and the river ports up into the Midwest—was lurching into the Roaring Twenties, the Jazz Age, the era of Prohibition, speakeasies, flappers dancing the Charleston and dancing around the edges of sexual liberation, the rich getting richer and thinking the boom would never end. But the flamboyant decadence that has defined that decade in the American imagination was a long, long way from Ayden, and not only in miles. In Ayden, as in much of the country, it was still more Booth Tarkington's America than Scott Fitzgerald's. But soon a bit of the Jazz Age—the music itself—would reach into places like Ayden through radio and phonograph records.

Loonis Reeves McGlohon and friend on the McGlohon farm, 1921.

All children are special, of course, but as the second child of parents whose first child had lived less than six months, Loonis was extra special. He was loved, nurtured, sheltered, protected—perhaps overly so. As an adolescent he wasn't permitted to drive a car. But he was not relieved of the responsibilities of school and work, and sharing the burdens of home and farm, and he did many of the kinds of things boys do and have always done. Many years later, as he remembered those days, he said, "Driving a car wasn't that important in Ayden."

In Ayden today the old downtown has been sapped by development along the roads connecting to the bypass, on the edge of town, as is the case in so many small and midsized towns. A way of life where chores and errands were a matter of walking—or, particularly for children and adolescents, riding bicycles—has been replaced by one that requires at least two cars per family, four-lane streets, and large parking lots. In downtown Ayden today small businesses alternate with empty storefronts. Edwards Pharmacy, where the soda fountain once drew teenagers from the high school just down the street, has relocated at a suburban intersection, where it competes with a chain drugstore across the way.

Downtown Ayden was about the same structurally when Loonis was a boy as it is today, but it was a busier and more interesting place. Ayden had a population of only about 2,500 people then, but its downtown was a thriving business district, just a short sprint from his front door. The businesses included the Princess Theater, Edwards Pharmacy, the Olde Towne Tavern, Worthington's five- and ten-cent store, a dry goods store, and the garage where his father worked. The church they attended was also there.

Just a block from their apartment was the school where Loonis completed the first through the fourth grades. Not much farther away was the yellow brick building that housed grades five through high school, which ended at grade eleven.

Not long after Loonis entered school, his parents bought a used upright piano, and he began to take piano lessons from Miss Virginia Belle Cooper, whose home was also just a short stroll from the McGlohons'.

In the early 1930s, Max McGlohon bought a house across and just down the street and moved his family there. Their new home was 469 West Third Street, a rectangular two-story house with a brick chimney, a tin roof, two big oak trees shading the front lawn, and a fig bush out back. There, at the end of the driveway, Max set up his own garage and became his own boss.

For the rest of his life, Loonis would remember his years growing up in that small, compact, shady, sheltering community, as part of a large extended family, as a happy time.

The church was an important part of his boyhood. Two churches, in fact. The McGlohons went to Sunday school and church every Sunday. They were members at Ayden Christian Church, a congregation of the Disciples of Christ. But some Sundays they went to his maternal grandmother's church a few miles out of town, in the Rountree community. Rountree Christian Church, founded in 1827, was the "mother church" from which the North Carolina Disciples of Christ denomination was organized. And for Loonis, it was a historic and significant church for another reason: "That's where I first had dinner on the grounds," he recalled.

Dinner on the grounds is a rural southern Protestant tradition in which members of the church bring food to lay out on long tables on the church grounds, for a congregational buffet dinner, or sometimes for a family reunion. The food and fellowship, the spirit of rural family and church life, formed an indelible memory for Loonis—one that he would later celebrate in a song called—what else?—"Dinner on the Grounds."

His grandfather and grandmother McGlohon's farm was the site of other rich boyhood memories. There was a comfortable, ten-room farmhouse, with tobacco barns and a smokehouse and other outbuildings, as well as other, smaller homes on the property. It had been known as the Dawson Place until Granddaddy Joe bought it, about the turn of the century. At one time, Loonis recalled, five of his father's brothers and their families lived and worked on the farm, as did some black tenant families.

The farm was where his lifelong appreciation of good southern cooking originated. On most Sundays, after church, Loonis and his parents and brother would go to the farm for Sunday dinner, another experience Loonis later recounted with relish:

Sometimes they would have twenty to twenty-five people there for Sunday dinner. There would be the family—uncles, aunts, and cousins—and they would invite people at church: "Come have dinner with us." Sometimes they would pick up two or four or even more extra people from church.

There was always plenty of food. Fried chicken. Hot biscuits. Mashed potatoes. Butter beans. Always butter beans. Lots of vegetables. My grandmother would can vegetables in the summer to eat in the winter. They grew all their vegetables. And the chickens.

Loonis also spent a lot of time there in summer, helping with chores, playing in the woods and fields, enjoying the simple, sensuous pleasures of rural life—including plenty of what commercial imitators later would advertise as "country cooking," which he later remembered with relish: "Lunch was dinner and dinner was supper, and corn bread and collards were served at one of those meals."

Growing and curing tobacco was a primary activity on the McGlohon farm, as it was all across eastern North Carolina, and the boys were expected to do their share in that process. Sometimes Loonis's job would be to break off the leaves and put them into the truck or trailer for transporting to the barn. Or he would hand the leaves, three or four at a time, to the worker who would tie them with twine and hang them in the barn to cure. Curing tobacco by fire in barns was a risky operation. Across the region a number of barns were lost every season when fires got out of control. Sometimes it would be his turn to stay up late at night to watch the fires, to monitor the heat and make sure the flames did not spread.

Occasionally on a sultry summer afternoon his grandfather would return home from the store with lemons and ice and make lemonade in a large bucket. Or his Uncle Sol would bring a few watermelons from the field and slice them into wedges on the edge of the porch so the children—and adults, too—could savor the cool, quenching sweetness. Loonis later admitted he sometimes got a watermelon on his own, breaking it open in the field and eating just the heart out of it.

He also remembered the wonderful smells of the smokehouse, and the tastes of the hams, pork shoulders, and sausages that came out of it. "One of the best meals I ever had was at an uncle's house on the farm, a mile or so from the big house," he said. "It was a cool fall night, raining, and my aunt had cooked country ham, rice, gravy, and biscuits. I can still taste that country ham. Country ham can be salty and kind of hard, but she knew just how to fix it."

A much less appetizing memory of the farm was hog-killing time. Loonis recalled that his friend Charles Kuralt, who experienced hog-killing time on his own grandfather's North Carolina farm, said that was when he realized he didn't want to be a farmer. "You had to wait for cool weather," Loonis said. "You couldn't do it when it was hot, because the meat would spoil. They had a big black pot over a fire and would boil the 'chitlins.' The aroma was very unpleasant to me. I was old enough to help. I carried wood for the fire, and water. Fortunately they never asked me to make the sausage."

Working and playing on the farm also provided an escape, perhaps, from the restrictions of his protective parents, and valuable experiences for a boy learning to be a man. Also valuable were the friendships he found there. The schools Loonis attended in town were for white children only, of course, and his boyhood friends in Ayden all were white. But his favorite playmates on the farm were Pot, Dee, and Sam, three boys from African American tenant families. Together the four of them—the slender, pale-faced redhead, freckling in the summer sun, and his three black friends—climbed trees, played along the creek that bordered the farm, and rode mules using burlap bags for saddles. Tobacco sticks were transformed by their imaginations into various tools and weapons, including swords for their make-believe duels. But it was a relationship that eventually had to end, and all of them knew it had to end, and they sensed when it had to end—even though they didn't really understand why.

"We were friends until I was into my teens," Loonis said. "It was strange. There was a common breaking-off of that relationship. It was as though all of us knew that relationship was coming to an end."

After that "breaking-off," Pot, Dee, and Sam visited Loonis in town one day. He enjoyed seeing them and remembered their visit for the rest of his life. But they would never again be his companions.

Those boyhood summer days on the farm left Loonis with idyllic memories, but for his grandparents and uncles trying to make a living from the land, times were tough and getting tougher, as Loonis would soon learn. Through the 1920s American agriculture was producing more crops than the market could absorb at prices that would provide family farmers a decent living. The federal government debated what to do about swelling crop surpluses and falling prices, but did little. The agriculture economy was becoming seriously depressed some years before the stock market crash in 1929 signaled the beginning of what would become known as the Great Depression. Caleb Joseph "Granddaddy Joe" McGlohon was one of many thousands of small farmers who mortgaged their land to buy time and cover the costs of planting the next season's crops. By the time he died, in October 1931, he had turned the farm over to two of his sons, Marvin and Sol. But in a national economy crippled by depression, they couldn't generate enough income to make the mortgage payments. In 1932, banks were foreclosing on farm mortgages at the rate of almost 20,000 a month, and that year the bank foreclosed on the McGlohon farm.

The furnishings from the big farmhouse were divided among the surviving children, including Max. The remaining family members who had lived on the farm scattered and found shelter as tenants on other farms. It was a cruel change from their good life on their own family's farm. Loonis's father, Max, and two of Loonis's uncles, Ned and Sol, took turns providing a home for their mother, Loonis's grandmother, Minnie McGlohon. She stayed with each for a few months, and then moved on to the next.

There was one chore left before the last of the McGlohons left the old family farm. Under the staircase was a large black iron safe that had been there when Granddaddy Joe bought the place. He didn't know the combination, so nobody had been able to open it. It was heavy and cumbersome, and none of the McGlohon brothers wanted to take it with them when they had to move. But before they left, they wanted to know what was in it. They managed to get it out into the yard. Loonis and the other grandchildren watched from a safe distance as his uncle Sol used dynamite to blow the door off the safe. Inside were cotton bandannas, probably once red but now a rusty brown, which crumbled into dust as they were brought out of the safe. Wrapped in each bandanna was a stack of Confederate bills and bonds—in all, hundreds of bills and bonds. The uncles gave them to the children, who used them for play money.

That year, 1932, Americans elected a new president, Franklin Delano Roosevelt, who promised a New Deal and relief from the Depression. In fact, full relief would be years away, but one of the new administration's initiatives was an area called Penderlea, almost one hundred miles south-southwest of Ayden, in Pender County. It was offering twenty-acre homesteads to farmers who had lost their land. Marvin's brother-in-law, Ray Smith, heard about Penderlea and moved there with his family in 1936. Marvin and Sol and their families followed the same year. Each homestead had a house with electricity and a bathroom, a barn, a corncrib, a smokehouse, a hog house, a chicken house, a pump house, storage tanks for hot and cold water, a refrigerator, a washing machine with a wringer, and some basic furniture. Loonis's cousin Edna Earle, Marvin's daughter, later recalled that the site itself was "a mud hole," but it was a considerable improvement over life as a tenant farmer.

Loonis was deeply saddened when his grandmother lost the farm, and he was very much aware of the economic depression. But his immediate family was surviving in Ayden, and he was going into high school and had other things on his mind. He enjoyed chemistry class in high school, and one Christmas he asked for a chemistry set, but didn't get one. He loved riding his bicycle around Ayden and out into the countryside and up dirt roads to swamps and creeks. He had not yet become an avid reader, but his father had some of Edgar Rice Burroughs's Tarzan books, and some of Zane Grey's Western novels, and Loonis read those. He also read some of the Hardy Boys mystery books, and a few of the classics, including Victor Hugo's *Les Miserables.* He read Margaret Mitchell's best seller about the Old South and the Civil War and Reconstruction, *Gone with the Wind,* which was published in 1936. He also read the Holy Bible, or at least many parts of it. His father read from the Bible often, sometimes aloud to Loonis, and said he had read it though several times.

Loonis did not travel widely or often as a boy. It was a special treat when, with his family, he visited his great-aunt—"a real citified lady," he recalled—in Raleigh, the state capital, to spend a weekend. "Raleigh was like New York City to me. I had older cousins. They could ride the streetcar down Glenwood Avenue and uptown, and I went with them. I remember there was a fourteen-story building there. I thought it reached to the sky."

One of his best friends in high school was Melba Gaylor. They often kept each other company after school, and sometimes went together with other couples to the soda fountain at Edwards Pharmacy. Melba later married and moved to New York City, where she lived most of her adult life. After she moved back to Ayden, as a widow, she was asked if she remembered Loonis having a girlfriend in high school. "He didn't need one," she said. "He had me."

Relatives often visited the McGlohon home in Ayden. One was his grandmother's brother, who lived on a farm a few miles away. Loonis remembered him as "the epitome of the southern gentleman, very tall and erect. I never saw him stooped. He always wore a white dress shirt, but not always a tie. He always wore a coat, except in the very hottest months, maybe July and August." On one occasion when Loonis was a teenager and his grandmother was living with them, her brother, her sister from Raleigh, and another sister from Smithfield visited the McGlohon home on West Third Street. "They sat on the porch at night and talked about when they were children," Loonis said. "I would give anything if I had had a tape recorder."

By then Loonis was beginning to discover the musician within him. He did not think of himself as a musician, and at that time he would never have even considered the possibility of a career in music. But he could pick out tunes on the piano and then put together the other notes that went with the tunes, forming chords. At first he played for an audience of one—himself—but soon he could play for others, which he enjoyed doing.

The interesting question now, looking back, is: What led an adolescent in Ayden, North Carolina, in the mid-1930s, in the musical direction in which Loonis McGlohon was headed? His first significant exposure to music was surely in the church. But even though church music would be an important part of his life, the music he was hearing in his head in those days, and trying to find on the piano, was not church music. Where did it come from?

Young Loonis knew the answer, of course, but so intimately that it's unlikely the question ever occurred to him. A more important question for him at the time, if he were inclined to ponder such questions, was where it would lead.

More than half a century later, as one of a panel of distinguished North Carolinians speaking at the East Carolina University Chancellor's Forum in 1991, Loonis talked about growing up in Ayden, in an impoverished region of a poor state, during the Great Depression. What he expressed was perhaps a uniquely American kind of optimism—the spirit of a young man in a young country:

"If our world was small," he said, "we didn't know it."

Then, perhaps intentionally using the flat rural landscape of his boyhood as a metaphor, he added: "Our horizon seemed endless."

It is within the soundscape of the home and its environs that children develop their early musical sensibilities, learning their culture's definition of music and developing expectations of what music ought to be. . . .

Within the larger community, hymnody at church services, marches at football games, and soul music at social dances contribute further to the children's education, as do concerts in performance halls and informal presentations in parks and at parades.
—Paul F. Berliner, *Thinking in Jazz: The Infinite Art of Improvisation*

When you're just learning jazz, everything is mystical.
—Wynton Marsalis, quoted by Berliner

Music : 2

"I grew up with church music," Loonis once said. The venerable hymns and anthems of Protestant worship were indelibly recorded in his mind long before he reached his teens, and for the rest of his life he could play many of them from memory. The church was where he first demonstrated a desire to play music. Years later, he did not remember the incident, but he remembered his mother and father telling him about it: "Mother and Dad said I was three or four years old, and we were in church, and they suddenly realized I wasn't in my seat but had slipped away and gone down and started banging on the piano. They were embarrassed. I guess that was my first public performance."

But church music was not the only influence.

Commercial broadcasting was born in America just a year before Loonis was born, when radio stations KDKA in Pittsburgh and WWJ in Detroit went on the air in 1920. Within a few years most American homes had radios, and entertainers such as Amos and Andy, Bing Crosby, Kate Smith, Burns and Allen, Jack Benny, Edgar Bergen, and Charlie McCarthy would become almost as much a part of many households as the people who lived there. Radio also brought symphonic music, light classics, and live dance band performances into homes in towns where those sounds had rarely if ever been heard before.

The first recording of a New Orleans jazz band—Kid Ory's—was made the year Loonis was born. General Phonographic Corporation recorded Mamie Smith, King Oliver, and Louis Armstrong for its Okeh label in 1924. Those were pre-electric recordings. By the following year electrical engineers had developed electric recording equipment and phonographs, and one of the first electric records was of Armstrong playing trumpet and scat singing on the tune "Heebie Jeebies," on Okeh Records.

Also the year Loonis was born, 1921, the great New Orleans trumpeter King Oliver took his band to Chicago for an extended stay "in residence" at Lincoln Gardens. The next year Oliver invited Louis Armstrong to join him there, and New Orleans jazz had made a major move, into the Midwest. To anyone living today, the significance of such a move might not be immediately apparent. But at that time, with only silent movies, no television, and with commercial radio and the recording industry each barely in its infancy, the only way most people could hear music was in person.

But soon the new recordings, played on radio and on home phonographs, would carry New Orleans music, and related styles of jazz that were developing elsewhere, including the blues-based jazz from Kansas City, all across the country. Bix Beiderbecke, a white cornet player who was often compared with Armstrong, formed his New Orleans–style band, the Wolverines, in 1924. Armstrong assembled his own band, the first of his "Hot Fives," in 1925 and began a series of historic recordings for Okeh, using the new electric recording techniques.

Meanwhile, what became known as the Harlem Renaissance was underway, as a remarkable group of African American musicians, artists, and writers took up residence in that New York City neighborhood and began informally but significantly networking and interacting. That environment began to draw musicians and bands from Chicago and Kansas City to New York City, where nightclubs, dance halls, theaters, and the new recording studios became laboratories for jazz experimentation. That process would continue there for the rest of the century, and most notably at midcentury, when a small group of musical revolutionaries stretched and strained the rhythmic and harmonic definitions of jazz to create a new music that was challenging and controversial and would be profoundly influential.

On Broadway, creators of revues and musical comedies were translating the European heritage of art music and theater music into a new American musical language. As part of that process, a few innovative composers were creating the modern American popular song, with works that set what would turn out to be irreplaceable standards for the genre. Between the time Loonis was born and the time he finished high school in 1938, the four greatest of those innovators—Jerome

Kern, Irving Berlin, George Gershwin, and Richard Rodgers—wrote the songs that first made them famous, including most of their best and most enduring songs.

In 1927, the year Loonis entered school, Warner Brothers produced a motion picture called *The Jazz Singer,* starring Al Jolson, which included a partial soundtrack. That ended the era of silent films, and over the next few years Hollywood studios began sending reels of film that carried music as well as moving pictures into theaters in almost every town—including the Princess in Ayden.

It was coincidental, of course, that those developments occurred in and around the year of Loonis McGlohon's birth; but it was not insignificant. If he had been born a few years earlier, his life might have turned out quite differently. The technical and cultural evolutions of the early 1920s—radio, electric recordings, sound on film, the emergence of jazz from a regional curiosity to a national and increasingly popular form of music, and the beginning of a repertoire of American popular songs—all came just in time to enrich the musical environment of his boyhood. The place where he was born and raised was a vast distance from the entertainment capitals, from Broadway and Hollywood, from the urban venues where jazz music was beginning to flourish, and it was even more distant in culture and ambience and attitudes than it was in miles. But over the next few years American small towns, including his, were suddenly plugged into the sources of evolving American culture and entertainment, through radios in the kitchens or living rooms of even the most modest homes, through phonograph records, and through motion picture soundtracks in the local theater. As those media exposed local and regional audiences to the sounds of the new big bands and dance bands, the bands went on the road to play for those new, eager audiences. Local and regional musicians formed their own groups, modeled on the new touring and recording bands they were hearing. Loonis was listening, and his young life was changed more than once, probably many times, by what he heard.

It was truly a time of miracles. It was miraculous to sit in a chair or on the floor, or lie on the sofa or in your bed, and from a veneered box with a couple of dials and a hole covered with fabric hear a famous dance band performing in some glamorous hotel ballroom in a great city hundreds of miles away. If you had one of those new phonographs you could play phonograph records, which were for sale at the dime store. A record was a rather heavy but fragile disk, ten inches in diameter, made of shellac and clay. On each side was a continuous groove that began around its outside circumference and continued its circular path until it ended along an interior circumference. A circular paper label imprinted with the name of the record company, the title of the song, some sort of identifying numbers, the musician or band or singer, and the composer(s)—and sometimes an indication of the kind of song it was (fox-trot, for example)—was glued to the center. There was a hole in the center to fit over the post of the turntable. The turntable turned at a speed of seventy-eight revolutions per minute while a needle sat in the groove of the turning disk, picking up the electric message implanted there last month or last year, by performers and engineers somewhere far away. The needle was wired into a system that converted the electric signal back into sound, audible through openings venting the speaker built into the phonograph. Music!

In the early 1930s, Loonis was expected to be in bed by 10:30 each night. Often the last hour or so before bedtime was spent by the radio in the living room, and what he would remember most vividly from those evenings was the music: "The first big band I heard was on radio. At 10 o'clock at night they had live broadcasts from the Edison Hotel and the Lincoln Hotel . . . fifteen-minute live broadcasts. The first one I heard was the Jimmie Lunceford band, and it was like a big light had turned on. I had never heard anything like that in my life. And then I heard Artie Shaw. I was very taken with that music. And later Tommy Dorsey, and Benny Goodman, on records."

The McGlohons' first phonograph was a wind-up model. His parents had a few phonograph records, including their favorite, "My Blue Heaven," by Gene Austin. It was a huge hit. Loonis heard it many times and later learned that the singer Gene Austin once lived in Charlotte for a while and named his daughter for the city. Loonis occasionally saved enough money to buy a record of his own, and he was learning what to look for on the labels—learning which performers, even which composers, would be on the labels of records he might want to hear.

From the perspective of a later era, of subsequent trends in popular music, perhaps it should be noted that Loonis was not some musical eccentric, searching out esoteric material that his friends would not understand or appreciate. Jazz was not the experimental, challenging, only marginally popular music it would become in the late 1940s. Jazz was part of the popular music of that era when Loonis was growing up—the kind of jazz known as swing, played for dancing, mostly by big bands, often with singers (called vocalists). It was a music based on the African American jazz that had developed in New Orleans and moved into the Midwest and the Northeast, polished and perfected by the great pioneering black bands led by Lunceford, Fletcher Henderson, Don Redman, Count Basie, and Duke Ellington. It was then adopted and brought to a larger audience and more profitable popularity by white bands, most notably those led by Benny Goodman and the Dorsey brothers.

Across the street from the drugstore in Ayden was a bank building with an empty room where someone had set up a phonograph, and teenagers could go there at night and dance. Loonis and his friends would have Cokes at the drugstore soda fountain and then go over to play records and dance, often to big band music.

Only white kids, of course, were welcome there. But, remarkably, some of the white teenagers in Ayden, including Loonis, sometimes desegregated a night spot operated by and for black patrons. It was a place Loonis later remembered as "a sort of primitive roadhouse, in what we in those days called Colored Town, and they played records. The records were different. They were blues records, and some early rhythm and blues. We didn't really know what it was called. But we would go there and dance to it."

That, too, signaled the small, tentative beginning of an important trend. It would be more than a decade, however, before rhythm and blues would become openly popular as dance music among white teenagers in the Carolinas. In the 1930s, like young people all over the country, Loonis and his friends in Ayden were dancing and listening primarily to big band swing music. The difference between Loonis and his friends was that when Loonis listened, he heard more than they did.

Although later, as a musician, he would have valuable mentors, initially nobody steered Loonis toward the music he would come to love and emulate. "There was nobody to teach me," he recalled. "I was self-taught."

A standard ten-inch phonograph record had about three minutes of music on each side, enough for one and a half or two choruses of a song, depending on the length of the song and the tempo at which it was played. The song that the record producer believed would be most popular and would prompt people to buy the record was on what was known in the trade as the "A side." On big band records it was often some kind of novelty tune, with verbal, instrumental or rhythmic gimmicks to grab attention or make it instantly, if temporarily, memorable—a raucous two-beat blues, for example, with honking horns and a humorous, maybe even risque, lyric. The "B side" was frequently something out of the band's standard repertoire, something that didn't immediately set your feet tapping or your mouth whistling, but that might reward more intense and repeated listening. Loonis was learning that he often preferred to listen to the B side. And if he particularly liked a record, he would listen to it over and over again, until every curve of the melody and every shifting layer of harmony would become as familiar as the words and tunes of those hymns he had heard and sung so many times in church.

He was also having some success finding those songs on his piano—picking out the melody, and then the notes that formed the harmonic structure in which the melody was set, and on which it moved.

For all that, or perhaps because of that, he was not, by his own account, a very good piano student when he was taking lessons from Miss Virginia Belle Cooper and Mrs. May Eure. The problem wasn't a lack of talent or the lack of a good ear for music, but too much talent and too good an ear. He later remembered that after watching his teacher play, he could "mimic her hands." He also "could play something without actually reading it. I think she knew that." Under their tutelage he learned the basics of musical notation and piano technique, and he learned to play simple tunes. But once he heard them he could repeat them without having to read the music. He could play them "by ear," so he did not need to learn to read music very well. He was too busy figuring music out for himself. And he wasn't bashful about it. By the time he was twelve years old he was playing piano for his Sunday school class, for friends and audiences at school, and sometimes on nearby radio stations.

There was a pianist in Ayden who was quite popular, "a hero to everybody," Loonis remembered. "He played a lot of arpeggios, and not very good songs. Everybody thought he was wonderful. My mother and dad thought I should take lessons from him. We became friends. But he said he couldn't play what I was trying to play. He didn't hear it. And what he played wasn't of much interest to me."

Loonis continued to find the music he was looking for on radio and on records, and occasionally he had an opportunity to hear it in person. While he was still in high school, some of the top touring black bands came to Greenville, just nine miles away, to play in venues for black audiences and dancers. Loonis had an aunt who lived in Greenville, and his parents, so protective that they wouldn't let him drive a car, nevertheless allowed him to spend an occasional Saturday night with her and go to a black concert and dance. He remembered hearing the great Count Basie band there, and the Lunceford band. The audience was segregated, of course. Loonis and the few other white spectators had to sit in the balcony, looking down on the stage, the dance floor, and the black patrons.

In the early autumn of 1938, Loonis, not quite seventeen years old, enrolled at East Carolina Teachers College in Greenville, just nine miles north of Ayden. Later East Carolina University, it was a state institution, in a state whose constitution requires that "the General Assembly shall provide that the benefits of the University of North Carolina and other public institutions of higher education, as far as practicable, be extended to the people of the State free of expense." So it was affordable even for students from families of modest means, and even in the continuing depression.

It is difficult to overestimate the importance of a school such as East Carolina in a state that was relatively poor and largely rural, as North Carolina was in the 1930s and 1940s. The state maintained two nationally recognized institutions of higher learning—the University of North Carolina, at Chapel Hill, primarily for the arts and sciences, and N.C. State College, at Raleigh, primarily for agriculture, engineering, and textiles—as well as the Woman's College of the University of North Carolina, at Greensboro. But East Carolina—like Western Carolina and Appalachian State, in the mountains hundreds of miles west of Greenville—provided

education that was both affordable and accessible for young people in the state's poorest areas. For children of working farmers and small-town blue-collar workers, whose homes were many miles from Raleigh and Chapel Hill, and perhaps even farther away in terms of cultural environment, those outlying state colleges provided life-enhancing opportunities. Although small, with about 1,500 students, the East Carolina campus was an important academic and cultural oasis in the tobacco fields of Pitt and surrounding counties.

East Carolina was the obvious choice for an inexpensive education for Loonis, not only because of the minimal tuition, but also because he could attend as a day student, staying through some semesters with his aunt in Greenville, and at other times commuting to and from home in Ayden. Although it was close to home, East Carolina was for Loonis, as college was meant to be, a different world. On a college campus, in a college town, opportunities to pursue his interest in music, to learn and to play, would expand significantly, as would his social and cultural horizons. Although he did not live on campus, he was an active participant in campus activities, particularly if they involved music. One of his earliest compositions was a ballad performed as part of a play written and produced by students.

Even though he knew by then that music was, as he later put it, his "number-one love," the idea of a career in music still seemed beyond any reasonable ambition. "It never occurred to me that music would be a career," he said.

He signed up to major in business administration, with a minor in music. He enrolled in two music classes—clarinet and first-year theory and harmony. He passed the clarinet class without difficulty. But in the theory and harmony class, he had problems. As he later explained,

> In my innocence I was alienating the professor.
>
> I made the mistake of going where my ear would lead me, and that really ticked him off. He would give us some chords to study, and then you had to use them. You would spell out the chords, and maybe I'd spell out, say, a C diminished. I probably didn't know that it was a C diminished, or whatever it was. I just spelled it out because the harmony sounded right. And he'd say, "Mr. McGlohon, we haven't studied that chord yet." I think he thought I was being a smart-ass, and I really wasn't.
>
> So I just dropped out. I flunked the course, and I never took another music course.

That was the end of his formal musical education, but outside the classroom, he would continue to expand his knowledge of music and stretch his abilities, largely under the influence of a new friend, a trumpet player named Spence Hatley.

As he had ever since he was a very young teenager, Loonis would play any piano he could find, for any audience willing to listen. "I played a million notes," he recalled. "As many notes as Vincent Lopez. And about as meaningless."

He was playing in that florid style for the lunchtime crowd of students in the East Carolina dining hall one day when a somewhat older young man walked up to him and said, "You know, you play the worst piano I ever heard in my life, but I think you have a lot of talent." That was how he met Spence Hatley, who had an aura of authority that probably came from being a working musician with his own quartet, which until recently had been on the road. The four musicians had decided they wanted to complete their education and had enrolled at East Carolina. From that first encounter over the piano, Hatley, a trumpet player in the style of Billy Butterfield, quickly became a mentor, almost like an older brother, to Loonis.

"You need to learn about space," he told Loonis. "I'll bet you don't read music, do you?"

Despite years of piano lessons, Loonis indeed did not read well. Hatley said Loonis needed to learn to read music and offered to teach him. Loonis said he didn't have any money to pay for lessons. Hatley persisted.

"How much could you pay me?"

Loonis calculated that he could skip dessert and save a nickel a day, or thirty-five cents a week. Hatley agreed to teach him for thirty-five cents a week.

Jazz musicians who had never learned to read well were not so unusual, of course. Many were self-taught. Few had been to college. Some of them had studied under a local teacher as children or teenagers, but, like Loonis, they played by ear, which in many cases limited their incentive to learn to read, or perhaps even made reading more difficult. Two of the most prominent examples would be the most popular jazz pianists of the next thirty years, Erroll Garner and Dave Brubeck.

Garner reportedly did not read at all. Brubeck majored in music at College of the Pacific and later studied composition and theory under Darius Milhaud at Mills College. But he acknowledged later in interviews that he had always been a poor reader, partly because, like Loonis, he could play by ear and memory, and partly because of vision problems. Garner mostly led his own trio or played solo, and Brubeck led his own quartet, so reading was not so important to them. But Hatley persuaded Loonis that to play in a band, particularly one that used professional arrangements, it was important to know how to read. So Loonis got serious about learning to read, and Hatley helped him with that, and with harmony, and with lessons in taste and restraint to curb his youthful flamboyance. And, despite the thirty-five-cents agreement, he never charged Loonis for the lessons.

He also made Loonis a working musician, and Loonis began to learn about a working musician's lot and life on the road—lessons that would influence some of the most important decisions of his life just a few years later.

In the period from the early '30s to the war years, the big bands were king and inspired the same adulation that rock bands enjoy today. The jazz fan and the young jazz musician had a very close relationship. Indeed, very often they were one and the same.
—Ira Gitler, *Swing to Bop*

On the Road : 3

Spence Hatley had signed on to play that summer with a big band—twelve or fourteen pieces—led by Jimmy Woodard, at a pavilion at Carolina Beach. He recommended Loonis to Woodard, and as the summer of 1939 began, seventeen-year-old Loonis caught a ride to the beach to begin his first professional gig as a big band piano player. He later remembered the place as "a big, wooden, open pavilion . . . a popular hangout for teenagers. The piano was awful." The musicians were supposed to get ten dollars a week plus a room at the Breakers Hotel, about a mile from the pavilion. "But it turned out that there was no contract for that kind of arrangement," Loonis recalled.

Saturday morning, after we had played a week, we waited outside Jimmy's room to get our money. Some of us didn't have any money at that point. We waited, and he didn't get up and he didn't get up. Finally about noon we decided to get him up. We knocked on the door, and then we found out he had left. He had 'suitcased.' He probably had gotten a little money Friday night, but not enough to pay us what he said we would make, so he just took it and left.

So we went to the manager of the pavilion. Spence took over as leader and talked to the manager. He said, "We're stuck here. You've got a band that hasn't been paid." The manager said he'd pay us a percentage of the "gate," and we could continue to live at the hotel free. Every night he would count the money and give us a percentage to divide up. One night we might get thirty cents apiece, or sometimes we'd get as much as one dollar. We stayed most of the summer, except for Spence. He took an offer later to go with the Dean Hudson band.

I think that was the first time I played for pay. But I still wasn't thinking about playing music for a living.

That same summer, Loonis had an opportunity to play at a club outside New York City, which gave him a chance to sample the city's musical offerings during one of the most fertile and creative periods in the history of jazz. He later wrote about that experience:

It was the summer of 1939, I was seventeen, and I was playing at a club called Bordnicks at Tuckahoe, New York, a town just north of Manhattan. We were off Monday nights, and I had saved a few dollars for a splurge in New York City.

There were four theaters that had stage shows in those days. If you checked the schedule in the newspaper, it was possible to catch maybe three live matinee shows if you didn't stay for the movie. On that day, I got lucky. I saw Mildred Bailey and Red Norvo at the Strand, Chick Webb and Ella Fitzgerald were at the Capitol, and I think Ozzie Nelson and Harriet Hilliard were at the Paramount. Ozzie and Harriet were very commercial, of course, but I was hearing a live band, and that's what mattered most to me at the time.

I had a late dinner at the Automat on Times Square, and I killed time walking until after nine o'clock, when I headed for Fifty-second Street. In those days, Fifty-second Street was a paradise for jazz fans. There were several clubs lining both sides of the narrow cross street: Onyx Club, Three Deuces, Kelly's Stables, Famous Door. Close by was the Hickory House, where a piano was raised high inside the bar, and it would be home for pianists like Marian McPartland and others. The clubs on Fifty-second were basement rooms, reached by a short set of steps, over which cloth marquees let passersby know who was playing inside. The rooms were small, dark, filled with small round tables (just big enough to hold drinks), and at one end, on a small stage, the greatest jazz players in the world performed for a crowd that could hardly be called standing room.

Some clubs allowed you to sit at the bar, where you didn't have to pay a cover, but where you were expected to keep drinks sliding down your throat all the time. I was underage, but that didn't matter to the bartenders. They were less impatient with me for sipping on a beer for an hour than they were the older guys. My age was obvious, and while the bartenders would wipe their bar cloths around my area when I was holding the glass in my hand, only occasionally would they say, "Ready for another?" I wasn't much of a drinker. Usually, there was a third of a glass sitting there when I left. In the second place, I couldn't afford more drinks. Beer was maybe twenty-five or thirty cents a glass back then, and I was lucky to be able to afford a glass in every club I visited.

I heard Ben Webster, the wonderful tenor player, who had gotten fed up in the United States with segregation. He went to Holland, lived there for a while, and finally returned to this country. He was a big man, and he played big. Probably more assertive than Coleman Hawkins, who had shared the jazz throne with him. He played standard tunes, and I knew each one. I was mesmerized.

On the same bill, I believe, although it may have been in another club, I heard Stuff Smith, a jazz violinist. I thought he was very interesting, but violin didn't seem to me to be a jazz instrument. Smith's virtuosity was compelling, and I had never heard a violin played like that. But to me, it still sounded like a violin, and I was foolish enough to think that instrument belonged only in a symphony orchestra.

At Kelly's Stables, Roy Eldridge, the Spirits of Rhythm, and Billie Holiday were on the bill. It was beginning to rain, and the night was getting late for a seventeen-year-old (who had to catch the subway back to Tuckahoe), but I had long admired Roy Eldridge, the wonderful trumpet player, who was later to become a star with the Gene Krupa band. Eldridge was a fiery player, but he also had the ability to play soulful ballads, and he played with sculptured lines and phrases that made you say aloud, "Wow!" The Spirits of Rhythm were just that, a wonderful rhythm section of piano, bass, and drums that had recorded with lots of different soloists.

Eldridge stretched his set out because he knew the star had not yet arrived. Finally, he looked down the narrow room and saw Billie Holiday come in the front door. Her raincoat was drenched from the pouring rain outside, and after shaking herself off, she walked over to the bar and sat on the stool next to me. When she asked the bartender if she could have a drink, he shook his head. "Sorry, your credit ain't no good here." She shrugged.

How I wished I had enough money to buy this famous singer a drink. I had just enough carfare to get back home, and a couple of dimes to spare. If only I had had a dollar or two in my pocket. She was friendly when I spoke to her. Maybe she was hoping I would spring for a drink, but she also had to see I was just a kid.

We had been there for a couple of minutes when Eldridge came over and said not too softly to her, "Billie, the damn people have been waiting all night to hear you. Where the hell have you been?"

"It's raining, man, and I gotta change before I sing," she told him.

"We gonna take a break," he said. "You get dressed. We need to do a show in ten minutes."

I didn't hear it, but her response was probably a standard Holiday obscenity. After he walked away, she got up slowly and disappeared, maybe upstairs to change. It was about fifteen minutes later that Eldridge introduced her as Lady Day, the incomparable Billie Holiday.

I think she wore a white gown, but I don't honestly remember. She walked onto

Billie Holiday. (1947 publicity photo.)

the floor to polite applause. There was only a handful of people in the room, and I was the only person at the bar. The room was dark except for the pin spotlight on her face. Billie Holiday never photographed very well, but in person she had an exquisite face. Her skin was cream and coffee, and her bone structure was perfect. Her hair was straight and shiny, and her mouth, as many writers have said, was very sensual.

When she sang, Billie was almost motionless. On up-tempo numbers, her fingers snapped, but quietly. There was no other movement. But the face! The face mirrored everything she was singing about. It was almost embarrassing to look at Billie perform, because it was as though you were seeing someone stripped naked. The pain, the sorrow, and yes, even the joy, was so obvious in her face, her mouth.

I saw Billie perform one more time, some years later, at her "Lady Sings the Blues" concert at Carnegie Hall. It was not too long before she died, and she looked wasted and thin. It was still a thrill to see the lady in person, even though she was still on drugs and she was being paraded like a freak.

But that first time, that night in the summer of 1939, was unforgettable.

That summer was only the beginning of Loonis's education in the life of a big band musician on the road. The next lesson came just a few months later. Spence Hatley had an offer to play with a band at a hotel in Pensacola, Florida, for a month during the Christmas and New Year's holiday season, and he said he could get Loonis a job there, too. Loonis, still just eighteen years old, got permission from his mother and father and persuaded his teachers to give him his fall-semester final examinations early. Then he, Hatley, and a singer named Lo Ramsey, who was also an East Carolina student, headed for Pensacola, where for a few weeks they would be part of a sixteen-piece band playing nightly at the elegant San Carlos Hotel.

The band was billed as the Sonny Charles band, but it wasn't the real Sonny Charles band. The leader called himself Sonny Charles, but that wasn't his real name. The band played stock arrangements of hit tunes and standards, including "Jersey Bounce," "One O'clock Jump," "Dipsy Doodle," "Marie," and "Stardust."

Most of the musicians were good enough to take improvised breaks, and some of them later moved on to play in some of the nation's top-name bands.

"The guy who played the role of Sonny Charles, supposedly this famous band leader, wore white tie and tails, and was very aware of his persona," Loonis recalled. "You couldn't tell when he was on the bandstand that he had a wooden leg.

"One night all of a sudden there was a big snap, a big loud noise. The brace on his false leg had broken and he just crumbled to the floor. We had to carry him off. I remember Lo Ramsey carrying off the leg, and a shoe and a sock."

After hours, some of the musicians moved to another venue. "Our last set was a dinner set, maybe seven until ten, so we finished early," Loonis said.

> Then some of us would go to an after-hours place. There were two storefronts. One had bolts of material in the window, very dusty. It was a cover for an illegal bar. You went in through the next storefront, next door. There were usually five or six of us, and we'd go there and play for drinks. I didn't drink, but I'd have maybe a ginger ale and a sandwich.
>
> It was a narrow room with a bandstand at one end. At the other end was like a window, with a stage set. It was a Hawaiian scene, all papier-mâché and plastic, very badly done. Every hour on the hour we had to stop playing so they could have a floor show. Everybody had to turn around and look at the other end of the room. Off to the side was a young guy who would flip a toggle switch on and off to make "lightning" in the Hawaiian scene, and another guy had a piece of corrugated tin he would shake. That was the thunder. They ran some water over it to make rain. Every hour everybody had to turn around to see the Hawaiian thunderstorm. That was it. That was the floor show.

When the after-hours gig was over, a lot of the band members would congregate in someone's room to listen to records featuring some of their musical heroes, the great jazz musicians of the 1930s. In the hours after midnight they would play the same records over and over, listening to the music, many of them dreaming of the time they would make records themselves.

Cousin Ralph's Punch : 4

Loonis returned to North Carolina from Florida with valuable musical and on-the-road experience, and with a couple of bottles of French champagne—gifts from an enthusiastic fan of the band. He was still too young to drink it legally, and in any case had chosen at the time not to drink alcohol, but he recognized the name on the label and appreciated the quality and value of the champagne. Instead of pouring it out, as his mother at first suggested, or giving it away, he stashed it in a cabinet in the kitchen of the McGlohon home, on a shelf high enough to hide it. He soon forgot about it and never thought about it again until many years later, when he was reminded of the champagne and learned what had happened to it, which became the subject of one of his favorite stories. Loonis insisted the story was true, but the cousin who first told it, and then Loonis, may have embellished it in the telling. It predates and presages the fictional Mayberry stories that would give another North Carolinian, Andy Griffith, eternal life on television. Loonis later put the story on paper, leaving us one more glimpse of the town, the people, and the home that shaped his early years.

Modest though it was, our home was always filled with company. One great aunt came every summer as soon as schools were let out, and she brought with her a couple of steamer trunks and two or three of her children. I had four first cousins, three of whom lived at our house and went to college at East Carolina University. One of them was Ralph Sellers. Mother was glad to have Ralph around, because by then I had finished college and moved on, and my father had passed away, and Mother could count on Ralph to help with chores around the house. One night she gave him a chore she had never suggested before.

It was about dusk on a humid August evening, and Mother had just come in from a Pocahontas Lodge meeting. She was running late and needed to change clothes and freshen up for the Christian Church Circle group that was coming there that night for a meeting. Mother found Ralph sitting in the kitchen studying, and she asked Ralph if he would help.

"I'm running late, Ralph, and the circle ladies will be here any minute. Would you mind making the punch for me? I've got to change my dress. It's a simple punch, and all you have to do is put one part grape juice to two parts ginger ale—there are bottles on the back porch. Mix them and get a block of ice and put it in the punch bowl—I'll put that on the dining room table—and then take a banana and slice it kinda thin and let the slices float on top. That's all. And put eight crystal punch cups around the punch bowl."

With that she hurried to her bedroom and starting getting ready for the circle meeting. Ralph got busy with the chore Mother had given him. He had heard her say before that the circle ladies had a custom of having punch or refreshments as soon as they arrived for the meeting. In recounting the story to my family and me a few years later, Ralph said that he mixed the punch, but instead of using ginger ale he used two bottles of champagne.

"Champagne?" I said. "That's impossible. There never was any champagne in our house."

Mother and Dad were both teetotalers. She would use a couple of tablespoons of scuppernong wine to baste her fruit cakes, but this small amount of wine she would "borrow" from a great uncle who made wine on his farm. To keep Dad from discovering that there was wine in the small fruit jar she kept in the kitchen cabinet, she labeled it vinegar. My father had an allergy to vinegar, and one sniff would bring on an attack of asthma. Or so he claimed. Mother knew she was perfectly safe in labeling her small cache of homemade wine as vinegar.

But Ralph insisted it was champagne he found and used in the punch.

"Impossible!" I said. "Where did you find it?"

"On the very top shelf in the kitchen."

Then I remembered. I had been playing with a band in Pensacola, Florida, during Christmas holidays. A drunk but apparently resourceful fan, a middle-aged man, had given every boy in the band a bottle of G. H. Mumm champagne. Alto player Max Johnson didn't drink. Neither did I. Max gave me his bottle, and I took both bottles home with me. Mother almost fainted when she lifted the bottles from my suitcase. She wanted them thrown away immediately, but I talked her into letting me keep them. I said that someday I might get married, and we could celebrate by having a toast. I am not sure she actually said yes, but I remember placing both bottles on the top shelf in the kitchen. The room had a ten-foot ceiling, so it was necessary to get a stepladder to retrieve anything from the top shelf.

Ralph continued his story. "I decided this would be the perfect time to slip some champagne to the old ladies."

"But did you have to give them my twenty-five-year-old G. H. Mumm?" I pouted.

According to Ralph, the ladies arrived that night and Mother ushered them into the dining room to have punch.

"How did you make this punch, Bertha?" Miss Kathleen asked. "It sure is good."

"Oh, you know how I make it—the same way all of you make this punch. Just grape juice and ginger ale," Mother said, pleased that the ladies seemed to be enjoying the punch.

"It's the best you ever made," Miss Addie said, and decided to have another cup.

Ralph swore that Miss Hortense, after each of them had enjoyed a second or third round, tipped the bowl to drain the last few ounces into her cup. By now, all of the ladies were very talkative, but they were finally persuaded to go to the living room and begin the meeting.

The night was humid and hot. Mother got half a dozen Tadlock Funeral Home fans and passed them out and left the door to the living room open so the air could circulate. That meant Ralph, listening from the dining room, could hear everything that went on in the meeting, which he later enjoyed describing.

One of the church projects was to take up money for a missionary project in Africa. Miss Addie said she thought that beads and jewelry would be more appropriate than money. The natives loved beads, she said, and these could be mailed to the missionary in Kenya. Besides, she pointed out, the natives would have no way to spend money.

Miss Susie disagreed about the beads. "I say let's send them clothing. I saw some pictures in *National Geographic,* and I want to tell you those natives in Africa were naked. Stark naked!"

The other ladies were shocked.

Miss Susie added, "You could see everything they had."

"Everything?" Mrs. Jenkins squawked.

"Yes, ma'am. And mothers were nursing their babies. Right out in broad daylight."

The ladies fanned faster and faster, and the giggling got louder, Ralph said.

At the time he told us this story, I figured Ralph was making up all or at least most of it. It seemed unlikely that he would have wasted two bottles of expensive champagne on ladies who probably had never tasted the stuff before. Of course, if he really had, the ladies would never have suspected it, because they knew Mother would never serve anything alcoholic.

It was about ten years later when I heard Mother and my wife's Aunt Daisy swapping recipes. Mother was telling her about a grape juice punch she usually made for church groups.

"One night," she said, "I must have done something different in the recipe. The ladies in the circle—well, Miss Addie has died since then—still talk about that punch. I don't know to this day what I did different."

When I heard that I knew Ralph's story had been true—or at least some of it.

Legends and Discoveries : 5

The next summer, after his sophomore year, Loonis headed north again, this time to work in a band led by Dan Genovese, which played weekends at a club in Banksville, New York. With him was another East Carolina student from nearby Glenbrook, Lois Hughes, who sang with the band. A brief newspaper item about their summer jobs notes that Lois was a singer and "Red" McGlohon was her accompanist.

Loonis's involvement in the music scene on the campus and in and around Greenville also brought him into contact with Billy Knauff, who became a close friend and later would play a major role in one of the most important decisions of Loonis's life. Knauff was a coffee company representative based in Greenville, but he also was a saxophone player and bandleader, and Loonis soon became part of the Knauff band, playing frequently on weekends.

One engagement that was particularly memorable—although Loonis didn't realize just how memorable until years later—was at a beauty contest. Here's the story, as Loonis wrote it:

My best friend when I was in college was Steve Hilley. His father was president of Atlantic Christian College in Wilson, so Steve was enrolled there. But he and I spent most weekends together because we were playing in the same dance band. We usually played every Friday night somewhere in eastern North Carolina, so Steve and I would spend the weekend at his parents' house.

Steve played alto saxophone, had a great sense of humor, and although I would not have called him a handsome fellow, he always had a lot of good-looking girl-friends. He went pretty much steady with one girl who was lovelier than the others, but he was always complaining to me that she chased him too much.

Somebody had talked his girlfriend into participating in the Miss Cotton beauty contest, for which we were providing the music. The pageant was in Tarboro, and the girl rode with Steve and me to the theater there.

Naturally the guys in the band were all pulling for Steve's girl to win. But I was afraid she might be at a disadvantage, given what was in vogue at the time. The movie version of Gone with the Wind *had made a great impact on style ever since the film was released a few years earlier. For formal occasions, most young girls dressed in Scarlett O'Hara style, with hoop skirts that ballooned out so far that no girl could stand within four or five feet of another girl wearing the same kind of gown. And Shirley Temple must have influenced hairstyles, because most girls had sausage curls all over their heads.*

Steve's girl didn't fit that pattern. She was from a poor background, and I guessed she was probably wearing a hand-me-down gown from an older sister. At least the dress wasn't inspired by Miss Scarlett. It was a clinging chiffon gown, classic in style and splashed with vivid Gauguin colors. Her auburn hair was shoulder length, only slightly waved. While many of the other contestants for "Miss Cotton" were full-figured—perhaps too full in places—number fourteen (Steve's girl) was slim, willowy, and a little taller than average. I couldn't keep my eyes off her, and Steve, the other guys in the band, and I were disappointed when the judges gave the title of "Miss Cotton" to a round-faced, very busty girl from Speed, a little crossroads community near Tarboro.

I don't remember who was named runner-up, but it wasn't Steve's girl. I do remember that Steve, his girl, and I talked very little about the pageant as we drove back to Wilson. It doesn't help much to say, "You should have won," even though that's what I was thinking. She hadn't even gotten an honorable mention in the contest. So much for the judges' taste. Just a few years later she would be recognized as one of the most beautiful women in the world. Her name was Ava Gardner.

In addition to playing with Spence Hatley's band, and later Knauff's, on campus or around the region or on summer and holiday trips, Loonis also took advantage of opportunities to hear his favorite bands and meet some of his musical heroes. He found ways to create some of those opportunities, such as getting himself appointed to the committee that booked bands for student dances and concerts. One weekend the committee had booked the new Claude Thornhill band—a white band, of course—for a 5 P.M. tea dance followed by an 8 P.M. concert. Dave Tough, one of the finest drummers of the swing era, was with the Thornhill band at the time. Loonis, taking advantage of his committee status to get acquainted with some of the touring musicians, mentioned to Tough that the great Jimmie Lunceford band was playing that night at a black dance hall in Kinston, about thirty miles away. The hard-swinging Lunceford ensemble was perhaps the definitive band of the early years of the swing era, and probably the most highly regarded among other musicians.

Tough became very excited and said that he and some of the other members of the Thornhill band would love to hear Lunceford. Loonis said he had some friends with cars, and maybe he could arrange for rides to Kinston after the Thornhill concert at East Carolina—which, Loonis suggested, Tough and his colleagues could cut a little short if they wanted to. Loonis lined up two cars, and after the Thornhill concert, he and Tough and several of the musicians headed for Kinston.

To show his appreciation, Tough introduced Loonis to the drummer in the Lunceford band, Jimmy Crawford, and asked Crawford to have Loonis sit with him on the bandstand. When Loonis talked about that evening years later, about being "right in the middle of that band," he said, "It was like playing in the band and hearing it all around you. That had to be among the top five experiences of my life."

Loonis's musical travels usually were limited to the area within an easy drive of Greenville, which was attracting an impressive array of big band talent in the late 1930s and early 1940s—black bands for black dances in tobacco barns and local dance halls, white bands for student dances and concerts at East Carolina and on other campuses. He also got to New York City at least twice. The great city probably dazzled him less with its skyline and famous landmarks than with the musical stars he was able to hear and see and even sometimes meet.

His success in making contact with the leading performers of the popular music of that era was remarkable, and he documented it with autographs. He began collecting autographs as a teenager and later preserved them in a small hardcover autograph book. Some autographs were written into the book, others were written on other pieces of paper and later pasted in. On each page Loonis wrote, in the meticulous block printing of a very young man labeling precious materials, the date of each autograph and the place where the signature was written.

The entries included a number of legendary big band and jazz musicians and singers who performed in eastern North Carolina during his college years: Jack Teagarden (Greenville Armory, April 8, 1940); Glenn Miller, Tex Beneke, Ray Eberle (Wilson, N.C., April 22, 1940); Jimmie Lunceford (Greenville Armory, September 20, 1939); Cab Calloway, Cozy Cole (Kinston, N.C., March 26, 1940); Ella Fitzgerald (Kinston, N.C., May 1940); Earl "Father" Hines (Greenville, March 28, 1941).

A trip to New York City in August of 1940, during the New York World's Fair, with stops at concerts at the Loew's State (Andy Kirk) and Paramount (Cab Calloway) theaters and several jazz clubs, yielded more treasured signatures, including Harry James, Andy Kirk, Helen Forrest, Mildred Bailey, Billie Holiday, and Mary Lou Williams. On another page is Benny Goodman's autograph, with no indication of the date or place.

In the back pages of the autograph book, in the same careful printing, Loonis wrote lists: "bands, trios, singers (girls), singers (male)." He may have been listing the groups and performers he had heard in person, or perhaps the bands and musicians he liked best.

In addition to the sudden, dazzling abundance of great live music, life at East Carolina also meant more extensive access to recorded music. Loonis quickly discovered a record shop in Greenville that catered to the student market. He browsed there whenever he had time, learning more about music, songs, songwriters, and performers simply by reading the labels of the thick 78-rpm individual records, or the covers of the albums. The albums contained two or more records by the same performer, group, or orchestra, or perhaps a longer symphonic or operatic work divided into the three- or four-minute segments the individual records could accommodate.

From sampling the music in the record store, and from music he heard in person and on the radio, he would discover what he liked most. For Loonis, it was not so much the performers as the composers who attracted his attention.

"I would hear something I liked and then look for other songs by the same composer," he remembered. "I was always looking for anything by Harold Arlen or Alec Wilder. And when I found one, it was like Christmas."

When you're young and seriously smitten by music and eagerly discovering its mysteries and magic, hearing a single special song, a single recording, just three minutes of music, can be a transforming experience. You listen to it over and over again, probably more intensely than most people ever listen to music, and you will never forget it. The shape of the melody, the harmonic structure, the rhythms, and the lyrics, if it has lyrics, become a permanent part of the soundtrack of your hopes and daydreams and, later, your memories. That surely happened to Loonis a number of times, with a number of songs, probably beginning at an early age. He once described the experience as "opening a door to places you never knew existed, or had only dreamed about."

Of all those special songs, the one that probably was most special was on a record he heard during his last year at East Carolina.

On June 11, 1941, the great clarinetist and bandleader Benny Goodman, by then known as the "King of Swing," assembled fourteen other musicians and a singer in a New York studio to record a few songs. The Goodman orchestra in those days worked through occasional changes in personnel, but whatever the immediate configuration, the collective level of talent was extraordinary. Goodman's legendary demanding leadership style did not exactly endear him to all his musicians, but it drove them to near perfection as a unit. The group that day included Cootie Williams, Billy Butterfield, and Jimmy Maxwell on trumpets; Lou McGarity and Bob Cutshall on trombones; a saxophone section of Les Robinson, Pete Mondello, Skippy Martin, George Auld, and Gene Kinsey; a rhythm section of Mel Powell, piano, Charlie Christian, guitar, Walter Looss, bass, and Sidney Catlett, drums; with Goodman on clarinet. The singer was Helen Forrest.

One of the songs they recorded was "Soft as Spring," with words and music written by Alec Wilder. It was not one of Wilder's better-known songs. Unlike some of them, it did not become a "standard." In fact, it was one of his earliest songs, probably written at least ten years before Goodman made the first commercial recording of it.

Wilder, born in 1907, scion of a prominent New York banking family, had an essentially lonely childhood and endured an unhappy prep school education. In the late 1920s and early 1930s he was living on his trust fund and hanging out at the prestigious Eastman School of Music in his hometown of Rochester, New York. Although he never enrolled there, he audited some courses, befriended students and faculty members, debated music and aesthetics with them, wrote music, and generally made himself a familiar figure on the Eastman scene, and a particularly yeasty addition to its creative ferment. According to Desmond Stone's biography of Wilder, "Soft as Spring" was written during that period, when Wilder returned to the campus from a drive into the country with a friend. Quoting Wilder's recollection of that day, Stone wrote: " 'We stopped on an unpaved country road and just sat there. Lilacs were in full bloom beside a deserted farm, and a joyous chorus of birds were celebrating life and love. My friend and I almost thumbed our noses at old age and all such dreary impossibilities.' Back at Eastman, Wilder rushed down to the basement and wrote the tune in an empty practice room."

Even without knowing that history, a listener would immediately label "Soft as Spring" as the work of a young songwriter. It is unabashedly romantic, with a languid, dreamy melody and spring-morning imagery that together create a dewy, pastel effect. Yet the tune is also clearly the product of an already sophisticated musical intelligence working out its rapturous springtime impulses with the kind of restraint imposed by a mature, well-calibrated schmaltz detector.

When twenty-year-old Loonis McGlohon first heard the Goodman orchestra's 1941 recording of the song—one side of a 78-rpm record—its impact was considerable. Knowing something about how Loonis's musical taste developed, and having some familiarity with the songs he later wrote, and with other songs that influenced him, it is interesting and perhaps instructive to speculate about what made that song and that recording so special to him.

He already had heard some of Wilder's "serious" music—the octets that were rarely performed but made a powerful impression on some listeners, including Loonis. But as far as he could recall, years later, "Soft as Spring" was the first popular song by Wilder that he had heard. Wilder would become an important influence on his music and in his career, and eventually a cherished personal friend, but in 1941 Loonis had no idea—indeed, would not have dared dream—that he and Wilder would become friends and collaborators. No, there was something there and then—something, probably more than one thing, about the song itself, and the recording—that made it one of those door-opening experiences.

Loonis later described "Soft as Spring" as "a very hymn-like tune, very simple and pure." Like many of the songs Loonis himself would write over the years, it begins with a deceptive simplicity. Its opening phrase is patient, with only four notes in the first two bars, but there are subtle surprises to come. At the end of each of the repeated eight-bar themes, the melody takes some unexpected twists, and even more so during the bridge.

And there is a somewhat unexpected chord in the fourth bar. It is not a radical or particularly daring harmonic change. But at that point the chord progression could have moved comfortably and expectedly back through the tonic triad—the major chord that defines the key in which the song is written. Instead, Wilder chose the diminished form of the dominant chord of that key. The effect is subtly dramatic, and given Loonis's growing interest in alternative harmonies and chord substitutions, when he heard it he must have thought "Aha!"—or maybe even "Wow!"

The arrangement probably drew a similar reaction. "Soft as Spring" was one of a number of songs arranged that year for Goodman by Eddie Sauter, whose new ideas were transforming the sound of the Goodman band in much the same way as young Gil Evans's writing was creating renewed interest in the Claude Thornhill band. In his liner notes for a 1953 Columbia Records long-playing album reissue of the Goodman orchestra playing Eddie Sauter arrangements, jazz critic George Avakian described Sauter's impact on the Goodman band and on big band music generally: "With the advent of Eddie Sauter's arrangements in 1940, the Goodman band began intermixing of scores which might not have swung quite so much as the [Fletcher] Henderson arrangements, but which contained a new concept of how to use the instruments of a dance orchestra. . . . Sauter . . . introduced to the Goodman sound new voicings and harmonies which added depth and richness previously unknown to Benny's music—or anyone else's, for that matter."

When Loonis heard the Sauter arrangements for the first time, they surely began to resonate in his imagination. He must have been enchanted by the spare, subtle, spacious setting Sauter provided for the pure tone and willowy lyricism of Goodman's clarinet, and for Helen Forrest's straightforward vocal. What he was hearing must have struck him as the sound of the future, maybe his own future. And indeed it was. Sauter's arrangements were at the leading edge of what would become known over the next few years as "modern jazz," the genre that would become the primary influence on Loonis's playing.

And perhaps the appeal of the song for Loonis was as much personal as it was musical. Maybe it was, in fact, springtime when he first heard it, and springtime on a leafy college campus can make any music seem a bit magical. Maybe when "Soft as Spring" became the song he wanted to hear over and over and then could not get out of his mind, the spreading oaks shading the East Carolina campus were tender green, the flower beds in front of the women's dormitories were bright and fragrant, and the white magnolia blossoms were luminous in the warm twilight. That is only speculation, of course. We don't know what season it was when he first heard that record. But here's what we do know: Whatever the time of year, it was the springtime of his life, and "Soft as Spring" is a love song, and when he first heard it, Loonis McGlohon had just fallen in love—for sure, for real, forever.

Couples who went together sat on the icebox.

—Nan McGlohon

Nan : 6

At a rural crossroads in Edgecombe County, North Carolina, some thirty miles from Ayden and about midway between Greenville and Wilson, is a place called Greenacre, where a fine old white house sits well back from the highway across a green lawn shadowed by tall pines and shaded by pecan trees. Greenacre is part of a farming community called Crisp, most of whose residents, less than five hundred in all, are surnamed Lovelace or Eagles or are related to one or both of those families. The head of the household at Greenacre, circa 1920, was Edward Young Lovelace. As a young man he had come from Halifax, Virginia, to work in a tobacco warehouse in Wilson, North Carolina. Eventually he moved the fifteen or so miles east to Crisp, where he became a tobacco farmer and a cotton gin and sawmill operator. He married Francis Pitt Eagles, and they had three sons and three daughters. The youngest of the six, Nan Flournoy Lovelace, was born August 24, 1921.

It is a broad house with two stories plus an attic with gabled windows, and tall brick chimneys at each end that gave it a comfortable, classic symmetry. Across the road were a general store and the offices where Edward Lovelace ran his businesses. Anyone seeing the house and grounds would guess that it had been a wonderful place to grow up, and apparently, for Nan and the other children of Edward and Francis Lovelace, it was. Nan's memories of Greenacre and her family and neighbors have almost as much of a children's classic storybook quality as the name itself.

Along with Nan's parents and five siblings, another member of the Greenacre household was Gladys Albritton. She had been raised in an orphanage and had come to live in the Lovelace home before Nan was born. When Nan arrived, Gladys was twenty years old. A few years later she became a practical nurse, staying with new mothers and their babies for a few weeks after they returned home from the hospital. But she continued to live with the Lovelaces and was an important influence in Nan's childhood. Over the years Gladys would remain, in all but the most literal sense, part of the family, and a part of Nan's life.

In Crisp, as Nan later described it, "everybody was related to everybody else." Her maternal grandparents lived just across the highway. There were aunts and uncles and cousins in every direction, and relatives from out of town frequently visited Greenacre. With three brothers and two sisters in the house, and cousins living in almost every house within sight, there was never a problem of finding playmates.

"We always had a good time," Nan recalled. "We stayed busy, and we always had a lot of company."

There was no country club or community swimming pool, but the Lovelace brothers dug out a swimming hole in the creek that ran through the pasture behind the house. It was a most welcome amenity in the merciless heat of eastern North Carolina summers.

Frances Lovelace played the piano and had a beautiful singing voice. Nan took piano lessons for a couple of years, and as a teenager she sang in the choir in the small, white, wood-framed Eagles Baptist Church.

Nan attended Crisp elementary school and then South Edgecombe High School, which Crisp shared with the nearby communities of Pinetops and Macclesfield.

Her sisters had attended Meredith College, a highly regarded Baptist institution in Raleigh. But Raleigh held no particular attraction for Nan. She had been there a few times, primarily to go to the dentist who was correcting her overbite. When she finished South Edgecombe High and it was time to go away to college, Nan chose not to go too far—just eighteen miles away, to East Carolina. It turned out to be a fortunate decision by almost any measure.

Nan entered East Carolina in 1939 to pursue a degree in primary education. She soon found it, as she would always remember it, "a great school." It was a perfect size. Most of the fifteen hundred or so students soon knew each other, and some, including three who became Nan's best friends—her roommate, Margaret Broughton, and next-door roommates Lois Green and Virgil Ward—would stay in close touch for the rest of their lives. The leafy, oak-shaded campus, with its big, glossy green magnolia trees across the front lawn, handsome brick buildings and rows of camellia bushes in front of the women's dormitories, was in its own way as pleasant an environment as Greenacre, and considerably more stimulating. In addition to classes and classroom assignments, East Carolina offered an array of social and cultural activities. Almost all the students had dinner in the dining hall. Few could afford to eat anywhere else. Almost every night after dinner students would walk from the dining hall to the Wright Building, a combination gymnasium-auditorium that was the center of student extracurricular life. There they would play phonograph records and dance—to hit songs from Broadway shows, and a lot of big band swing music for jitterbugging. Because there were more young women than young men on those occasions, the informal dances were "girl-break"—that is, it was the girls' prerogative to break in on a dancing couple and take the place of the girl. After an hour or so of dancing, the students would stroll back to their dorms to study. They had to be in their rooms by 10 P.M. on weeknights. The curfew was a bit more lenient on weekends.

Military facilities across eastern North Carolina were increasingly busy as the nation prepared for the possibility of becoming involved in the war in Europe. The Greenville campus was a popular destination for young men in uniform—particularly from the Cherry Point marine base just over fifty miles away—on leave or weekend passes, looking for dates.

In addition to the nightly socials, there were formal dances each year, to which the men wore suits and ties and the women wore long evening dresses.

The Wright Building also was where Nan and her fellow students heard concerts and danced to some of the top bands of the era, including those led by Glenn Miller and Tommy Dorsey. And Eleanor Roosevelt spoke there. Nan's mother visited her on that occasion to hear the First Lady.

All of that must have seemed almost dazzling to a girl from Crisp, even one as bright and quick as Nan Lovelace. But Nan was a pretty strawberry blonde full of soft-spoken charm, and a lot of the young men around campus must have found her a bit dazzling, too. One who caught her eye, in return, was the boy with the curly red hair from nearby Ayden who was always playing the piano.

One day she was walking to class when she was stopped by an older woman who asked how to get to the library. After Nan pointed the way, the woman asked if Nan knew her son, who was a student there.

"You might have heard of him," the woman said. "Loonis McGlohon."

"The one who wrote the song for the play?"

"Yes, that's him."

"I've heard of him," Nan said, "but I haven't met him yet."

Soon after, she did meet him. He asked her to go to a dance, but she already had a date for the occasion. Later he asked her out again, and they began dating regularly.

Nan soon learned that dating Loonis McGlohon was not like dating most other young college men. Loonis was working his way through college and earning spending money by playing any paying gig he could get. On weekends, when most college couples were out having fun together, Loonis usually was playing piano for some event, or playing for a dance with Billy Knauff's band. But Loonis was different in other ways as well. Nan realized he was obviously very talented, and she appreciated his bright smile, his wit, and his great sense of humor. Unlike a lot of musicians, he was a good dancer. And he was very much a gentleman, and rarely in a bad mood.

So Nan and Loonis dated mostly on weeknights. They would talk in the parlor of her dormitory, Wilson Hall, or meet at the informal "girl-break" dances in the Wright Building. ("If I got mad at Loonis," Nan recalled, "none of my friends would break on him. He would be stuck with the same person.") Or they could walk to the movie theater or the drugstore.

In her sophomore year, a few months after they started dating, she found out how serious he was about their relationship. She had gone home for a weekend, and a young man she had dated in high school drove her back to the campus. Loonis saw them arrive and later, somewhat to her surprise, he expressed his displeasure at seeing them together, and his dislike of the young man. Along with that display of jealousy, Loonis also was a protective boyfriend. Although he was usually pleasant and polite and rarely spoke a harsh word to or about anyone, if someone used profanity in Nan's presence, Loonis would ask him not to use that kind of language "in front of my girl." Nan was impressed.

Behind Wilson Hall, beside the dining hall, was a large icebox, with a drinking fountain attached. The icebox somehow had attained a particular and unusual kind of significance for East Carolina students of that era: If a couple sat together on the icebox, it meant they "went together." As Nan recalled years later, "That's when people realized you were going steady." Soon after Loonis objected to Nan's catching a ride with an old high school boyfriend, Nan and Loonis began sitting on the icebox.

It was a profoundly innocent time to be young. Just a few years earlier it had been party time in America, an era of postwar exuberance, swift, astonishing accumulations of wealth, cultural experimentation, and artistic revolution. Young women had bobbed their hair, worn thigh-baring dresses, smoked, drunk illegal liquor, danced the Charleston, proclaimed their sexual emancipation, and generally thumbed their pretty noses at the mores and morals of their parents' generation. And just a couple of decades after Nan and Loonis passed through East Carolina, the birth control pill and other factors would launch a second sexual revolution, which accompanied a general youthful rebellion against traditional institutions and conventions. Generation gaps would cleave families and shred the fabric of American society. But between those excesses—between the Roaring Twenties and the traumatic Sixties—the Great Depression squelched the nation's flamboyant, rebellious spirits, and a battered middle America reasserted itself.

(For example, in response to the complaints of religious and other organizations to the salacious offerings of the Hollywood studios, and the even more salacious behavior of some of their star performers, the motion picture industry had cleaned up its act. It cleaned it so thoroughly that for the next thirty or forty years, married couples in movies always slept in twin beds, and lips remained sealed even during the most passionate on-screen kisses.)

So for Nan and Loonis and most of their fellow students, it was a sober and innocent time, but apparently no less exciting for that. Alcohol was not a major factor in student social life, on or off campus. College campuses were largely free of illegal drugs and would remain that way for more than twenty years. Nan and the other young women at East Carolina wore proper dresses and skirts to class and on campus. By most accounts, few students were sexually active. Kissing was serious business. Cigarettes were the great vice among the ladies of East Carolina College. "We smoked," said Nan's friend Lois Green Brown, when asked if she and her friends ever did anything "sinful" while they were in college. "We smoked in the dorm room, we smoked in the bathroom," she confessed.

If there appeared to be some conflict between the innocence of their college generation, and the darker, edgier environment of the jazz scene in which Loonis was increasingly immersed, it seems to have been no problem for Nan and Loonis. For Loonis, the attraction of the jazz scene was not about lifestyle or rebellion; it was about music. For Nan, it was about Loonis, which meant it was about music for her, too.

One weekend Nan went to a resort town on the North Carolina coast where Loonis was playing in a band in a beachfront dance pavilion. After the band had finished playing for the night, Loonis and Nan walked on the dark beach, the damp wind in their faces. Maybe the sky was full of stars, or maybe there was moonlight on the ocean. Or maybe not. Either would have been nice, but it would not have made any difference. They paused, and Loonis said, "I love you, Nan." It was the first time he had said that to her.

"I love you, too, Loonis," she said.

They stayed a long time on the beach that night.

Beyond the sheltering environment of the campus and the happy distractions of student life were the grim realities of lingering economic depression and the growing probability of American involvement in the war spreading across Europe. Those were among the hazards that awaited Nan and Loonis and their classmates as they moved toward graduation.

President Roosevelt's New Deal was creating a priceless legacy across the nation: building schools, hospitals, theaters, and other important facilities; sponsoring useful conservation projects; providing opportunities for artists of all kinds to pursue their visions, which would enrich the national culture and lift the spirits of the people both then and for generations to come. It was putting a lot of unemployed people back to work, and for a while it had raised the nation's hopes for economic recovery. It marked a permanent transformation in American politics and government. But for all the good it was doing, it had not achieved its ultimate goal, which was to revive the national economy. There were encouraging signs of progress in the late 1930s, but as a new decade began, businesses and farms continued to fail in North Carolina and elsewhere, and many thousands of Americans still struggled to survive.

Across the Atlantic, Germany, defeated in the first world war just a couple of decades earlier, had rebuilt its military power. On their radios and in their newspapers, Americans learned of the Nazi regime's swift and brutal conquests of its neighbors. They heard and read analyses of the European crisis and speculation about the possibility of American involvement. They listened to debates between those commentators and politicians who insisted it was not and should not be America's war, and those who warned against a false sense of security and said America could not simply sit back and do nothing as a ranting dictator took over an entire continent. On newsreels in movie theaters Americans saw ominous, frightening images—goose-stepping German troops on parade, and thousands of German people massed in the streets, cheering the inflamed rhetoric of Adolf Hitler, whom Americans increasingly viewed as a charismatic but evil madman.

By the fall of 1940, as Loonis McGlohon and Nan Lovelace began sitting together on a significant icebox on a small college campus in eastern North Carolina, German warplanes were bombing England, America's mother country, a people with whom Americans shared language, lineage, and a priceless heritage of human rights and political freedoms. It was increasingly obvious that the United States would have to go to war, and soon. In September of that year, the U.S. Congress had voted to authorize the first peacetime military draft in the nation's history.

For college graduates of the early 1940s, the future seemed to offer an unhappy choice between graduation into a feeble economy that offered little opportunity for good jobs or, at least for the men, going abroad to fight a war from which they might never return. But Nan and Loonis would remember it as a happy, hopeful time. When you are lucky enough to be young, in college and in love, it is probably easier than it ever will be again to live in the present. You can change the world when your time comes, if it needs changing. For now the future is somewhere out there, beyond your control, and in any case it may change before you get there. If you make plans, you make them based on your own hopes and dreams, your perhaps naive confidence in your own talent and intelligence and determination, all of which seem to define the future more reliably than a stubbornly stalled economic cycle or the aggressions of a distant tyrant.

So Nan and Loonis made at least tentative plans. They began talking about getting married—eventually. First Loonis had to finish college and graduate, and it seemed likely that when he did he would be facing military service. Nan assumed all plans were on hold until the war was over—or at least until Loonis's part in it was over. And who could know what might happen by then?

But on a summer evening in 1941—they both were in summer school that year—they were sitting beside a pond behind the home of their friends Marguerite and Billy Knauff when Loonis presented Nan with a diamond engagement ring. Surprised and delighted, she rushed inside to show the ring to Marguerite. Marguerite had already seen it. She had helped Loonis pick it out.

While Americans watched the ominous events in Europe, the decisive impetus for American involvement in a second world war came from the other direction, when the Japanese attacked the U.S. Pacific Fleet at Pearl Harbor, in Hawaii, on December 7, 1941. Loonis was drafted but got a deferment to finish college. When he received his degree in the early summer of 1942, his father, mother, and fiancée took him straight from commencement exercises to the bus that would carry him a hundred miles or so southwest, into the central North Carolina sandhills and pine forests, to Fort Bragg. There, for a few hot, miserable weeks he would learn the basic skills of a soldier—which, as it turned out, he would not need. Loonis would serve his country for the duration of the war but, appropriately, as a musician, not as a warrior.

Early the following summer, on a ten-day leave, Loonis returned to North Carolina to marry Nan. The ceremony was held at 5 P.M. on June 19, 1943, in Crisp, in the small, hot, humid sanctuary of Eagles Baptist Church. With his curly red hair, Loonis appeared very much at home with the Lovelace family. All of Nan's brothers had the same kind of curly red hair. The resemblance prompted one of her mother's friends at the wedding to say, "Oh my, she's marrying her brother!"

The *Ayden Dispatch* reported that the bride wore "a wedding gown of white Chantilly lace and maline. The skirt fell in folds forming a train. Her fingertip veil of illusion was draped from a tiara of Chantilly lace and satin. She carried a white prayer book on which a white orchid showered with baby's breath and stephanotis was fastened."

Film was scarce because of the war, and there were no pictures taken of the wedding. A friend from Rocky Mount had one roll of film, and from that there would be one photographic record of the day, a picture of Loonis and Nan on the steps of the Lovelace home.

The bride and groom had little time for postwedding festivities. They were
showered with rice as they left Greenacre and headed for Rocky Mount to catch a
7 P.M. train to Richmond, Virginia, where they had reservations at the elegant Jefferson Hotel. The train was packed with soldiers. As it headed north in the summer
twilight, Nan and Loonis were sitting on their suitcases, which would be their only
seats for the rest of the trip—except during dinner. They lingered in the dining car
until they were asked to leave to make room for other diners. Part of Nan's wedding
trip wardrobe was a white straw hat. Every time she moved her head, rice fell from
the hat. People noticed, and smiled. Finally she took the hat off.

Somewhere between Rocky Mount and Richmond the train stopped. As Nan
and Loonis later recalled, it "broke down." By the time it was moving again, it was
hours behind schedule. Nan and Loonis finally reached the Jefferson Hotel at
about 2 A.M. By then the hotel had decided the McGlohons weren't going to show
up, and had cancelled their reservations.

But wait—there was a room available. Mr. and Mrs. McGlohon could stay there after all. Their protracted wedding day finally ended.

In that same year, by the way, Loonis's favorite composer, Alec Wilder, collaborated with Mortimer Palitz and lyricist William Engvick to create one of the finest songs ever written, "While We're Young." It ends with this affirmation:

> So blue the skies,
> All sweet surprise
> Shines before our eyes
> While we're young.

Sixty years later, there seem to be very few true honeymoons anymore. But anyone who knew Nan and Loonis would have no doubt that theirs—for three days and nights of sweet surprise in June 1943, in a fine hotel in Richmond—was the real thing.

Making a Life : II

It was the only time I've ever had a tan.

—Nan McGlohon

The Wild Blue Yonder : 7

During World War II it was not unusual for the army and navy to divert talented athletes, entertainers, and musicians from other military duties, including combat. Their abilities were put to use, on the home front and abroad, boosting morale and spirit among the troops and encouraging patriotism and support for the war effort through the media and in personal appearances.

When Spence Hatley was drafted, he became part of a military band organized by a warrant officer named Leo Driggers. Hatley told Driggers that it was the worst band he had ever heard. If you want a real band, Hatley said, you've got to get some real musicians, and I know some you can get.

Driggers apparently had influence in high places, and in the summer of 1942 he began to get some of the musicians on Hatley's list transferred from other bases around the country to join the band, which was assigned to the 345th Army Air Force training field in Marianna, Florida. One of the draftees transferred was Loonis McGlohon, who was in basic training with a field artillery unit at Fort Bragg.

When Loonis was called into the sergeant major's office and told he was being transferred to an air base in the Florida Panhandle, he knew nothing about what had happened. But he was pleased to be leaving the field artillery, and even more pleased when he learned he was being assigned to a band.

Accommodations at Marianna were in temporary, unpainted structures scattered through a grove of very large, old pecan trees draped with Spanish moss. Loonis thought the moss hanging from the old tree limbs and the raw buildings in the deep shade created a rather eerie ambience.

The fifty or so musicians there staffed four musical units: a large marching band, a large concert band, an eighteen-piece dance band, and a five-piece combo. Loonis played clarinet in the marching band, glockenspiel in the concert band, and piano in the dance band and quintet. The dance band played for special dances at the Officers' Club, and the quintet played there every other Saturday night. Members of the dance band and the combo were fitted with tuxedos by a tailor Driggers brought in from New York. The concert band played for occasional rallies in nearby communities to promote the sale of war bonds.

A few months after Loonis and Nan were married, Loonis found a small apartment just outside the base, within easy walking distance of the barracks. In the early fall of 1943 Nan joined him at Marianna. She got a job teaching kindergarten in a day care center for children of military couples. Loonis spent most nights at the apartment and reported to the barracks early each morning.

Despite their duties at the Officers' Club and at bond rallies, most of the time the musicians had little or nothing to do. The marching band, which was the primary justification for the large number of musicians on hand, rarely performed. As a result of that inactivity, officers in charge of the base began removing some of the musicians and assigning them to other duties. But Warrant Officer Driggers was resourceful, and he found ways to bring in new musicians to replace those who were transferred.

Often when creative young people are gathered in one place for an extended period without enough to do, they become bored and eventually busy themselves with activities of their own design. The turnover in the band's ranks gave Loonis, Hatley, and a few others an opportunity to exercise their creativity in ways that the Army Air Force never intended. They decided to "initiate" the new musical recruits.

The first to be initiated was a young man named Ronnie Graham, a jazz enthusiast who played piano. Loonis and his co-conspirators decided to pretend they were fans of country and western music, a genre that in those days was an anathema to most jazz fans. They found some country and western records, and through the day and evening they would play the records and talk about the country and western stars. Graham quickly decided that he had landed in the middle of a bunch of hillbillies, and he began trying to find someone in the group with whom he might have more in common, at least musically. But everyone was in on the game. Every time Graham would approach someone he had not already identified as a country and western enthusiast, that person would immediately ask Graham which country singer was his favorite, and had he heard some new country and western recording. Graham finally concluded that everyone in the barracks was a country music fanatic. The twanging music and the endless idolatrous chatter about country singers soon got on his nerves.

Finally they told him, much to his relief, that they were just playing a joke to initiate him into the band. Relieved, Graham complimented them on their performance. They were subtle, he said, making it all seem very natural at first, and then as he kept trying to find someone who wasn't a country music fan, he gradually began to feel it was all some kind of bad dream.

Graham was eager to help with the next initiation, and he turned out to be the most creative prankster of all. With his help, the initiation tricks became considerably more complex. The initiation team began devising scenarios that would convince a newcomer that everyone in the unit was crazy—and eventually cause him to doubt his own sanity.

For example, when a new recruit named Battinger, a trumpet player, arrived late one afternoon and was being introduced to everyone, he found that one of the musicians he met, named Luther Fricks, had a pair of silk stockings hanging above his bunk. (Loonis had "borrowed" them from Nan, and given the scarcity of silk stockings during the war, she was not pleased when she found out.) Fricks was standing by his bunk stroking the stockings and inviting others to stroke them. Battinger declined.

The weather was warm that night, and all the windows in the barracks were open. When Battinger went to bed, about 10 P.M., a violin player began walking back and forth outside the barracks, underneath the pecan trees and the Spanish moss, playing "Hearts and Flowers," very out of tune. No one except Battinger seemed to notice. Everyone acted as though it was quite ordinary.

A few hours later another band member stumbled into the barracks, waking everyone. He was dragging an automobile axle that appeared to have matted hair and blood on one end. "I killed me another MP tonight," he said. Ronnie Graham, who could shed tears at will, began to cry. Otherwise, nobody seemed concerned about the fate of the MP.

The next morning when the first sergeant came into the barracks, Loonis was searching for his wallet. Someone must have stolen it, Loonis said. The first sergeant asked how much money was in the wallet. Fifty dollars, Loonis said. All right, said the first sergeant: Everybody up by his bunk for inspection. He walked down the row of bunks, asking each person if he knew anything about Loonis's wallet, and lifting each mattress to look underneath. En route he declined an invitation to stroke Fricks's silk stockings. When he got to Battinger, the newcomer obviously was outraged that he might be a suspect. But the first sergeant, who was playing his role to perfection, gave Battinger a knowing nod, as if to say, don't worry about this, everybody here is nuts except you and me.

Next to Battinger was the bunk of a vibraphone player named Watson Klincewicz, known as Klink. The first sergeant lifted the mattress and found Loonis's wallet and two others. The first sergeant was in on the game, of course. He said, "That's not nice, Klink. These are your friends. You don't do that to friends. It's not nice."

Ronnie Graham wept and agreed that what Klink had done wasn't very nice.

Battinger was furious. "What kind of place is this?" he asked. "You've got a kleptomaniac in here and all you do is tell him it's not nice?"

The conspirators realized if Battinger got away from the group by himself he might start talking to someone about what was going on in the band, so later that day they told him they weren't allowed to go to the PX by themselves. They were required to go together, in formation. If you needed razor blades or cigarettes or anything else from the PX, you had to wait for the group trip.

A short while later, when the first sergeant lined everyone up for a march to the PX, he told them, "If any of you get ice cream today, it has to be tootie fruitie. No chocolate, vanilla, or strawberry. Everybody has to get the same thing. If everybody asks for something different, there are so many of us it will just confuse the girl there. So today it's tootie fruitie."

Meanwhile, someone asked Battinger where he had lived in Atlanta. Battinger explained that he had never lived in Atlanta, had never even been to Atlanta. A little later someone else asked Battinger if he missed Atlanta. Again, Battinger denied any knowledge of Atlanta.

Every day at mail call Graham would weep and wail because he had no mail from his family. Each night the violin player walked beneath the pecan trees, playing "Hearts and Flowers" out of tune. During the day he would talk about the job waiting for him with the Metropolitan Opera after the war.

Another band member collected twigs for several days and built a fort with them, just outside the barracks door. Then he set fire to the fort and squatted beside it, warming his hands.

A guitar player took a shower and put his clothes on without drying himself, so that he appeared to be soaked with sweat. He put some toothpaste in his mouth. Standing just outside the barracks, he began foaming at the mouth, as though he were having some kind of seizure. Battinger saw him and shouted that someone should get a spoon to keep the man from swallowing his tongue. But someone else said no, leave him alone, he enjoys this.

Over the next couple of days Battinger began looking in vain for somebody in the band who was normal. A clarinet player named Artie had been assigned to stay aloof from all the strangeness, so Battinger decided Artie might be sane. The next time he had an opportunity to approach Artie when nobody else was close enough to hear, Battinger asked him if he found the other guys a little strange. Artie ignored the question and interrupted.

"Do you like steam?" Artie asked.

"What?"

"Steam. Do you like steam?"

"Steam?"

Artie took a quick glance around the room. "There's nobody looking," he told Battinger. "Let's go down to the latrine and stoke the boiler and put some coal in it until it goes like this—whoosh!—and you see all that steam come out."

An army veterinarian, Captain Swale, lived next door to the McGlohons, and although officers and enlisted men weren't supposed to socialize, he and Loonis became friends. When Loonis told the captain about the tricks being played by the band members, Swale said he didn't believe him. Loonis offered to demonstrate, and asked if he would like to help.

Loonis and the other pranksters realized Battinger at some point was likely to go to one of the officers and describe what was going on, and that might lead to some kind of inquiry or inspection. To preempt that possibility, Loonis recruited Captain Swale to play the role of a psychiatrist who periodically inspected the unit. Loonis drew the captain a diagram of the barracks, indicating the name of the person at each bunk, and what each person's problem was: kleptomania, silk stocking fetish, seizures, uncontrollable weeping, whatever.

On the day of Dr. Swale's inspection, each of them stood by his bunk, and Swale stopped and talked with each one. He asked Ronnie Graham if he had heard from his family, and Graham started crying and said he had not. Swale asked Fricks where he got those beautiful silk stockings.

When he got to Battinger the doctor said, "I'm sorry, your name is . . . ?"

"Sergeant Battinger, sir."

"Oh, yes. Battinger," said Swale. "You were transferred here from Atlanta."

All of Battinger's pent-up confusion and anger exploded. "I'm not from Atlanta," he screamed. "I've never been to Atlanta."

"Yes, I understand," said Dr. Swale, soothingly. "Obviously there are some unpleasant memories from Atlanta that you aren't ready to face. But we really need to talk about how you can get that anger under control."

Now Battinger looked as if something in his head was about to snap. The group decided they had pushed him far enough. They explained what was going on.

Soon Battinger was ready to help initiate the next unsuspecting new arrival.

Their three years in Florida were a pleasant time for the newlywed McGlohons. They didn't have a car, but when Loonis had a weekend off they usually could get a ride with another couple to one of the nearby Gulf Coast beaches. Nan, who al-

ways had tried to keep her redhead's pale ivory complexion out of the sun, got into the spirit of Florida living and found herself for the first time in her life with a suntan. Or maybe it was just an increase in the density of her freckles.

They made one trip home to North Carolina. Once, when Loonis had a three-day pass, they went to New Orleans, and on another extended leave they took the train to New York City. It was in early May, and still cold in the Northeast. The change from Florida weather to the chilly streets of New York was a shock, and they didn't have the right kind of clothes to keep them warm. Walking around on Broadway, they would stop and stand outside the doors of a theater to catch some of the warm air when the show was over and everyone was coming out. They saw a couple of Broadway shows and, of course, went to a few jazz clubs, where a musical revolution was underway.

His musical service in the Air Corps also provided some valuable musical experience for Loonis. In the small combo and dance band he polished his piano skills. He was rehearsing and playing with, and learning from, other talented musicians, and he had opportunities to try his hand at arranging. His relationships with the other musicians would be of value in later years, providing musical contacts across the country.

After the war a number of the musicians from Marianna went on to jobs with major jazz bands operating out of New York and Los Angeles. Ronnie Graham became an actor and screenwriter, and the in 1970s he wrote a number of episodes —and appeared in a few—of the hit television series *M*A*S*H,* an irreverent comedy about doctors and nurses in a field hospital during the Korean War. His experiences at Marianna, and the antics of his colleagues there, obviously influenced some of his contributions to *M*A*S*H.*

Loonis got a job with a big band being organized in New York City, but before claiming his place in that organization, he visited Billy Knauff in Charlotte. The visit lasted longer than he had intended, and Nan joined him there, and their plans took a detour that became permanent. They never got to New York.

If swing was jazz that went to the public with open arms,
bebop was jazz that seemed to have turned its back on its audience.
—John Fordham, in *Jazz*

Bebop : 8

In the early 1940s, while Loonis, Spence Hatley, Ronnie Graham, and others were at Marianna, a few jazz musicians who hadn't been drafted, most of them black, and mostly in Harlem, were playing new and controversial rhythms and harmonies. Some of that new music was being recorded on new and still obscure labels, and a few of those records made it all the way to the barracks at Marianna. It was a sound that challenged the imaginations of the best of the young musicians there, including Loonis.

Reflecting the austerity of wartime, the new music was being created mostly by small groups instead of big bands—two or three horns at most, with a rhythm section of piano, bass, and drums, and sometimes a guitar. That meant lower costs for club owners. It also meant less financial, administrative, and logistical problems, and more flexibility, for bandleaders. A quintet could be put together on short notice, and different musicians might rotate on and off a particular band, depending on who was available. The arrangements were shorter and the improvised solos were longer, so less rehearsal was required. The focus narrowed from a collective style and sound to individual creativity and virtuosity.

An even more important change from the big band era was in the content of the music. It was, like much of the jazz that preceded it, built on the blues and on the great popular songs of the first half of the century, and played against a standard 4/4 beat. But within that beat the musicians shifted the accents in new and eccentric ways, and they stretched and embellished the harmonic fabric of traditional blues and standard tunes. They extended the intervals of the chords from the usual basic triads and sevenths out to ninths, elevenths, and beyond, which created a more dissonant sound and a larger framework for improvisation. They inserted more "passing" chords into the existing structure, requiring faster changes, making the music more difficult to play and creating a richer, denser texture. And in some cases they substituted different chords for the ones in the original compositions. Those more complex rhythmic and harmonic structures challenged the improvising musician, pushing him farther away from the original melodies and traditional variations and clichés.

The result was an aggressively modern, vigorous, almost startling music. It could be almost unbearably intense, or relaxed and playful. It could be exquisitely lyrical without being sweet or sentimental. At times it seemed to approach the aural equivalent of a nervous breakdown.

It became known as bebop. There is no consensus about the origin of the term. Perhaps it was coined by one of the handful of young jazz critics who were aware of the new music and were writing about it in publications such as *Down Beat* and *Metronome*. Maybe it was a fragment broken out of a bit of scat singing. Whatever the source, the term was a good fit, and it stuck. It echoed the rhythmic eccentricity of the music. It was as if, in its two syllables, with the stress on the first, the essence or spirit of the music was distilled into a single word.

Bebop evolved from the restless experimentation of a number of musicians, perhaps beginning as early as the late 1930s, and certainly underway by 1941. Emerging as the leaders of the movement by the early 1940s were a handful of extraordinarily talented musicians, including the alto saxophonist Charlie Parker, known as Yardbird, or simply Bird; the South Carolina–born, North Carolina–educated trumpeter John Birks "Dizzy" Gillespie; and pianists Thelonious Monk (born in Rocky Mount, North Carolina), Al Haig (who was white), and Earl "Bud" Powell. In those years they were in and out of big bands and in and out of Harlem, where they played in various combos and in various clubs along Fifty-second Street, often moving after the last set to another club to jam until dawn.

They played for pay, but they also played for the sheer excitement of being on the edge of something new, and their late-night energy and creativity were often fueled by drugs, alcohol, or both. Some, like Gillespie, avoided the excessively self-destructive behavior. Others, like Parker, an authentic genius and a musician of stunning conceptual as well as technical virtuosity, effectively committed slow suicide and died young.

There probably were several motivating factors in the creation of bebop. The primary innovators were gifted musicians who were tired of the restrictions of big band arrangements with limited solo opportunities. They were tired of playing the same "hits" audiences wanted to hear every night. They wanted more space and freedom for self-expression.

Some musical and social historians believe bebop was a reaction to racism in the musical marketplace—more specifically, to the successful white exploitation of swing, a music created primarily by black musicians out of the African American experience and African American culture. In a society where racial segregation and discrimination were still the norm, white musicians had access to more up-scale venues and white audiences, and thus to more lucrative concert, recording, and broadcasting contracts. While many of the black musicians who created swing struggled to make a living with their music, the white musicians who copied them —the great white bands of Benny Goodman, the Dorsey brothers, and Artie Shaw, for example—were prospering. So the black creators of bebop were moving beyond swing. They set out to play something too difficult for white musicians to copy. And although there were white musicians capable of playing the new style, there also were a lot of competent swing players who could not, or were not willing to do the hard work of learning it.

The beboppers also seemed to deliberately defy many of the conventions of commercial jazz. Although some customers danced to some bebop, a lot of the music was played at tempos too fast for dancing. And there was no pandering to the audience. They were playing music to please themselves and to impress their colleagues. The listeners could make what they would of it.

Bebop began as a sort of in-group cult music, in part because it was played primarily in a small area of New York City. Also, the American Federation of Musicians, demanding better pay for its members, shut down the recording industry for a couple of years in the early 1940s, at the precise time bebop was ripe for recording. So it was music played for musicians, and for a relatively small coterie of enthusiasts, some of whom understood and were moved by the music, and others who simply wanted to be "in," or part of the latest "scene."

The record industry was back in business in 1944, and a few small, pioneering labels began recording the new music. In 1945, Gillespie and Parker led a small group in an engagement at a club called the Three Deuces—an occasion that, according to Ira Gitler, in his book *Swing to Bop,* "made history." Concerts at Town Hall in the spring of that year further exposed the new music and its most celebrated practitioners.

It was about that same time that Loonis and Nan made a trip to New York and heard the new music as played by Bird and Dizzy at the Three Deuces. Loonis was awed by the virtuosity of the players, and the music was like a new language to be learned. Just as he had sensed that the Eddie Sauter arrangements for Benny Goodman a few years earlier foreshadowed the direction his music needed to go, he recognized that the new music called bebop represented another test he would have to pass in order to get where he wanted to be.

(As much as he was impressed by the technical skill and ideas of the beboppers, Loonis was also "knocked out," as he later described it, by the intermission pianist, a young man newly arrived from England who happened to be blind. His name was George Shearing, and years later he and Loonis would become close friends.)

But as awareness of the new music filtered out across the country, bebop—not only the music, but also the sartorial tastes of the hipsters, and the vernacular that developed among jazz musicians of the time—became the subject of satirical and even mocking treatment in the national media. It was not very popular, and the people who played it didn't seem to care. Even the jazz genre itself soon moved beyond bebop, using bebop innovations in more accessible forms—at first primarily West Coast or "cool" jazz, a softer, more relaxed version of bebop that was, compared to the original, relatively easy listening.

But that is the beginning of another story, about the transformation of the popular music business over the next two decades. The point for now is that bebop is an important part of the story of Loonis McGlohon and his career, for at least two reasons.

First, although Loonis was never categorized as a bebop musician, he and almost every other musician in the second half of the twentieth century who played jazz, or played or wrote popular music in a style influenced by jazz, used a harmonic and melodic language expanded and enriched by bebop. It is hard to imagine Loonis writing "The Wine of May" or "Songbird," for example, without the influence of bebop.

Second, bebop was one important factor in the eventual declining popularity of jazz. The music Loonis learned to play in high school and college was America's popular music, a genre that dominated the hit parade and the lists of best-selling sheet music and records. By the time he became an adult seeking to make at least part of his living as a musician, the music he played was still popular on college campuses and among the generation that had come home from the battlefields of World War II, but it was increasingly being relegated to a niche. It was, to be sure, a rather large and important niche, in which blues and popular music had converged to create a true American art form. But in terms of popularity and commercial viability, it was a niche—and a shrinking niche.

Meanwhile, its rejection by the mass audience notwithstanding, bebop was ultimately irresistible. Even as bebop, as a term, a category, an image, all but disappeared from America's cultural consciousness, the music itself infiltrated the larger soundtrack of American life. It influenced almost every subsequent kind of music, not only in the various directions jazz evolved, but also rock music, lounge music, retro pop music, Broadway music, and elevator music. You hear its echoes in film scores, in theme music for television dramas, in television commercials. You sometimes hear it in the background music piped into offices, department stores, and restaurants. Most important, you hear it in almost all the "serious" music composed since its supposed demise. The uncompromising innovators who created and played it in the 1940s, for their own excitement and for a tiny audience that never really grew much beyond the capacity of those smoky, shoebox jazz clubs on Fifty-second Street, would be astonished at its ubiquity more than half a century later.

In 1954, when Charlie Parker died at the age of thirty-four, the graffiti immediately began appearing in Harlem and elsewhere: "Bird Lives." Indeed. The amazing thing is, almost half a century later, he still does, and so does bebop.

Somewhere there are bright lights,
You don't have to go too far . . .
But I like it here, I like it here.
—"I Like It Here," words and
music by Loonis McGlohon

Charlotte : 9

It was 1946, and Loonis, honorably discharged from military service, was planning to go to New York City. A group of musicians had split off from bandleader Tony Pastor to form a new band, and through an agent they had offered Loonis a job. He accepted the offer. He would go to New York, find an apartment, and Nan would join him there. Then he would go on the road with the band and make his living as a musician. A few years earlier that would have seemed like a dream coming true. But now there were other dreams, and second thoughts.

Billy and Marguerite Knauff had moved to Charlotte, where Knauff had taken a job with the postal service and was putting together a dance band. He was finding a number of good musicians returning home to the Carolinas after duty in military bands. Many of them were looking for opportunities to play but also wanted to settle down and didn't want to go on the road. Knauff had a "day job" and didn't plan to tour. With his band they could not earn a living, but they could make some extra money playing close to home, in Charlotte and around the Carolinas. As Loonis was getting ready to go to New York, Knauff telephoned him and asked him to come to Charlotte for a few days to help him organize and rehearse his new band. Loonis agreed to come for a weekend.

He moved in with the Knauffs, worked with the band, and stayed longer than he had planned. Knauff persuaded him to extend the visit even farther and invite Nan to join him. Loonis played a few gigs with the band, and at the Knauffs' urging he and Nan began to think about staying in Charlotte instead of going to New York.

Like so many bright young people who had gone from small southern towns to college and seen enough of the wider world to whet their ambitions, neither Nan nor Loonis apparently gave much thought to returning home to live. There were few economic, social, or cultural opportunities to lure them back to Ayden or Crisp, except as visitors. But they valued their roots and were not at all inclined to disavow where they came from, or its shaping influence. Nor were they inclined to move any farther from those roots than opportunity and ambition might require.

Both of them had grown up surrounded by large extended families, and family was important to them. Nan and Loonis wanted children, and they wanted their children to grow up, as they had, connected securely to family and place. Their backgrounds were small-town and southern, imbued with certain regional values and attitudes. The subsequent popularization of humorous and sentimental stereotypes of small-town southern life—the fictional Mayberry on television, for example—ignored some unpleasant realities, but in other respects much of it was quite realistic. There was a gentleness in personal relationships, a relaxed pace of life, a sense of community, and of responsibility for each other.

Some of that stereotypical southern way of life was a consequence of the hot, humid climate from late spring to midautumn (and nothing was air-conditioned in 1946). Some of it persisted from a traditionally agricultural economy, attuned to the rhythms and whims of nature and the sequence of changing seasons, which were not subject to acceleration in the service of commerce. Other differences are not as easy to explain. Whatever the reasons, there was a more patient tempo, and a soft buffer of courtesy and tolerance in relationships between individuals, whether friends or strangers, white or black. Even in passing encounters between busy strangers there was time for eye contact and an exchange of friendly greetings. There was respect for the dignity and wisdom of age, and reverence for traditions, religious and secular.

All of those blessings and benevolences of life in the American South were undermined to some extent by widespread, persistent poverty, and most of all tarnished by the terrible sin of racism. In those early postwar years the South and many of its defining characteristics were about to be transformed, for better and for worse, by industrialization, technology, education, and social revolution. But growing up southern in the first half of the century could shape people's hopes for the future in very different ways, depending on their race and circumstances. Nan and Loonis probably were readier than most white southerners in the late 1940s to move beyond the shameful heritage of slavery and away from racism and discrimination. But other than that, growing up southern had left them a lot of emotional and cultural baggage that was no burden at all, and that they had no desire to unload.

That baggage was part of what was weighing Loonis down as he contemplated leaving for New York. And it was part of what made Nan and him feel at home rather quickly in Charlotte, although it was a long way, and not just in miles, from Ayden and Crisp.

Charlotte was in their home state, but neither of them had been there before their visit to the Knauffs. It was the largest city in the Carolinas, and according to the 1940 census its population had edged past the 100,000 milestone, to the applause of the chamber of commerce and other civic boosters. It sat in a gentle rolling piedmont landscape just a few miles from the South Carolina line; it was about midway between the state's eastern tip, which jutted into the Atlantic Ocean, and its western flank in the Appalachian Mountains. Just two hours to the west, and in those days visible in clear weather, were the Blue Ridge Mountains. Just four hours east were barrier islands and beaches.

Charlotte itself had no seaport or navigable river to attract commerce, and no beaches or scenic mountain vistas to attract tourists. But it seemed that the lack of those natural assets only made the city more determined to amount to something.

What it did have were significant transportation connections, an economically advantageous location, a strong manufacturing base within its own borders, and an even more important, growing ring of manufacturing facilities in the surrounding region. Running through the center of the city was U.S. Highway 29, which stretched from Washington, D.C. to Atlanta and in those days, before the construction of the interstate highway system, was called the "main street of the South." Alongside that major highway was the main line of the Southern Railway. On the edge of town was a small airport. Those connections made Charlotte an important regional distribution center by truck, rail, and air. Plants in smaller communities within sixty miles or so of Charlotte produced much of the nation's textile products and furniture. Charlotte provided financial, accounting, and other professional services, as well as a shipping and receiving hub for that growing two-state regional manufacturing economy. With three significant hospitals and a growing medical community, Charlotte was also a regional center for health care. Its bustling downtown business district featured a few buildings that, without stretching things too much, could be described as skyscrapers. Downtown's big department stores and elegant specialty shops made it the shopping center of the region.

Most important for Loonis were the city's communications industry and its limited but lively entertainment scene. Charlotte was home to the South's first radio station, WBT, which broadcast news and entertainment across the region. As a pioneer in radio, Charlotte also had become a significant broadcasting and recording center for the Southeast's indigenous country and bluegrass music.

People came to Charlotte from across the region to see first-run movies and stage shows at downtown theaters, for live entertainment at the Armory Auditorium, and to cheer for the city's minor league professional baseball and football teams.

There were two good newspapers—the afternoon *Charlotte News* and the morning *Charlotte Observer*. The *Observer*'s out-of-town circulation rivaled its in-town numbers and was another element linking the city to the surrounding region.

Although it would be many years before a dining establishment in North Carolina would be able legally to sell liquor by the drink, "brown bagging" and beer and wine were legal, and Charlotte had several nightclubs and supper clubs that employed jazz musicians.

Charlotte was not New York City, nor was it Ayden or Crisp or Greenville. For Loonis, it must have seemed a compromise of sorts, and it was appealing in other ways as well.

The end of the war brought sighs of relief, prayers of thanks and cheers of victory, and young men returning home to marry sweethearts and create families and earn a living in a nation converting its awesome wartime capacity of human and material resources to peacetime uses. In that national environment, Charlotte had an aura of expectation, ambition, and opportunity, an urban energy that appealed to young people looking for a place to plant roots and build careers. At the same time, it was still very much a southern city, where most people talked rather slowly, softly, and sweetly, even when they talked business.

Loonis's few days in Charlotte stretched to a few weeks. The Knauffs' home was a five- or six-room house on Cumberland Avenue, shared with Marguerite's invalid mother, an aunt, and the three Knauff children, so when Loonis and Nan were there it was a tight fit. Nan returned home after a short visit, then traveled back and forth a few more times, waiting for Loonis to make a decision. Loonis called the agent in New York and asked if he could have a couple of weeks more before reporting for work. The agent said the band had to have a piano player right away; either come on now, he said, or forget it.

Knauff urged him to forget it and stay in Charlotte and play with his band. Loonis would need a day job, of course. What he earned on weekend engagements with the band was a lot less than a living. And he and Nan would need a place to live. Knauff said he could help Loonis get a job at WBT radio. He knew some people there, including the boss, Charles Crutchfield.

Finding an apartment turned out to be more difficult than finding a job. Charlotte was flooded with people coming home from military service and with young people moving in from the surrounding towns and farms. The postwar building boom had barely begun, and apartments and affordable homes were in short supply. The Knauffs said Loonis and Nan could stay with them until they found a place, but that wasn't a satisfactory situation for either family.

In his college years Loonis had enjoyed a taste of life on the road with a band. It had been a good experience then, but he realized now it wouldn't be a good way of life for someone with a wife and children. As much as he loved New York, and in his few earlier visits had always felt at home there, he wasn't sure it was the place he wanted his children to grow up—and certainly not with a father who was never home. So, despite the uncertainties, he and Nan decided to make Charlotte their new home.

It is interesting to speculate about what their lives would have been like, and what other directions his career might have taken, if he had gone as planned to New York and become a full-time musician. The band that was waiting for him became known as the Ralph Flanagan Orchestra and achieved some success touring and recording. But he did not go, and although he must have thought occasionally over the years about what might have been, there are no indications that he ever seriously looked back.

Knauff arranged an appointment for Loonis with Charles Crutchfield at WBT. They had a pleasant visit, but Crutchfield said the station already had a music director and he had no other openings that Loonis might consider. Disappointed,

The Billy Knauff band in the late 1940s, with Loonis McGlohon at the piano. The singer was Delores Mantes.

Loonis began searching the classified ads in the newspapers. He got a job with a trucking company, but lost it after a couple of months. Then he had an interview with Southern Railway for a position in the freight office. When he left the Knauff home for the interview, Nan predicted to Marguerite that if Loonis returned in a cab, bringing gifts for everyone, it would mean he had the job. A short while later, Loonis arrived in a cab, with flowers for Nan and Marguerite. He was now an employee of Southern Railway.

They were still staying with the Knauffs. Finally a real estate agent arranged for them to look at a vacant apartment. Loonis was in bed with flu, so Nan went alone to see a Mrs. Brown, in a two-story, four-unit apartment house on Walnut Avenue. Mrs. Brown said she loved Nan's red hair. Nan told Mrs. Brown that her husband, Loonis, also had red hair. That apparently clinched the deal. Mrs. Brown loved red. She said her husband had recently died, and that the McGlohons could rent her apartment.

That turned out to be something of an exaggeration. In fact, Mrs. Brown stayed in the apartment. The McGlohons would have only a small bedroom, and would have to share bathroom and kitchen privileges with Mrs. Brown, and with a young widow who was renting and living in the dining room of the apartment.

When Loonis and Nan moved into their new quarters, they noted that everything in the apartment that could be painted was painted red. The curtains were red; there was red oilcloth on the kitchen table.

Mrs. Brown told them her late husband had been a private detective, and because of some of the things in which he had been involved, she did not want anyone to know he was dead. His razor and shaving brush and soap remained in the bathroom, and when Loonis asked if he could move it out of the way, she said no. She told Nan and Loonis that if anyone telephoned and asked for her husband, they should simply say he was away. And people did call, at all hours of the night and day. When he answered the telephone and the caller asked for Mr. Brown, Loonis would say Mr. Brown was away. If the caller asked when Mr. Brown would be back, Loonis would say probably not anytime soon.

Nan cooked their meals, and while she and Loonis ate, Mrs. Brown and the other tenant would stand in the kitchen and watch them. As soon as they finished eating, Mrs. Brown would quickly take any leftovers from the table and feed them to a neighborhood dog. They had been living there barely a week when Nan told Loonis she was going home to Crisp until he could find another place for them to live.

Loonis kept looking and found a vacancy—a bedroom with bathroom—in a boarding house on Kingston Avenue, in the Dilworth neighborhood. He also got his name on the list for one of the new houses the Crosland company was building in a development called Westover Hills, and in a few months, in 1947, the McGlohons moved into a new suburban home. It was small and basic, but to Nan and Loonis, after years in a small apartment, months squeezed in with the Knauffs, a few days with Mrs. Brown, and a few more months in a boarding house, it must have seemed palatial.

In the 1940s William Henry Belk, founder of the Belk department store empire, built a few small Presbyterian chapels to serve the population spilling out into new residential subdivisions of the growing city. One of them was in Westover Hills, and Nan and Loonis joined the congregation of the new Westover Hills Presbyterian Church near their new home.

The church did not have and could not afford to hire an organist or music director. When the pastor learned that Loonis played piano, he asked him to serve as volunteer choir director. Having no experience with choral or sacred music, beyond singing hymns in the congregation during church services, Loonis at first declined the offer. But the pastor was persistent, and Loonis apparently had never been and would never be intimidated by any kind of musical or other creative challenge. He finally agreed to give it a try, and that turned out to be a significant decision: For almost all the rest of his life, whatever else he was doing, he would be a church choir director.

His secular music career was expanding beyond the weekend gigs with the Knauff band. He had organized a trio with bass and drums to play for occasions that did not require and could not afford a big band. Meanwhile, he continued his day job in the freight department of Southern Railway, where, apparently because of his ancestry, he had picked up the nickname "Scotty."

Only a few blocks away, on Tryon Street, the "main street" corridor through Charlotte's uptown business district, was the Wilder Building, home of radio station WBT. It was Charlotte's first radio station, the local CBS affiliate, the most powerful and the dominant station in the market. Its prestige and significance took a major leap in the summer of 1949 when it put the Carolinas' first television signal on the air, with the call letters WBTV. The station was a magnet to ambitious and talented young people seeking a career in communications, and to someone with Loonis McGlohon's tastes and talents. It was only a short walk for Loonis to the Wilder Building Soda Shop, where he could take a morning break with some of the young men from the WBT-WBTV staff. His contacts there, and his growing local stature as a musician, finally produced an opportunity for him to move his reputation and his music to a level beyond the local club and private party scene, and to a new and larger audience.

A network shift to daylight savings time in the spring of 1955 cut off CBS programming to WBTV at 10 P.M. Station management solicited ideas from the staff for local programs to fill the hour between 10 P.M. and the 11 P.M. local news. One suggestion, probably offered by producer Norman Prevatte or Mark Rascovich, the station's set designer and all-round creative handyman, was for a program featuring some of the city's talented jazz musicians. Prevatte asked Loonis if he would put together a small band for a fifteen-minute show on television, Monday through Friday nights. Loonis eagerly agreed.

From now on the postwar world's job would be
not just to dance to jazz, but to listen.
—Jerome Klinkowitz in *Listen: Gerry Mulligan*

Making the Scene : 10

The big bands and swing music never really recovered from World War II. In the late 1940s and early 1950s, some of the best of the former big band vocalists, such as Frank Sinatra, Doris Day, Rosemary Clooney, and others, were back on the hit-music charts with prewar standards, new ballads, and novelty tunes, accompanied by studio orchestras, sometimes with full string sections and lush, almost symphonic arrangements. Although a few big bands survived, many musicians had to look for other vocations. Some found work in recording studios. A few, including the bebop pioneers, continued to pursue careers in jazz, seeking other opportunities for expression, other venues, other audiences.

While bebop was taking jazz to a place where a lot of its audience would not follow, a parallel development was taking jazz out of the dance halls and smoky Harlem nightspots and into concert halls, new California jazz clubs, and onto college campuses. It was a more restrained, relaxed, and often more lyrical approach to many of the same musical ideas being explored in bebop. But labeling or describing it was tricky. It was variously known as "modern jazz" (a term of "built-in obsolescence," as the British jazz pianist and critic Brian Priestley has pointed out), "West Coast jazz" (although much of it was performed and recorded in New York City), "cool jazz" (although some of it had considerable warmth), and "progressive jazz." Adding to the confusion was the fact that all of those terms, with the possible exception of West Coast, could be used generically to include bebop.

This other new direction for jazz was frequently characterized by a studied attitude of emotional insouciance, both in the playing and in the personal style and behavior of the players. Paradoxically, that had the effect, at least with the best players, of making the music emotionally more intense. Perhaps what was left unexpressed somehow added weight to what was expressed. But generalizations are inadequate to capture the almost infinite varieties of a music as personal and individualistic as jazz. There were a few bebop musicians who were the epitome of cool, and there were musicians who were not at all cool who are in the very front row of the pantheon of modern, or postswing, postwar jazz. Beginning in the late 1940s, that kind of "modern jazz" acquired a substantial audience, particularly among young people in urban centers and on college campuses.

The development of the long-playing (LP) record provided space for as much as forty-five minutes of music on one twelve-inch disc, allowing jazz musicians to record extended improvised solos, including "live" performances taped in clubs and concerts. That expanded capacity and the new high-fidelity recording and playback equipment greatly enhanced the appeal and shifted the market for recorded music, including jazz.

In the early 1950s, jazz pianist Dave Brubeck's somewhat stiff, percussive, classically flavored style got little respect from the critics, but his quartet, with the very cool but very lyrical alto saxophonist Paul Desmond, became the most popular group in the short history of modern jazz. Their college tours drew sellout crowds, and recordings of some of those concerts climbed onto the charts. Brubeck himself was featured on the cover of *Time* magazine, an event considered a historic breakthrough for jazz.

Other modern jazz performers were enjoying remarkable popularity—not comparable to the popularity of the top big bands at the height of the swing era, but far exceeding anything Gillespie, Parker, and the other originators of bebop had achieved. Pianist Erroll Garner's ebullient *Concert by the Sea* album became a best seller in the mid-1950s, and Garner's composition "Misty" became a hit tune for a number of players and singers. A young baby-faced lyrical trumpet player named Chet Baker was known as the "James Dean of jazz" and gained a cult following, fragments of which still existed at the end of the century, after his death. Another young trumpeter, the moody, intense, charismatic Miles Davis, attracted attention with his experimental Birth of the Cool band. By the end of the 1950s Davis was on the jazz best-seller lists with quintet recordings and as a concerto-type soloist backed by a large band arranged by Gil Evans. Jazz-influenced singers and vocal groups were also an important part of the 1950s music scene, including June Christy, Chris Connor, the Four Freshmen, the Hi-Los, Nat "King" Cole, and Frank Sinatra.

Jazz was no longer primarily music for dancing. It was for listening, for "digging." Young people looked elsewhere for dance rhythms. In the years just after World War II, a medium-tempo shuffling dance that became known as the shag evolved from earlier jitterbug and African American dance styles among teenagers in the Carolinas. It began to the beat of rhythm and blues records on jukeboxes in beachfront pavilions. Shag music eventually became a genre of rock and roll called "beach music," but originally it was basic rhythm and blues performed by black artists, whose recordings were identified in southern record shops under the category of "Colored" or "Race."

But while rhythm and blues and later rock and roll were increasingly the dance music of young Americans in the 1950s, jazz persisted as the background music of college life and the after-hours music of urban and urbane young adults. Much of the music written for films and television shows in those years employed the harmonic innovations of modern jazz, and much of it was played by jazz musicians. Henry Mancini's award-winning scores for motion pictures and television were heavily influenced by jazz, and his songs became part of the jazz repertoire. There were regular jazz features and reviews in leading men's magazines such as *Esquire* and *Playboy*. Boston jazz promoter George Wein launched his Newport Jazz Festival, which became a major national event. American jazz was even more popular in Europe than in America, prompting a number of outstanding musicians to move abroad.

In the late 1950s at the Open Kitchen, a popular Italian restaurant (and pizza pioneer) just a short walk from the new WBT-WBTV studios on Morehead Street, you could play records by Miles Davis, Ahmad Jamal, and other jazz stars on the jukebox.

Indeed, the period from the end of the war until sometime in the 1960s was arguably the last golden age of American jazz, and Loonis McGlohon launched his musical career just in time to be part of it. If he had come along a few years later he would have had a more difficult time building a following and a reputation for his music.

Charlotte was not exactly a hotbed of jazz music, and nobody made a living playing jazz in the Carolinas. But the city offered plenty of opportunities for good musicians to play for pay, and since the gigs normally were at night, it wasn't difficult to take advantage of those opportunities and still hold a day job. There were frequent dances in the city and the surrounding region, sponsored by college groups, civic clubs, social clubs, professional and business associations, and country clubs. There were charity balls, wedding receptions, and other private parties. For more regular nightly or weekend gigs, there were restaurants that featured live music (often just a pianist), and several successful "supper clubs," where people came to dine and dance, including the Pecan Grove, the El Morocco, and the Lodge. Some of the musicians you could hear in and around Charlotte in those days had worked in nationally known bands but had gotten tired of life on the road and had come to Charlotte to raise families and pursue more stable careers.

Loonis quickly became a prominent part of that scene. His musical talent and taste were obvious. The fact that he carried neither a chip on his shoulder nor a

Loonis at the piano, early 1950s.

big ego made him popular with other musicians, but his personality stood out from the crowd. He had a flashing smile, a quick wit, and southern-style good manners. He was charming and articulate in talking to audiences or meeting people between sets. In addition to playing with the Knauff band, he put together a trio with bass and drums, often augmented by a saxophone or a vocalist or with Jim Stack on vibes. He also organized a nine-piece band for occasions that called for, and could afford, a larger group.

The nine-piece band played two joint concerts with the Charlotte Symphony in 1965 and 1966, under sponsorship of the Charlotte Jaycees, to raise money for the proposed "Parkshell"—a band shell to be built in Freedom Park. The trio was much in demand for events such as the Symphony Association's Candlelight Ball, the annual meeting of the Central Charlotte Association, and special events and fundraisers for other civic and cultural groups.

Loonis developed a number of programs for broadcast and live performances tracing the roots of jazz in southern church music. One of his earliest performances on that theme—"Origins of Jazz in the Church"—was in February 1964 at St. Andrew's College in Laurinburg, North Carolina, with WBTV announcer Clyde McLean as narrator.

Among the musicians frequently associated with Loonis in those days were drummers Earl Blankenship and Jim Lackey, bassist Creighton Spivey, saxophonists George LeCroy and Matt Wingard, trumpeters Jim Dooley and Bill Hodges, trombonists Joe Belk and H. P. Polk, and singer Lo Ramsey (a friend from East Carolina days now living in Gastonia). In the 1960s he often featured singer Linda Perez, a talented teenager and McGlohon protégé.

Of all his regular musical associates in the 1950s, the one who would have the longest tenure was Jim Stack, who would continue to work with Loonis in recording sessions and concerts for the rest of Loonis's life. Stack, a native of nearby Monroe, North Carolina, was a fine pianist but also very gifted on vibraphone, and in the late 1940s he was recruited to play vibes in the Knauff band. Stack was a bit younger than Loonis and recalls being "a little bit awed by him." He watched Loonis's hands, the way he played chords. He admired his taste and his knack for coming up with good songs for their repertoire and also admired Loonis as a songwriter who created "fresh melodies" and wrote songs with "no clichés." Stack and Loonis shared a thirst for new musical ideas, which frequently were not-so-new ideas adapted to new musical purposes. They sometimes got together at the McGlohon home to listen to music by the French impressionists Debussy and Ravel and the British composer Frederick Delius.

In addition to club and private party gigs, Loonis was also quick to put his musical talent and organizational abilities at the service of worthy causes. In the 1950s he wrote scripts and original music for several annual "Jaycee Jollies" musical productions, which were major fund-raising projects for the local Jaycees. The first one, in 1957, was called *On the Square* and took a satirical look at Charlotte's local government officials and some leading citizens. Directed by Loonis's WBTV colleague Norman Prevatte and staged in the city's new Ovens Auditorium, with sets by a brilliant young artist and designer named Jack Pentes, it was a huge success. The all-amateur cast included a number of local broadcast personalities and some prominent Charlotteans. Local newspapers published extensive coverage of the many weeks of preparation and of the performances.

The Jaycees' 1958 musical comedy was called *The Hornets' Nest,* which was and is a familiar term in Charlotte. During the American Revolution, Lord Cornwallis, commander of the British forces in the South, called Charlotte a "hornets' nest" because of the fierce armed resistance his troops met there. But Loonis's script wasn't about Charlotte history. It took another satirical view of current events, this time the city's efforts to annex a reluctant farmer's property. The McGlohon-Prevatte-Pentes team once again created a hit show with a cast of amateurs that included WBT's Wade St. Clair. Billy Knauff was music director. The *Charlotte Observer*'s arts editor, Dick Banks, who never let boosterism dull his critical faculties, called it "lavish entertainment of almost superb quality." The 1959 show, *April Green,* was another great success for Loonis and his team.

When the Charlotte Junior Woman's Club decided to launch an annual fashion show called *Serenade to Autumn* in the mid-1950s to raise money for its favorite causes, Prevatte was recruited to direct, with Loonis as music director. The show attracted the Belk department store as a major sponsor, and Loonis continued to provide music for it for many years. He also recruited nationally known singers to appear in the show, and he was named producer of *Serenade to Autumn* in 1973.

He wrote the official song of the Miss North Carolina Pageant and for many years produced the pageant for the state's Jaycees. Over the years he organized and played in concerts for the March of Dimes and other charitable causes, often using his contacts and his WBT-WBTV leverage to bring in big-name performers for those events. All those activities won him many friends and admirers outside the immediate audience for jazz music.

Loonis had written his first songs—at least the first to be performed, as far as we know—as a student at East Carolina, for a student play. For the rest of his life he never stopped writing music, and he was especially prolific during his first two decades in Charlotte. By the 1960s he already had written hundreds of songs, including several that were recorded by other artists and some that would be performed for years to come, such as "Dinner on the Grounds" and "The Wine of May." In 1969, singer Misty Moore recorded four of Loonis's songs—"I'll Let You Go," "You Stayed Away Too Long," "Don't Mail the Letter," and "When Summer Dies"—for the Pzazz Records label.

All the while, like other Charlotte musicians, he had a day job—first with the Southern Railway, and then, fulfilling an ambition he had pursued since first coming to Charlotte, with the radio and television stations WBT and WBTV.

It was an incredible place. There was no competition.

We could have done anything. . . .

Everybody ate, slept, and breathed their work.

—Loonis McGlohon

WBT/WBTV : 11

In 1920, an amateur radio operator in Pittsburgh began playing phonograph records and sending the music out through his transmitter. The music could be heard and enjoyed on nearby crystal sets. This novel use of radio, some twenty years after the first radio transmission of the human voice, demonstrated the medium's entertainment potential. Within the year, in Pittsburgh and Detroit, the first commercial radio stations were on the air.

That same year, amateur radio station 4XD was established on the dining room table of F. M. Laxton's home on Mecklenburg Avenue in Charlotte. In 1922, what began as 4XD was granted the first commercial broadcasting license in the Carolinas by the U.S. Department of Commerce. It would operate with an authorized power of 100 watts, under the call letters WBT.

For a while it was the only radio station in its market, and it would dominate, enlarge, and help shape that market for more than forty years. Its authorized power increased to five hundred watts in 1925. In 1929 it was sold to the Columbia Broadcasting System and became part of the CBS national network; its signal was boosted to 10,000 watts, and four years later to 25,000, and by the mid-1940s to 50,000. The network sold the station in 1945 to the Jefferson Standard Life Insurance Company of Greensboro, North Carolina, but WBT maintained its CBS affiliation.

Through the years of the Great Depression and World War II, WBT brought almost instant news to people hungry for news, and entertaining diversions to a population in need of entertaining diversions, in homes throughout the Charlotte region. Its local announcers and performers became household names in the Piedmont Carolinas.

In Charlotte and in the small textile mill towns and rural communities of the Piedmont, people had their morning coffee and their breakfast while listening to

Grady Cole on WBT. Cole was a cigar-chewing, cigar-smoking announcer with a spittoon by his chair, a rich, gritty, instantly recognizable voice, and a down-home style. He read the morning farm reports, played records, provided news and weather information. A very effective pitchman, he put his personal imprimatur on his sponsors' products and services, endorsing them in his own style of straight-talking sincerity. He plugged amateur boxing and other local activities on the air and often in person.

Grady Cole's morning show was a comfortable fit with the region's largely rural landscape and character, a reminder of its agricultural heritage and traditions. In contrast, the CBS news reports, soap operas, nighttime dramas, and musical and comedy programs brought a cosmopolitan diversity of voices and cultural influences into the living rooms, kitchens, and bedrooms of Charlotte and the surrounding area.

And if Grady Cole soothed listeners with accents of a familiar and lingering past, some of the other local announcers in the postwar years were pointing the station and its market toward the future, toward more urbane and sophisticated interests and tastes. In the 1940s and 1950s some of the more familiar names included Doug Mayes, Fletcher Austin, Lee Kirby, Phil Agresta, Bob Bean, Clyde McLean, Alan Newcomb, Kurt Webster, and Bob Raiford. Some of them were to some degree parochial in style, but none played to any regional stereotype, and their voices and programming ideas made WBT a station that would have been a significant and successful broadcasting presence anywhere in America. Indeed, by the 1950s the WBT directional nighttime signal could be heard from Canada to Cuba and along the entire East Coast of the United States.

Such was the reach of the station beyond its immediate market that in the early 1950s, Kurt Webster, the station's nighttime disc jockey, began playing a previously obscure recording of a song called "Heartaches," and it became a national hit. In February of 1955, *New York Times* radio critic Jack Gould listed Webster's successor, Bob Raiford, as one of the top disc jockeys in America. Raiford's musical tastes leaned strongly toward jazz-influenced popular music by recording artists such as Frank Sinatra, Nat "King" Cole, Jeri Southern, Chris Connor, June Christy, and the Four Freshmen; on Saturday nights he hosted an all-jazz program.

Perhaps the best examples of the range of the WBT programming spectrum of that era were those Carolina mornings with Grady Cole at the microphone, reading farm reports, chewing a cigar, and using the spittoon on the floor by his side, and those late Saturday nights with Bob Raiford, a bottle of White Horse Scotch within easy reach, spinning progressive jazz for an audience that included Floridians and New Yorkers.

In those optimistic postwar years, WBT's local programming projected Charlotte's image across the region as an urban center, a place of action and opportunity, rooted in the rural Carolinas but reaching beyond the parameters of its heritage. The very paradigm of the pre–television era radio station, licensed by the federal government to use the public airwaves in the public interest, it offered something for almost everyone.

In 1949 it added the Carolinas' first television station, WBTV, under the same roof, and two years later began doing live telecasts from its own studio. Until 1955 both the radio and television stations operated from the Wilder Building in uptown Charlotte, in those years before sprawling suburbs and shopping malls when uptown was the commercial, cultural, and political heart of the city and the region.

Although Loonis McGlohon had never made a conscious decision to seek a career in broadcasting, he realized, in those first few years in Charlotte, that WBT would be a great place for his day job. With a shared interest in music and entertainment, he developed a natural affinity for the people he met from the WBT staff, and some of them obviously were looking for ways to make use of his talents. In early 1955 when Norman Prevatte asked him to put together a small band for a nightly music show on WBTV, the opportunity was both less and more than Loonis had been hoping for. It didn't mean he could trade his job in the railway freight department for a full-time position in radio and television—yet. But it meant he would be performing on the still new and immature but obviously powerful medium of television—and on the only station in the market.

Years later, Bob Raiford would remember driving to work at night and seeing "that blue glow" through the windows of houses along the way. People were watching television, and that meant they were watching WBTV. If they were watching television at 10:15 P.M. on a weeknight in the spring of 1955, they were watching and hearing Loonis McGlohon.

The show was called *Nocturne.* It featured a quartet led by Loonis on piano, with Creighton Spivey on bass, Earl Blankenship on drums, and Jim Stack on vibraphone. The instrumentation was similar to that of the popular quintet led by the blind, British-born pianist, George Shearing. The result was often similar to what had become known as the "Shearing sound"—the vibes carrying the melody over block chords from the piano, achieving a lightly swinging, "cool," almost crystalline effect.

Although Bob Raiford was employed as a radio announcer, he was the obvious choice to be the "host" of *Nocturne.* Raiford, from nearby Concord, North Carolina, was still in his twenties. With his nighttime radio show, he was identified with the kind of music Loonis and his group played. And in addition to the rich

The Nocturne *set in the WBTV studio, 1955: announcer Bob Raiford, Loonis at the piano, vocalist Carrie Smith, Jim Stack on vibes, Creighton Spivey on bass, and Earl Blankenship on drums.*

baritone voice and relaxed, naturally articulate style that had earned him such a significant position in radio at such an early age, Raiford looked good on camera. He was tall and slim and knew how to dress.

Although there was little time for planning or rehearsals, Prevatte and Loonis weren't content simply to have a few musicians play a few minutes of music. They tried to come up with a theme for each show, and the theme was sometimes visual as well as musical. The multitalented Mark Rascovich built sets for the show. If the theme was Paris, for example, songs associated with that city and with France would be played against a background of the Eiffel Tower and French travel posters.

For variety, Raiford occasionally read poetry with Loonis and the group providing a musical background. Loonis sometimes brought in a saxophone player or

a local vocalist for the show, and Raiford also sang a few times. On one occasion, using a couple of suitcases as props, he sang "Sentimental Journey."

The show was telecast live, as were most television programs of that era. There was no videotape, and kinescope recordings were of poor quality, so there was no opportunity to do retakes or edit out mistakes. By the standards of modern television production, *Nocturne* was pretty basic, even amateurish. For its time and place and circumstances, however, it was ambitious and admirably creative. Most importantly, the music was good, and the show made Loonis McGlohon an increasingly recognizable name among jazz fans in the Carolinas.

Loonis and his new show got an early boost in the *Observer Forum,* the "letters to the editor" column of the *Charlotte Observer.* A woman who signed herself Jessie May wrote to complain about *Nocturne:*

One of the Nocturne *theme sets, this one about Paris. (Photo courtesy of Bob Raiford.)*

A couple of weeks ago they had some sort of dancers on there that I sure wouldn't want my children to see. Nearly every time it's got some kind of drinking going on, or they try to be real mysterious about it all, and that is real easy for the fellow who talks so you can't understand what he's saying, and looks like he's asleep or something.

I can't see any reason for the program at all, and all my friends can't either. . . .

After all, this TV is mighty important in our lives. We ought to at least keep it as decent as possible.

Over the next few days, several fans of the show came to its defense in the *Forum.* Some excerpts:

Someone who evidently only watches cooking schools, weathermen and commercials comes along and starts griping about what we believe to be one of the best produced local TV programs in Charlotte—five boys who do a very good job of putting over a restful 15 minutes of good music.

In a way, I'm glad Jessie May openly bared her feelings about WBTV and *Nocturne,* for she gives me an opportunity to say what I think about this program. It's wonderful!

Nocturne happens to be, in my opinion and that of my friends, about the nearest approach to adult entertainment WBTV has yet produced. It has achieved a rare combination of atmosphere, intelligence and subtleness, far above the average level. In fact, out-of-town associates of mine have often commented about the "network quality" of the show.

The totally inept and ridiculous letter concerning the TV show *Nocturne* has inspired me to reply. . . . In the opinion of the copious number of people I've talked with, *Nocturne* offers entertaining, refreshing music activated by showmanship and made more interesting because it is not of the sameness that is apparent in so many programs today.

Nocturne probably gained a lot of audience as a result of that exchange, as people tuned in to see what all the controversy was about. A high-powered professional public relations campaign could hardly have gotten the new show more exposure than its critic, Jessie May, did. Or was that in fact what it was? There were a lot of clever people on the WBTV staff. Could one of them have been Jessie May?

That same spring, WBT and WBTV moved from their increasingly cramped offices and studios in the Wilder Building to a large, impressive new building designed for radio and television operations, on West Morehead Street just beyond the southwestern edge of uptown Charlotte.

Through the 1950s Loonis segued from performing on WBT and WBTV for talent fees and working as a de facto part-time staffer to full-time employment there. The official change came on February 28, 1957, when Loonis resigned from Southern Railway to take a position at WBT-WBTV. It was a change he had been hoping to make for several years, but it's worth noting that he hadn't been simply marking time at Southern Railway. His letter of resignation brought this response from C. M. Kimball, assistant to the vice president of Southern Railway System:

> Scotty, I had hoped to see you in person to express to you not only our Company's sincere appreciation for your loyal and faithful service, but also my personal gratitude for the very interested, faithful and dependable service you have rendered in discharging the duties assigned to you and our Department. . . .
>
> It goes without saying that the latchstring both to our hearts and offices will always be awaiting your visits and we trust that you will drop by to see us at every opportunity.

When Loonis told Nan the good news that he had been offered a job at WBT and had accepted, she asked him how much it would pay. He didn't know. Hadn't asked. Probably didn't care.

WBT provided Loonis opportunities to develop, expose, and exploit his talents—including some talents that nobody, including himself, knew he had. He and his new colleagues created a string of new television and radio shows, many featuring his piano playing—*Spectrum, Studio Party, Melody Fair,* and *Tempo in Jazz* were a few.

He loved the people at the station, many of whom already were old friends, and he fed off their enthusiasm, energy, and creativity. A favorite lunch spot for the staff was the French restaurant in the Mecklenburg Hotel, near the railroad tracks on the western edge of uptown Charlotte. It was a plain room with white tile floors and the feel of a Paris bistro. Lunch table conversation among the WBT-WBTV crew was always about the station, about radio and television, about new programming ideas. With the dominant radio station and the only television station in the market, they didn't have to worry about competition for audience shares. They were free to experiment, to try new things, and management, in the form of Charles Crutchfield, encouraged them to use that freedom.

Although some employees found Crutchfield gruff and intimidating, Loonis viewed him with respect and affection and considered him a visionary. Crutchfield had started his broadcasting career as a teenager in Spartanburg, South Carolina. He had already worked at radio stations in Greensboro, North Carolina; Columbia, South Carolina; Augusta, Georgia; and Charleston and Greenville, South Carolina, but he was still barely in his twenties when he arrived at WBT as an announcer in 1933. He was a small, neat, well-dressed young man, and with his slick dark hair and a small mustache, he was considered rather dashingly handsome, in the style of some of the more elegant male movie stars of the time, such as William Powell. He soon began to move up in the management of the station even as he continued his successful announcing career. He had a natural talent for commercial announcements on behalf of all kinds of products, including patent medicines. One of his most memorable on-the-air jobs—and an interesting contrast with his otherwise starched-collar, urbane image—was as the announcer for a late-afternoon WBT show featuring a local country music group called the Briarhoppers. Crutchfield always opened the show with the same line: "Do y'all know what time it is? It's Briarhopper time!" At which point the Briarhoppers would launch into their theme song, a foot-stomping up-tempo version of "Wait 'til the Sun Shines, Nellie."

When Jefferson Standard Life Insurance Co. bought WBT from CBS in 1945, Crutchfield, at thirty-three, became the youngest manager of a 50,000-watt radio station in the country. Crutchfield encouraged his young staff to break new ground. WBT created and produced the kinds of programs normally left to the networks or to stations in major markets. One was *Radio Moscow,* which in an era of cold war anxiety and anticommunist fervor gave listeners an idea of what was going on behind the iron curtain. Another was *Project 60,* a weekly documentary that tackled a variety of subjects. Loonis found that Crutchfield "would let you do what you thought you did best. If you came to him with an idea, he'd say, 'Go for it!'"

It was the kind of atmosphere in which Loonis thrived. He quickly made himself a useful musical handyman, providing background music for various programs—sometimes with appropriate recordings from the WBT library, and sometimes composing and performing it himself. He became a regular on the *Pat Lee Show,* a sort of radio version of the newspaper "women's page," broadcast every morning. He and Pat Lee would chat for a moment and then Loonis would tell her what he was going to play, and play it—usually a ballad or love song, often in the lush, richly arpeggiated style made popular by Erroll Garner. For a while Loonis also had his own morning show, featuring his trio.

Loonis also began programming the music for the WBT announcers who played records on the air—including Grady Cole, whose taste in music was not exactly contemporary or jazz-oriented. When he chose his own music, Cole tended to play records by Guy Lombardo or Wayne King. He wasn't always pleased with

Loonis's selections, and when he would play one he would sometimes announce it as "another Loony Tune." The boss apparently agreed with Cole. At one point Crutchfield advised Loonis that he was hearing too many Four Freshmen and Stan Kenton records on the Grady Cole show. But Loonis's musical tastes were generally appropriate for the station's image. That image became consistent around the clock in the spring of 1961 when Ty Boyd, a young, energetic announcer whose boyish enthusiasm was tempered by a wry, hip sense of humor, replaced the legendary Grady Cole as the morning voice of WBT.

The station's longtime music director, Clarence Etters, retired in January of 1960, and Loonis replaced him, under the title of "music supervisor." The new job put him in charge of cataloging and maintaining the station's tremendous library of recorded music, which had been accumulating for almost forty years. There were thousands of old 78-rpm records in mint condition, including rare classics such as Ethel Waters singing "I'm Coming, Virginia." There were newer 45-rpm "extended play" single records and albums, and the even newer 33⅓-rpm "long-playing" records. In all there were about 350,000 selections—classical, semiclassical, Broadway, Dixieland, big band, blues, popular, modern jazz, country, folk—and Loonis was their ecstatic custodian.

Loonis also took advantage of the *Project 60* documentary format to create programs. Some were for Thanksgiving and other holidays. Others were on musical subjects. On one, in 1959, Loonis interviewed Billie Holiday by telephone, just a week, as it turned out, before she died.

Another was a two-part series on jazz piano players, featuring their recordings and Loonis's commentary. A few days after that series aired, Loonis received a letter from George Wallington, one of the featured pianists. Wallington said he had been on vacation in a rented cabin in the woods somewhere in the Canadian province of Quebec and was playing around with an old Emerson table-model radio when he heard a voice announcing "George Wallington playing 'Billie's Bounce.'" Wallington, a rather obscure bebop pianist who had played with Dizzy Gillespie in Fifty-second Street clubs, was surprised to hear one of his recordings played on the radio, and found it even harder to believe that he was hearing it on a North Carolina radio station.

To demonstrate appreciation of Loonis and his talent and promote his avocation as a jazz pianist, WBT and Jefferson Broadcasting in 1963 produced a long-playing album called *Loonis McGlohon and the Trio Play*. The trio consisted of Loonis, Butch Ward alternating with Jim Lackey on drums, and Creighton Spivey alternating with Rusty Gilder on bass. The album included five songs written by Loonis: "Dinner on the Grounds," "Chicken Scratch," "Spring Has Sprung," "Sunday Blues," and "The Wine of May." The other selections were the standards

Special guest Jose Ferrer with Loonis (seated), Jim Stack (middle), and Creighton Spivey (right).

"Summertime," "Laura," "When the Saints Go Marching In," "Once upon a Summertime," "Lullaby of Birdland," and "I've Grown Accustomed to Her Face." The popular *Charlotte Observer* columnist Kays Gary wrote the liner notes. The record jacket was designed by Jack Pentes, the Charlotte artist whose set designs had helped make Loonis's "Jaycee Jollies" productions such a success; Pentes would be a significant collaborator with Loonis on future projects. Without the marketing and distribution capabilities of a major record company, *Loonis McGlohon and the Trio Play* never had much chance at commercial success. But Jefferson's influence in its industry and Loonis's growing reputation got it some airplay around the country, and it earned several favorable reviews from regional and national jazz critics.

Loonis also began to develop ideas for more ambitious television shows, and in the process won the first of a steady stream of awards and honors that would continue for the rest of his life.

The early 1960s saw the beginning of significant social change on many fronts. Young people were caught between the conventional expectations of their parents' generation and the influence of historic changes in traditional social mores. Loonis was serving as adult adviser to the senior high fellowship group at Westover Hills Presbyterian Church at the time, and he wrote a script for a thirty-minute television show called *Both Sides of the Coin,* aimed at helping teenagers sort out their attitudes and values. It won first place in the 1962 television script-writing competition sponsored by the Communications Division of the Presbyterian Church U.S.

Two years later he won the Three-Star Award of Merit from the National Federation of Music Clubs for a February 1964 *Project 60* radio program on American composers Stephen Foster, Samuel Barber, George Gershwin, and Alec Wilder.

East Carolina College took note of Loonis's achievements, honoring him as its Alumnus of the Year in 1964. (He would be so honored again in 1983.)

In 1968 he and the jazz singer Marlena Shaw were cited for "distinguished public service" by the Presbyterian Church U.S. for a television show called *Come Blow Your Horn,* which traced the roots of jazz in church music and was broadcast in all major markets across the nation.

Another award-winner was his 1978 production *The Rowe String Quartet Plays on Your Imagination,* which won a Peabody Award, perhaps the broadcasting industry's highest honor, and an Iris Award from the National Association of Television Program Executives. The Catholic Church USA also honored Loonis and the Rowe String Quartet program with a Gabriel Award.

Later that year he produced *Songs of the Soul,* which traced the evolution of African American church music in Georgia and the Carolinas and featured the black folk singer Odetta. It was an ambitious production, filmed at St. Helena Island and St. Johns Island on the South Carolina coast, in Savannah, and in eastern North Carolina. Bob Wisehart, the entertainment editor of the *Charlotte News,* wrote that it was "quite simply the best locally produced television program I've ever seen."

Obviously Loonis had found a productive new outlet for his restless creativity, and he continued to conceive and produce outstanding programs for the rest of his career at WBT and WBTV. After the 1960s he increasingly focused on television. WBT radio no longer provided opportunities for innovative local programming such as *Project 60,* nor did any other successful commercial radio station except, perhaps, for a few in the major markets.

Some people predicted that television would mean the end of radio, at least as a commercial entertainment medium. But commercial radio survived, and a lot of

From left, George Shearing, Ty Boyd, and Loonis in the 1960s.

the credit for its survival goes to the increasing percentage of automobiles with radios and the development of suburbia and the interstate highway system, which meant Americans were spending more time in their cars. Another thing that helped radio survive was the growing teenage appetite for hearing the latest hit rock and roll records. While those factors saved radio, they also changed it.

Just as Loonis was fortunate to come along while his kind of music was still popular among a significant share of the youth and young adult market, he also was fortunate to be part of an important broadcasting organization during those last few years of eclectic, creative commercial radio. By the mid-1960s, families no longer gathered around the radio at night for drama and news. Housewives who were home during the day could watch their favorite soap operas on television. Radio stations increasingly were programmed for automobile listening and for teenagers' tastes in music—or for other specific genres, particularly country and western. "All music, all the time," or some variation of that theme, was a common promotional slogan for successful radio stations by the end of the decade. WBT continued a more traditional kind of programming through most of the decade, and declined to play much rock music, promoting itself as an adult alternative and thus a more attractive advertising medium. But teenagers controlled the radio dials to a significant extent, and they were no longer the only market segment looking for rock music. The first generation of teens raised on rock and roll was now out of school, into the workplace, starting families, moving into the demographic category of young adults. The young adult audience that most advertisers wanted to capture was increasingly a rock music audience.

By the late 1960s WBT could no longer take its traditional dominance of the market for granted, and it was no longer winning the audience ratings race in the youth and young adult demographic categories that so many advertisers wanted to reach. The station finally began to change with the times and play more of the music younger listeners wanted to hear. In 1971 WBT switched from a "middle-of-the-road" music format to a "Top 40" (mostly rock) format.

Loonis himself was now in his forties and had aged out of the radio advertisers' primary target audience. More to the point, there was not much need for his musical knowledge or taste or creativity in the kind of radio station WBT inevitably was becoming. By the early 1970s he had become the radio and television stations' director of community relations, and later he was in charge of special projects. From that position he would launch yet another important chapter in his career and claim yet another identity—as public citizen and successful champion for a multitude of worthy causes.

Whatever gap was left by commercial radio's abandonment of its role as a significant information source and a medium of diverse musical and cultural dissemination would be filled to some extent by public radio networks and stations, financed by government arts monies, foundation grants, and listener contributions. That was where Loonis would again be involved in radio production and performance in a significant way a few years later.

Meanwhile, his willingness to put his talent at the service of the radio and television stations, his colleagues there, and the community at large brought a steady series of challenges to Loonis's versatility as a musician and composer.

When country singer Tommy Faille, a regular soloist on WBTV's *Arthur Smith Show*, launched his own musical television show, Loonis somewhat reluctantly signed on as the pianist. As much as he liked the country musicians he had met at WBT and WBTV and respected their talent, it wasn't his kind of music. He agreed to play with Faille for at least a couple of reasons. One was the money. Another was his friendship with Faille, and the fact that Faille needed him: neither Faille nor any of the other musicians on the new show could read music.

Loonis was active in the 1968 Charlotte–Mecklenburg County Bicentennial celebration. He and his trio and band provided music for a number of bicentennial events. He helped organize a Bicentennial Jazz Festival, a two-night event at the Charlotte Coliseum, produced by the nation's leading jazz impresario, George Wein. It featured some of the most prominent jazz musicians in the country, including Dave Brubeck, Thelonious Monk, Herbie Mann, Gary Burton, Nina Simone, Cannonball Adderly, and Joe Zawinal. And Loonis wrote the score for *Hornets' Nest*, a historical musical drama with a script by Mecklenburg County native and novelist Legette Blythe.

Part of that *Hornets' Nest* score would turn up again in the service of community pride and celebration eight years later. In March of 1976, the basketball team of the University of North Carolina at Charlotte was in New York City to contend for the National Invitational Tournament (NIT) championship. UNCC was relatively new to big-time college athletic competition, and its teams, nicknamed the Forty-Niners, had no fight song. WBT-WBTV executive Jim Babb asked Loonis if he could come up with something appropriate. Loonis took the first four bars of a piece he had written for *Hornets' Nest* and created a song called "This Is the Day." He took it to a meeting of the Charlotte Chamber of Commerce where, to his piano accompaniment, one of the most unusual vocal ensembles in the city's history gave the song's, and their, premier performance. The impromptu chorus included Charlotte mayor John Belk, UNCC chancellor Dean Colvard, and banker and chamber chairman Luther Hodges, Jr.

Loonis sent a full arrangement of the song to the UNCC Pep Band, already in New York City for the NIT. At a dinner hosted by WBT and WBTV at Friar Tuck's in New York City, Coach Lee Rose and his Forty-Niners heard the new fight song for the first time, on tape.

For a moment at mid-century, lowdown southerners rewrote popular culture....

The explosion of rock 'n' roll ... was part of a cultural revolution that recoded music, language, dress, dance and values.
—Pete Daniel, in *Lost Revolutions: The South in the 1950s*

Rock : 12

While Loonis was establishing himself as a musician in Charlotte, high school and college students in the Carolinas were dancing to rhythm and blues (R&B) records by black artists, and to black R&B bands that played the campus party circuit. Younger teenagers were getting into a sort of sanitized version of R&B called rock and roll (or rock 'n' roll), much of it performed by young white musicians. What galvanized that new and initially rather pale—no pun intended—imitation of a traditional blues form was the appearance in the mid-1950s of a young white man who sounded at once like a black blues singer and a bluesy country singer, who wore his dark hair swept back in long ducktails and made suggestive movements with his hips when he sang, whose lips often curled in a sort of sensuous sneering smile in a broad, open face that otherwise wore an expression of childish innocence.

His name was Elvis Presley, and his early recordings and personal and TV appearances touched something deep and obviously ripe for tapping in that generation of teenagers. He projected an image—clothing and hair and body language—that summed up a decade of emerging adolescent rebellion. He was, wrapped into one almost instantly larger-than-life persona, all the slouching drugstore cowboys parents warned their teenage daughters to avoid. His music took rock and roll to a different level—higher or lower, depending on your point of view. Earlier rock music had mostly hinted at something really different and, from an adolescent perspective, daring. It teased its young audience. Elvis was no tease. He was the real thing. And he transformed popular music in America and abroad just as profoundly as did, years earlier, the great Broadway composers, the movement of New Orleans jazz into the Midwest and New York, or the big bands and Bing Crosby and Frank Sinatra. In addition to his personal impact, musically and visually, he had tools those earlier musical innovators had lacked: television, hi-fi, LP records, and radio stations increasingly catering to the teen market.

Elvis Presley made rock music impossible to ignore. Suddenly his music was everywhere. His records dominated the best-seller charts. He became a movie star, despite an embarrassing lack of acting ability. Indeed, to an older sensibility, there was always something embarrassing about Elvis Presley, and the fact that his young fans didn't see it that way was unsettling to their elders. Parents suddenly sensed that they and their children saw the world very differently, and they wondered if they really knew their children at all. The very ground, now vibrating to a hard rock beat, was shifting beneath their feet.

As older people watched and listened to the new music, the more sophisticated among them were mildly bemused by what they assumed was just the latest passing teenage musical fad; but others were outraged or even a bit frightened by the aggressive rhythms, and by the blatant sexuality of many of the songs and singers.

Generational differences in musical tastes are understandable and unexceptional. But surely there has never been anything in the history of music that so captivated one generation of young people and so thoroughly offended and confused their elders as did rock and roll. Loonis McGlohon hated it. And why not? Almost everything he cared about in music was mostly or wholly lacking in rock and roll.

Graceful melodies? There were some, most notably in the music of the Beatles and the Beach Boys in the 1960s. But many rock songs had no melody at all—just a lot of grunts and chants that occasionally changed pitch.

Fresh, sophisticated harmonic patterns? Most rock songs used three or four chords at most, alternating over and over, monotonously.

Intricately rhymed, intelligent (if often sentimental) lyrics? Many rock songs had as few different words as they did chords. Many of the words weren't words at all, but just sounds or syllables—"shboom, ya de da, bim bam, ugh ugh, yeah, yeah." The other gaps left by the almost subhuman inarticulateness of rock lyrics were often filled by repetition of the word "baby."

For Loonis, music, if it was up-tempo, was supposed to swing. Rock, by definition, didn't swing. That didn't mean it had no rhythmic pulse. In fact, sometimes it seemed rhythm was all it was. But it was rock rhythm, and that was different. The difference had nothing to do with tempo. Whether slow, moderate, or fast, rock rhythm was earthy, thumping, even raunchy; modern jazz rhythm had more of a flowing, floating quality, almost ethereal. (To hear the difference, listen to, say, Elvis Presley's recording of "Hound Dog" and Frank Sinatra's version of "I Get a Kick out of You." Both will have you tapping your foot, but one is rocking and the other is swinging. Loonis preferred the latter.)

So in the beginning, Loonis hated rock and roll, but he assumed it would not last. If he had known then how rock was going to dominate the popular music market for the rest of his life, he would have had even more reason to hate it, because it pushed his kind of music farther out to the margins of popular taste and commercial appeal.

It's a bit ironic that just as progressive jazz was giving American popular music a harmonic and melodic vocabulary as rich as any in the history of Western music, American popular music suddenly regressed to the musical equivalent of baby talk. In a marketplace where record sales were increasingly influenced by adolescents, and adolescents increasingly dominated the radio audience, the recording industry increasingly produced music geared to immature tastes and immature emotions. The traditional arbiters of musical taste were no longer consulted. The entertainment media were romanticizing the phenomenon of teenage rebellion. But teenagers didn't actually have to take the risks involved in real rebellion against anything. They could just listen to rock music and feel that they were rebelling, while remaining safe and secure under their parents' roofs. Teenagers determined what was popular, but their choices were heavily influenced by radio station playlists, some of which were, in turn, heavily influenced by illegal payoffs from record companies or their representatives to radio station programmers.

So as jazz became more complex, popular music resisted and went back to its most basic elements in the form of rock and roll. And coinciding, as it did, with the explosion of recording and playback technology and the adolescence of the baby boom generation, rock became the most financially significant development, and the most easily manipulated for profit, in the history of music.

Both its ancestors—rhythm and blues, and country and western—were authentic indigenous styles of American music. Each had its own legitimate aesthetic values. Each had its own heroes, who created their music out of authentic experience and their often raw but very real talent. Rock and roll eventually would develop its own aesthetics and produce its own legitimate artists, the first being Elvis Presley. But a large part of it was a hybrid created for pandering and exploitation, using hairspray and hype—and illegal payoffs to radio station programmers—to turn youngsters with minimal musical talent or training into overnight stars. It tipped the popular music industry, always a delicate balance of art and commerce, into the same category as any other kind of mass-market manufacturing.

Wary adults worried that sexual and drug-related messages were somehow encoded into rock recordings, either by the use of euphemistic terms that teens understood and adults didn't, or by hiding them in the background vocals where they weren't obvious to a casual listener. Part of Loonis's job as music director at WBT was to make sure nothing of that kind got on the air. When it occasionally did, he would hear from some alert listener or from his boss, Charles Crutchfield. It's interesting to speculate that if Loonis had believed rock music had any significant musical value, he might have felt just a bit uncomfortable in the role of censor. Probably not. But given his distaste for the entire genre, he had no reservations about keeping suggestive material off the air.

In the 1960s, as rock music was taking over the airwaves (but not at WBT, yet), he expressed his opinion of it in a script he wrote for a radio program titled "Ninety-eight Cents Worth of Trash." Narrated by Clyde McLean, who shared Loonis's sentiments on the subject, the script pointed out that many rock singers couldn't carry a tune, but that the deficiency was hard to notice because frequently there was no tune, and the musicians accompanying the tuneless singers were often off key. Meanwhile, the script pointed out, good singers and instrumentalists were looking for work. The show also criticized rock for lack of taste and for vulgarity. The situation was so bad, Loonis wrote, that of the hundreds of new recordings received at WBT from record companies every week, the station could find only a handful fit to play. In an editorial prompted by the radio program, the *Charlotte Observer* noted that the case against rock music was a commentary on "a culture and a set of values as well. Rock-and-roll," the editorial continued, "is carefully calculated garbage. . . . The disturbing thing is not that it came upon the scene; it is that it has stayed so long."

And it would stay much longer. Indefinitely, in fact. In 1976, many years after Loonis wrote and WBT aired "Ninety-eight Cents Worth of Trash," the influential entertainment critic Rex Reed wrote in the *New York Daily News*: "Songwriting used to be an honorable, even artistic industry that enriched our culture and shaped our lives. Today, music publishers have been replaced by record company executives and, except for politicians, I can't think of any group of people in America who display more ignorance, hostility or greed. It is almost impossible to hear one decent song on the radios or juke boxes of America without the aid of earplugs." Loonis clipped the column and pasted it into his scrapbook. Despite Reed's problem with syntax, or saying what he really meant to say (was he really suggesting that you could hear decent songs on radios and juke boxes if only you would wear earplugs?), his words did not exaggerate the bitterness and even outrage that Loonis felt.

As rock matured and developed its own aesthetics and nurtured its own genuine talents, and as his own children grew into their teens and were, of course, rock fans, Loonis mellowed a bit on the subject. He acknowledged the quality of some rock songs, particularly a few by the Beatles, but he recognized that those rare gems stood out only in the context of their generally tasteless and tuneless genre. Compared to the great songs of earlier generations, they did not deserve such extravagant appreciation. They sounded great because everything else was so mediocre. He also appreciated the crisp, brassy arrangements played by Chicago and Blood, Sweat, and Tears, which were reminiscent of the big band sounds of his youth.

In later years Loonis acknowledged rock music as a fact of life and, when asked to condemn the taste of its fans, was quick to defend people's right to listen to whatever pleased them. But he never really made his peace with it, and there was really no reason why he should have. In the last year of his life, he told at least one friend, and probably more, in an attitude of wry astonishment edged with just a trace of bitterness, that in the music department of Borders bookstore he had noticed CDs by a rock group called Butthole Surfers. He would shrug and acknowledge that he must have been becoming an old fogy. But he continued to wonder why anyone of any age should accept, much less encourage and pay good money for, that sort of debasement of popular culture.

Rock music had transformed the market in which he composed and performed, and the medium in which he worked, in ways that were neither favorable to his own best interests nor acceptable to his aesthetic tastes and personal values. He had good reasons to dislike it.

It's a quiet town where the warm red sun
Makes the grass grow green where the children run;
It's a place for fun when the work is done. . . .

It's a southern town with a shady street
Where you always nod to the folks you meet;
It's a town where springtime is long and sweet,
And Charlotte is her name.
—"It's a Quiet Town," words and
music by Loonis McGlohon

Home Base : 13

Doris Betts, the distinguished novelist and teacher, once told an audience of students and parents at the University of North Carolina at Chapel Hill that a university "is not a place to learn to make a living, but a place to learn how to make a life."

The distinction Ms. Betts was asserting is not limited to the issue of how and to what purpose young people spend four or more expensive years at an institution of higher learning. The larger point is that making a living is not the same thing as making a life. For most people making a living is certainly part of making a life. But making a life involves vastly more.

Some people seem to understand that distinction intuitively, and some never figure it out. Loonis obviously understood it. Making a life, for him, would involve music, no matter how he made his living. Making a life would involve Nan and the children they wanted and the kind of home they wanted, even if that meant he would not make a living playing music.

When he and Nan decided to establish a home and family in Charlotte, he passed up what in retrospect we know was a reasonably good opportunity for fame and possibly even fortune as a musician and composer. They chose to live where they believed they had a chance to make a life for themselves and a family—the kind of life that would be consistent with their own values and tastes.

The world of jazz and popular music is seductive and destructive, a glamorous path littered with wasted lives and wasted talents, of genius that explodes on the scene brilliantly and then self-destructs. Loonis planted his roots in a place and a way of life that helped immunize him against the toxic elements of an artistic pursuit and a creative environment he otherwise embraced passionately. If he had been driven by genius, by an obsession with his art, the decision would have been different, or he would eventually have regretted it. But for all his talent and his love of music, that was not the totality of who he was. He was a multidimensional, enviably whole person. If that meant he would never be one of the great jazz pianists of his time, it also meant he was arguably a more admirable human being and enjoyed a longer and richer life than most of those who might claim that title.

That was the kind of person Nan had fallen in love with; that was the kind of person who had fallen in love with Nan. And while he changed and grew, he never stopped being that kind of person.

So he had no regrets, and—again, in retrospect—it is easy to understand why. He attained considerable fame as a musician and composer in his own city and state, and even though he lived some distance from the environments in which his kind of music thrived, he also earned, within his musical niche, a fair measure of renown nationally and even internationally. There was no fortune, of course, but steady employment with a large, prosperous organization, ample opportunities to supplement his regular salary by playing music, and royalty checks from songs he had written added up to a comfortable living.

Meanwhile, Charlotte provided opportunities to make a life, opportunities for the whole person, that someone of his inclinations might never have found as a full-time musician living in New York City and/or on the road: the opportunity to raise children the way he and Nan had been raised, the opportunity to be part of his community, to play a role in solving its problems, enlivening its culture, and shaping its character and destiny. As the whole person he was, he needed those opportunities, and he embraced them with gratitude and commitment.

After family, music would come first, but there were plenty of other things that mattered, too. As a husband, father, employee, citizen, person of faith, he was as intense about meeting his responsibilities, being of service, doing the right thing, as he was about finding the right shape of melody, the right chord, the perfect words for a song lyric.

Choosing to live in Charlotte, then, was never a matter of sacrificing the career that might have been. It was a matter of making a life. And few people have ever done it more wholly, more wholesomely, more richly, or more successfully.

For all the sometimes dazzling distractions of his career, at the center of that life he and Nan made was, always, family.

The family began to expand in July of 1947 when Nan gave birth to their first child, a son. They named him Loonis Reeves McGlohon Jr. and called him Reeves.

The second child was Frances Lovelace McGlohon. Like Nan's mother, Frances Lovelace, she would be called Fan. When they brought baby Fan home from the hospital in November of 1952, it was obvious that the house in Westover Hills was no longer large enough for the McGlohons.

Nan and Loonis decided they wanted to build a house. They chose a lot on the southeastern edge of the growing city. Charlotte's rapid suburban development would transform the area over the next few years, but at the time the McGlohons' property was on a narrow gravel lane on densely wooded terrain surrounded by open fields and pasture, with only a few houses in the vicinity. In a nearby subdivision called Sherwood Forest, Nan saw a house she liked. It was a three-bedroom brick ranch. She pointed it out to their contractor and asked him to build one like it on their lot. They moved into the new home in 1957, and the following year, in July, their third child and second daughter was born. Her name was Laurie Leigh McGlohon, and they would call her Laurie.

The house was unimposing, unpretentious, simple, lovely. It would be home to Loonis for the rest of his life, and it fit him well. In summer it was blessed with deep shade. In autumn it was surrounded by brilliant red and gold foliage. Loonis and Nan planted flower beds and gardens that blossomed every spring. In every season the house was a place of music and laughter, bursting with the energy of bright youngsters growing up, warmed by the good aromas from Nan's kitchen.

For several years after they moved into the new home, the McGlohons drove back across town every Sunday to Westover Hills Presbyterian Church, and Loonis made the trip again in midweek to rehearse with the choir. As the children grew older and began to be active in youth activities at churches that were closer and more convenient, they persuaded Loonis and Nan to join a church nearer home. They visited and then joined Carmel Presbyterian Church. Another member at Carmel, and a congregational leader, was the Lance snack foods executive Pete Sloan. Carmel was still a young church, and Sloan quickly recruited Loonis to be its choir director, apologizing for the fact that the church could not afford to pay him. Loonis took the job. Carmel grew and prospered over the years, and well-paid music directors became commonplace among comparable Charlotte churches. But Loonis insisted on continuing to serve as a volunteer choir director, without salary, for some thirty years, until his age and health problems prompted him to relinquish the position.

Almost from the day it was completed, the McGlohons' new home was opened to a fairly steady stream of often fascinating guests. Many of them were celebrities, major or minor, in Charlotte for a concert or a charity fund-raiser organized or produced by Loonis, and he would bring them home for dinner, or to spend the night, sometimes unannounced. Nan and the children learned to deal with such intrusions with remarkable grace, and some of the unexpected guests became lifelong friends who stayed in touch and returned to the McGlohon home at every opportunity.

One of the things that drew them back was Nan's cooking. It occurred to her early on that these were people well acquainted with restaurant food, both gourmet and mediocre. They didn't need any more filet mignon or lobster. She fed them the same fare Loonis and her family loved, southern country home cooking, and most of them loved it and were eager to come back for more whenever they had the chance.

For his children, Loonis's multiple careers and many enthusiasms meant advantages in some respects, handicaps in others. His busy schedule meant he was not always available to participate in the children's activities. Some fathers count on weekend time with their kids, but Loonis was usually working on Friday and Saturday nights. He often had to play gigs that kept him from attending Friday night football games when Reeves played tackle for the East Mecklenburg High School Eagles. And Loonis otherwise was not much assistance in whatever athletic ambitions his son might have harbored. Loonis obviously was blessed with a rare kind of coordination: hand-brain, hand-ear, whatever motor skills might be required for someone to improvise, to hear music, or conceive music in his head, and then play it instantly on the piano. But that was the extent of his motor skills. You hear of boys who wish their fathers had more time to play ball with them. But when Reeves and his friends were shooting baskets, Reeves was always hoping his Dad wouldn't come out to play.

Perhaps the fact that he felt he had too little time to spend with his children made him reluctant to spend whatever time he had imposing discipline. He was quick to lecture but slow to punish. The role of disciplinarian was largely left to Nan. The only exception was when Nan herself was in some way the object of a child's offense. Loonis was tolerant of almost anything the children did, Reeves recalled, except being unkind to their mother.

Left to right: Reeves, Fan, and Laurie McGlohon in their senior portraits.

Although Reeves, Fan, and Laurie were very much aware that their father wasn't always on hand when they wanted him to be, they also knew he would always be there if they really needed him. He worked hard to be supportive even when he couldn't be present, and when he missed some occasion that involved them, he would ask them for a full report at the next opportunity. Most important of all, as Reeves put it, the children never questioned their father's love, or their mother's, and never had cause to worry about the stability of their family. They grew up knowing they were loved and feeling secure.

Loonis also gave his children a gift few fathers could provide: He wrote songs in honor of some of their special occasions. One that became known outside the family was "Grow Tall, My Son," written for Reeves. For Fan's sixteenth birthday, in 1968, Loonis wrote a song called "Birthday Candles." Eight years later the same melody, under the title "Waltz for a Toy Ballerina," won the 1976 North Carolina Composer of the Year Award for Loonis. Laurie's sixteenth birthday song was "Wear the Sunshine in Your Hair."

Loonis worked hard to instill his musical standards in his children, with limited success. They certainly grew up with a greater appreciation of classical music, jazz, and popular standards than most children of their generation, but they also embraced their generation's music, which was rock and roll. Loonis reluctantly accepted that, and his position as music director at WBT gave him access to new record releases, which meant opportunities to make points with his kids. Once, when the Beatles released a new record, Loonis brought a copy home, making Fan and Laurie the first among their peers to hear the new music. There were strings attached, however. Loonis required the girls to listen to one side of an Ella Fitzgerald LP before he would let them play the new Beatles record.

Loonis and Nan probably hoped one or more of their children might turn out to have some of their father's musical talent. But there was never any apparent genetic explanation for Loonis's musical abilities, and he was not able to pass them along. He tried giving piano lessons to Reeves, but gave up after two or three sessions, and Reeves never took lessons again. Fan took piano lessons for ten years and Laurie for six, but neither showed any inclination to play professionally. Laurie's instruction ended one night when Loonis went to hear her in a recital. There was something of a buzz on that occasion because the well-known pianist Loonis McGlohon was in attendance. Perhaps his presence made his daughter nervous. Whatever the reason, she was obviously miserable, and so was her performance. After the recital, Loonis walked up to her, gave her a hug and said: "You don't ever have to do that again. Let's go get an Icee."

Soon grandchildren were becoming frequent visitors to the McGlohon household. First were Max and Allan McGlohon, Reeves's sons. Fan and her husband, Ervin Caldwell "Skipper" Smith, provided Graham and Laurie. Laurie and her husband, Lawrence Edward "Larry" Shouse, provided Edward and Hilary. Then there was Brooke Shepherd, daughter of Reeves's wife, Peggy.

Loonis and Nan had added a swimming pool behind the house, which became a major attraction for the grandchildren and a center of family activities. Loonis chronicled their activities on film and videotape, documenting each grandchild's progress in swimming and diving from summer to summer.

The pool was also the site of the annual New Year's Eve fireworks display. Fireworks sales were illegal in North Carolina, so Loonis would load the grandchildren into his car on the last day of each year and drive across the state line into South Carolina to buy an array of rockets and Roman candles. Grandsons Allan and Edward were usually in charge of the pyrotechnic display, which drew family, friends, and neighbors. Nan would remind the boys to be careful. Loonis always assured her that they knew what they were doing. Maybe they did. They never set themselves or the house on fire.

Christmas was Loonis's favorite holiday and his favorite occasion. More than any other holiday it has become a special time for children, and for Loonis it seemed to bring out a childlike capacity for wonder and pure joy. He was a sentimental man, and he loved the Christmas story, the traditional images and carols, and the popular songs of the season. He wrote a number of Christmas songs, including "That's What We Love about Christmas," with Carroll Coates; "Christmas Is Just about Here"; "Be a Child at Christmas"; "Christmas Child"; "Christmas Is Love," with John Lamont; "A Christmas Memory"; "The Day after Christmas"; "I Know It's Christmas"; "I'd Like to Go Back Home for Christmas"; "It's Christmas Time"; and "Christmas Back Home," for which he wrote the lyrics to a tune by Hugh Martin.

He often said that his favorite song, the song he most wished he had written, was Hugh Martin's "Have Yourself a Merry Little Christmas." Once, when asked why he considered that such a fine song, he noted the symmetry of the melody and the way the words and music work together to express the emotional message of the song. For example, in the phrase "Hang a shining star upon the highest bough," the melody rises to hang the word *star* on the highest note of the song. But it was also a favorite because it was a Christmas song.

Christmas was so special at the McGlohon home that the children, even after they were grown and married and had children of their own, continued to be there for the occasion. Years after leaving home, Reeves and Fan and Laurie returned each year to hang their stockings, and after each of them married, stockings were added for the spouses.

One Christmas tradition at the McGlohon home was Loonis's Christmas eggs. He would drain eggs and decorate the shells to hang on the tree. Another tradition was the rule that nobody went near the tree on Christmas morning until Loonis went in alone and lit the candles. While he was handling that duty, Nan usually was in the kitchen, plugging in the coffee pot and putting a sausage, cheese, and egg casserole she had made the day before into the oven. Then everyone would go in to open presents while breakfast was cooking.

Another Christmas culinary tradition was Loonis's annual Christmas cake. He never used a recipe, so the results were rarely predictable. In later years, he turned the actual mixing and baking over to granddaughter Brooke. Each Christmas Eve they would run Nan out of the kitchen and create a dessert for Christmas Day. Loonis would instruct Brooke to add a cup of this and a pinch of that. The finished product was always at least edible and sometimes quite good.

And at Christmas, as on other special occasions, Loonis turned photographer, trying to capture all the magic moments of each year's family Christmas activities.

Vacations usually meant going somewhere Loonis and his band were working, but that didn't necessarily mean they were less than enjoyable. Those combination vacation-gig destinations included fine resort hotels in Myrtle Beach, Asheville, Colonial Williamsburg, and New Orleans, and later abroad.

Other family trips were educational. Loonis seemed always to have some purpose in mind other than simply relaxing and having fun. Laurie remembers a trip to the New York City World's Fair in 1964, when she was five years old. Her father pointed out a larger-than-life-size sculpture of the crucified Jesus lying across his mother's lap—Michelangelo's *Pietà*. As they stood looking at it, he said, "Don't ever forget this." She didn't. Years later she saw the sculpture in Rome. Laurie would study art and become an artist and art teacher.

Loonis's idea of appropriate educational opportunities for children was broader, probably, than that of most parents, reflecting his own eclectic tastes, his curiosity, his openness to the fascinating variety of human experience, of the larger human family.

When Reeves was a teenager, the local schools were still largely segregated by race, and a white youngster's exposure to black people was very limited. There was a large old black neighborhood called Brooklyn at the southeastern edge of Charlotte's central business district. Many of its residents lived in poverty, in shamefully primitive conditions. The neighborhood was infested with rats, and in cold weather the air was thick with smoke from the coal fires many homes used for heat. The acres of slum housing almost in the shadow of the new office towers being built uptown were an embarrassment to an ambitious, growing city, and beginning in the late 1960s the city used federal Urban Renewal money to raze Brooklyn and relocate its residents.

Prior to the demolition, Brooklyn's most important and beloved neighborhood institution was a church, the United House of Prayer for All People, part of a denomination headed by a Bishop Grace, also known as "Daddy" Grace. When "Daddy" Grace came to Charlotte to conduct services, it was a great day in Brooklyn, and local news media often covered the event. Loonis may have attended some of those services. Given his inclinations, and his interest in black church music as part of the root system of jazz, it would not have been surprising.

When "Daddy" Grace died, Loonis took young Reeves to the funeral service at the United House of Prayer for All People. It was a memorable experience for Reeves. The ceremonies were elaborate, even regal, full of music and wailing. One of the most memorable things about the experience, for Reeves, was how totally comfortable his father was in that environment.

Beginning in the late 1970s, as the McGlohons became more prosperous, Loonis took great delight in taking his family to Europe. In the summer of 1978 he and Nan rented two flats in London for a ten-day vacation, taking Laurie, then a rising junior at the University of North Carolina at Greensboro, and Reeves and Fan and their spouses. It was the first of a number of such trips, continuing through the 1990s. Other destinations with Nan, and sometimes with one or more of the children, included Scotland, Ireland, Paris, Rome, and Japan. Some of the trips included Loonis's scheduled performances or recording sessions. Others did not. In addition to the occasional overseas gigs, his incentives were his own enjoyment of travel to great cities and interesting places and his joy in sharing those experiences; but on those occasions Reeves, Fan, and Laurie also felt their father was making up for some of the times he hadn't been home or hadn't been able to attend events in which they were involved.

Loonis planned their trips meticulously. He wanted to give everyone the full advantage of their opportunities. He made reservations at the best restaurants, got tickets to the latest hit plays. Once when they arrived in Rome, Loonis instructed everyone to be up and ready to go at 7 o'clock the next morning. He took them to St. Peter's and into the Sistine Chapel. Laurie remembers that early morning excursion vividly. "There was just us and one guard. It was incredible. You could hear a pin drop. He had planned it that way. Later in the day it would be wall-to-wall people. He wanted to get there early so it would be just us, so we could experience that moment."

Fan recalls a visit to London that included dinner at the Savoy before going to the theater. With them was a singer, Robert Habermann, who was a protégé of Loonis's friend Margaret Whiting. They were seated in a small dining room. Fan had been recording the high points of their trip with a video camera, but when she started to videotape the room where they were dining, a waiter asked her to stop.

"Madam," he said, "We don't videotape in the Savoy."

Haberman said he thought that was "rather stuffy." But Fan took a different approach.

"I'm from North Carolina," she said. "I want to be able to show my friends the wonderful places I've been. Can't I please . . . ?"

She got permission to continue. Later she was advised that the reason the Savoy didn't allow any photography of any kind in the restaurant was because the management wished to respect the privacy of men who sometimes dined there with their mistresses.

Son-in-law Skipper Smith shared Loonis's passion for travel. Once a destination for a family trip had been determined, Skipper and Loonis would trade articles and information about the upcoming journey. Son-in-law Larry Shouse was the designated driver on most of the family trips, including excursions through the small towns of Ireland and the roundabouts of England, with the steering wheel on the right-hand side of the car. The only mishap with a vehicle during all the

McGlohons' foreign travels took place in the Cotswolds of England, when Larry let Reeves take the wheel of a rented minivan. Ten miles and a missing side mirror later, Larry took the wheel again.

One of the most memorable trips Loonis and Nan made was in the early summer of 1977. They were in London, where Loonis was performing, and he wanted to take Nan to Paris for the day. He had set aside about $600 for such extras during their stay. Before they boarded the flight to Paris at Heathrow, Loonis tried to exchange some of his dollars for French currency. The teller advised him to wait, because he would find a more favorable exchange rate in Paris. When they arrived in Paris, Loonis reached for his money and discovered that he no longer had it. Either he had left it in London, or it had slipped out on the plane, or somebody had stolen it. And because he had the cash, he had left his credit cards in the hotel in London. The airline reluctantly let him get back on the plane and look for the money, but he didn't find it there. Reluctant to worry Nan by telling her what had happened, he said he had misplaced about $40. He had $11 and change in his pocket, so he spent $4 on train tickets and decided to continue with his plans to show Nan around Paris.

He took her to one of his favorite spots, Saint Chapelle, a tiny chapel older than Notre Dame, with the oldest stained glass in Paris. They walked to the Galleries LaFayette and past the Opera to the Louvre. Every time they passed a restaurant, Loonis would glance at the menu posted by the door, looking for something they could afford to eat. They finally settled on a place where they could get cheese sandwiches and a couple of glasses of water.

All along the route he kept stopping at phone booths, trying to reach his friend Jacques Poulain, who was with Hertz car rental in Paris. If he could reach Poulain, he could borrow some spending money. But Poulain was in meetings, and Loonis was never able to get in touch with him. After several other adventures and misadventures, Loonis and Nan made their way back to the airport and returned to London.

The next morning he finally confessed to her that he had lost all his cash before they got to Paris. Nan said she had begun to suspect that.

"I'm so sorry," Loonis told her. "We could have had such a good time if we'd had some money."

Suddenly Nan turned pale. "I forgot. I had $150 in my pocketbook."

When they got back to Charlotte, Loonis's account of the trip made a good column for his friend Dot Jackson, who wrote for the *Observer*.

Of all the lessons the McGlohon children learned from their parents, most important were the things Loonis and Nan taught by example. One was a work ethic. Another was an absolute fidelity to commitments. They saw their father, after a full day at the office, spend the evening writing music and take one night a week for choir practice. He usually worked on weekend nights. There were several occasions when he turned down more lucrative or prestigious offers rather than try to get out of a prior commitment. Benny Goodman once called to ask him to sit in with the Goodman band during a stop in the Carolinas. Tempting as the offer was, Loonis declined without hesitation. He was already committed to play for a wedding reception in Charlotte. And no matter how late a Saturday night gig kept him up, he was at church directing the choir on Sunday morning.

Time for the children and time for his music were precious to Loonis, so he sometimes rushed through other chores. In spring and summer when the grass was growing fast, he sometimes would come home from work and quickly mow the lawn without pausing to change clothes. When he became aware that Loonis cut the grass while still in his suit and tie, his good friend Julian Massey decided to poke a little fun. One late afternoon Loonis came home to find Massey in tuxedo and black tie, mowing the McGlohons' lawn.

Another characteristic the McGlohon children learned to live with was their father's frugality. Although friends usually found him quick to pick up the check at lunch or dinner, his children knew Loonis was reluctant to spend money. Special circumstances such as family trips to Europe were exceptions, of course. His first car was a hand-me-down from Nan's mother. When he finally decided he could afford to buy a new car, he eschewed all the extra-cost options. He was a musician working for a broadcasting station, but for years he drove a car without a radio.

There is no doubt that one of the most important keys to Loonis's success as a musician, composer, broadcaster, and active citizen was the home environment Nan provided. It was reliably a place of refuge and respite, a place where an extraordinarily busy person could revive and refuel and write music. The home reflected Nan's good taste and graciousness as well as Loonis's creative interests. She bit her tongue and smiled, usually, when he brought home unexpected strangers for dinner, or even to spend the night. The children, in the years they lived there, provided a lively but largely stress-free counterpoint to the usual serenity of the household.

There were frictions, of course, as there are in every family, but they were remarkably rare and usually minor and quickly forgotten. One that has lingered larger in memory than most began when Nan's mother died, having willed her piano to Loonis. Nan was thrilled to be getting the piano. Her mother had played it well, as had one of Nan's sisters, and Nan had played it as a child. She considered it a fine piano, a treasured piece of family heritage. She also knew that Loonis had been wanting a new piano, and knowing his reluctance to spend money, she thought he would be the grateful recipient of her mother's thoughtfulness and generosity.

It was, instead, an awkward and difficult moment for Loonis. Grateful as he may have been, Loonis did not want his mother-in-law's piano. He already had his heart set on something better, and was prepared to pay for it. Meanwhile, not knowing Loonis's intentions, his bosses at WBT took Nan's mother's piano and had it reconditioned and polished up for him. Loonis decided the best thing to do was sell the piano and use the proceeds to help pay for the new piano he wanted.

Nan was uncharacteristically prickly. "You're going to sell Mother's piano?" she asked, in a tone and manner clearly indicating that to do so would be unthinkable.

Loonis tried to explain. He appreciated his mother-in-law's gift, but he was a professional musician; he made his living playing and writing at the piano. It was time for him to own a really good piano. He wanted, deserved, needed, a better piano than the one he had just inherited.

In her mind Nan probably understood and appreciated what he was saying, but in her heart she was hurt and angry that he didn't think her mother's piano was good enough for him—that in fact he had intended to sell it. And in her mind and heart she was determined that he was not going to sell it.

Word of his parents' unusually bitter disagreement got to Reeves, who was living in Raleigh at the time. He telephoned Nan and told her he had decided to buy a piano and wondered if they might be willing to sell him the piano her mother had left to Loonis.

"If you want it," said Nan, "you can have it. But if your father tries to sell it to you, don't you dare pay him a penny."

So Reeves took possession of his grandmother's piano. Whether any money changed hands in the process remains a family secret.

Loonis bought the new piano he wanted.

At the McGlohon home, life, and music, continued.

The man is a saint, and a genius with it.

—Alec Wilder, talking about Loonis McGlohon

Good Deeds : 14

Loonis McGlohon would emphatically deny any claim or even aspiration to saint-hood. He was endearingly human, and thus flawed, capable of attitudes and be-havior that would hardly qualify as saintly. But he was also a very good person by almost any definition, and he certainly had some saintly characteristics. One was the urge to be of service, to do good.

Almost from the beginning of his life in Charlotte, Loonis was eager to donate his musical talent to the service of any good cause in the community. In almost any month of any year, he was involved in planning, organizing, producing, or playing in a benefit concert of some kind. In the 1960s he helped produce and promote several concerts to raise money to build a band shell in Freedom Park, which would serve as a venue for his own and other musical groups during the annual Festival in the Park. The band shell also would provide an outdoor stage for other occasions, including, for many years, the Charlotte Symphony's free summer pops concerts. He also participated in benefit concerts for the March of Dimes; and for Holy Angels Nursery, the Catholic Sisters of Mercy facility for children with birth defects—a lifelong cause of *Charlotte Observer* columnist Kays Gary. Loonis brought in the jazz singer Marlena Shaw in 1970 for a free concert at Ovens Auditorium, with free transportation provided for the low-income residents of Model Cities neighborhoods. The Junior League *Serenade to Autumn* fashion shows, for which he provided music and which he later produced, raised money for charities. For some of those occasions he was paid, as appropriate, but he was always happy to donate his time and talent.

One of the most ambitious McGlohon projects, *A Child's Christmas,* was spon-sored by Observer Charities, Inc., the philanthropic arm of the *Charlotte Observer,* which raised money to support a summer camp for underprivileged children and other good causes. Loonis wrote the script and new music to be used along with traditional carols. The show, presented four times in mid-December of 1972, featured a cast of 150, many of them children. Various ethnic groups and nationalities were represented, in appropriate costumes and with appropriate music—including Japanese, Greek, African, and German. Tying it all together were the characters from *The Wizard of Oz*—Dorothy and her companions from the yellow brick road. Set designs were by Jack Pentes. Loonis also put together and wrote arrangements for the twelve-piece orchestra, which he directed.

But music was only part of his civic repertoire. The urge, the need, to serve—to serve his friends and his community and beyond—was part of him. It was never a matter of jumping through the civic service hoops in order to enhance his status in the community. He was, after all, a musician, a songwriter, and on the creative side of the broadcasting business—not a young executive trying to climb the corporate ladder.

Long before his job description put him into the community service business, community service was simply part of what he did. And when he became director of community relations and head of special projects for WBTV, he took those positions as a mandate to put himself and his company even more aggressively in the service of the community. WBT and WBTV already had built a strong reputation for corporate citizenship, but Loonis would push it to a higher level.

It would be difficult to enumerate the good deeds done and good causes served, small and large, by Loonis and, at his initiative, by the company that employed him. They were simply part of his day-to-day work for more than twenty years, and it would be an impressive list. But some of the more prominent efforts are worth recalling.

In the late 1960s Loonis learned about a national organization called Big Brothers of America, which recruited adult male mentors to work with fatherless boys. It seemed to him a good idea. There was a chapter of Big Brothers in Atlanta, and Loonis, on his own time, spent a couple of days there learning about how it was organized and how it functioned. He returned to Charlotte and recruited a committee to establish and raise money for a Big Brothers chapter. Soon they added Big Sisters, to serve girls in single-parent homes. Loonis served on the board of Big Brothers for many years and was its primary fund-raiser. At one point he had Nan trying to mass-produce her famous pepper jelly to sell to raise money for Big Brothers and Big Sisters.

Another Big Brothers–Big Sisters benefit, an annual auction, led to an unsolved mystery in the McGlohon household. One day in the early 1970s Loonis was in his office talking on the telephone to someone about the upcoming auction. A record company representative had stopped by his office, probably trying to get one of his company's new releases on the WBT playlist. When Loonis hung up the telephone, the rep, who had overheard part of the conversation, asked about the auction. Loonis told him it was to raise money for Big Brothers and Big Sisters, and added that he was particularly glad he had stopped by. Having heard the man on other occasions claim to know Elvis Presley, Loonis said he was counting on him to donate a record autographed by Elvis to the auction. It would bring big money, Loonis said, and for a very worthy cause.

The rep called a few days later to say Elvis certainly wanted to help and would donate, not an autographed album, but an outfit he had worn in performance. Great, said Loonis. He waited, and the auction was held without anything from Elvis, and then two days later the package arrived. It was a silver dinner jacket and black pants, the sort of thing Elvis wore for concerts at that point in his career, and Elvis's signature was inside the jacket. It surely would have brought hundreds, maybe thousands of dollars at auction. But it had arrived too late. Loonis decided to keep it for the following year's auction. He stuffed it back into the box and took the box home and put it in the attic. The next year, when planning began for the auction, Loonis climbed into the attic to get the Elvis outfit. It wasn't there. Nobody ever figured out what happened to it.

In the early 1970s the federal court ordered the Charlotte-Mecklenburg Schools to use pupil assignments and busing to desegregate every school in the system. The community, in one of the proudest chapters in its history, met that challenge, desegregated, and maintained a high-quality, nationally respected school system— but not before it endured some ominous moments. There were a few outbursts of violence in a few schools before things settled down and community pride and support took over. During those few weeks of racial friction, with the future of the local public schools and the city's reputation in the balance, Loonis contacted some of his friends in the entertainment world and persuaded them to come to Charlotte. He took them to some of the more troubled schools where they could meet with students and encourage them to work together, to support their school, to put their education first. It helped.

In the fall of 1974 there was a bit of open space in the middle of the first block on the north side of East Trade Street, just off the center intersection of Charlotte's downtown business district. In a few years the entire block would become the site of the Bank of America world headquarters office tower and the North Carolina Blumenthal Performing Arts Center. But at that moment there was still a drugstore on the corner and the side entrance of the Belk Department Store flanking what was one of the few undeveloped plots in a rapidly redeveloping inner city. The vacant lot had become a hangout for vagrants and panhandlers. Loonis decided it should be a park. He invited a designer named Joe Sonderman and somebody from the city parks department to lunch uptown and then took them to the site on

East Trade Street and suggested that it would make a fine park, maybe with a gazebo and a kiosk. Again, a committee was formed under Loonis's leadership to pursue the idea. The property was owned by Davidson College and a family trust, and the owners agreed to make it available for a park for a few years, knowing it would eventually be purchased as part of a larger development. Sonderman provided a design and the committee raised some private money to cover the $50,000 cost of landscaping, planting, and construction. Loonis presented the proposal to the city council in October, asking the city to take temporary control of the land and maintain the park. The park was dedicated the following spring.

Three years later Loonis was instrumental in establishing another park. This one was Pearl Street Park, a green oasis between busy Independence Boulevard and a new high-rise apartment building for senior citizens. Loonis's friend and colleague Pat Lee had advocated putting a park there, to provide a buffer between the adjacent traffic corridors and to give the elderly residents of the high-rise some pleasant, peaceful green space to enjoy. When she died that year, the Charlotte Junior Woman's Club took up the cause and recruited Loonis as coordinator of the project. Again, the effort was successful.

The Salvation Army cited the two parks, the establishment of Big Brothers and Big Sisters, and his service on the boards of Big Brothers and the National Conference of Christians and Jews in presenting an award for community service to Loonis at its annual Civic Appreciation Dinner in March of 1981.

In late 1984, Loonis read about poor people starving and dying of thirst in a drought-stricken region of Africa. The problems could be relieved, he learned, if people there had the equipment to dig wells—hardly a high-tech or extravagantly expensive solution. It seemed ridiculous to Loonis, who had spent part of his boyhood dependent on wells for water, that people should be dying in 1984 for lack of something so basic. He recruited WBTV and NCNB (formerly North Carolina National Bank, later NationsBank and eventually Bank of America) as cosponsors of a project called Water for Africa. It raised $100,000, which paid for forty wells and an irrigation system in Kenya.

A humanitarian campaign on a much smaller scale probably meant more to Loonis at a personal level than any of his other good deeds. He had become a friend and admirer of the Charleston civil rights leader Septima Poinsett Clark in the mid-1970s when she helped him with research on a television special on the music of the black southern church—Negro spirituals. Ms. Clark had marched and been arrested as a civil rights activist in the 1960s. She had been a close friend and adviser to Dr. Martin Luther King Jr. She was a legend in the South Carolina low country where she had been born and spent most of her life.

Loonis wanted guidance and access to some of the black churches on the Sea

Islands just outside Charleston, where the old dialects and traditional spirituals could still be heard, and someone suggested he contact Septima Clark. They met. He immediately felt that he was in the presence of greatness, of nobility, of amazing grace. She, in turn, was charmed, and she realized Loonis was a person of honor and goodwill, and that his interest in the music and culture he wanted to film for television was real and respectful. She took him around the islands where she had worked as a teacher, where pastors and congregations otherwise might have been wary of the redheaded white man and the television crew.

Loonis delighted in describing the experience. He could not have had a more effective introduction. At one church, where Ms. Clark did not know the pastor, she and Loonis walked in and she introduced herself. The pastor, said Loonis, was so awed by the presence of the legendary Septima Clark that he literally had to grab the edge of a table to keep from falling.

Septima Clark in front of her home in Charleston, South Carolina, in 1985. (Photo from and courtesy of The Charlotte Observer.)

They stayed in touch from time to time, but a decade later Loonis learned that Ms. Clark, then eighty-seven years old, was all but destitute. The situation was a result of one of those outrageous scenarios that keep coming back to haunt the South, to remind us that the sins of slavery, racial discrimination, and segregation were so profound that we seem destined to live with the consequences indefinitely. Ms. Clark taught in the impoverished public schools on the Sea Islands near Charleston for many years. In 1956, two years after the U.S. Supreme Court declared racially segregated schools unconstitutional, she was fired when she admitted being a member of the National Association for the Advancement of Color People (NAACP). She lost not only her job, but also her state pension. Some twenty-five years later, after she had been elected to two terms on the Charleston school board and received a Living Legacy Award in 1979 from President Jimmy Carter, the state acknowledged its error with back pay of $20,000. According to Ms. Clark and her advocates, that was only a fraction of what she was due.

An editorial in the *Charlotte Observer* in February of 1985 described her plight: "For much of this century, Septima Clark has fought against poverty, illiteracy and discrimination with quiet dignity. Today, at 87, she is barely subsisting in her crumbling Charleston home; a Social Security check is her only income. And though Ms. Clark isn't complaining, we're thankful that Charlotte jazz musician and composer Loonis McGlohon is acting on her behalf."

Loonis wrote to about seventy friends asking them to contribute to a fund to help Septima Clark pay off her mortgage and meet other needs. That initial effort brought in only a few hundred dollars. Loonis then asked a few other people in Charlotte who knew or knew of Septima Clark to get involved. They organized a luncheon at Johnson C. Smith University in honor of Ms. Clark, and Loonis staged a benefit concert. By late March they had raised $8,000. It was enough to make a difference in what would be the last two years and nine months of her life.

Septima Clark had a stroke in September of 1987 and died three months later. During her last few weeks she lay mostly peacefully, slipping in and out of consciousness. People who were with her say that from time to time she would sing, softly, one of those old spirituals from her childhood.

Songs and Singers : III

*It's increasingly difficult, but I attempt to keep an open mind
and a hungry heart, a constant need for wonderment and magic.*
—Alec Wilder, in a letter to Whitney Balliett of the *New Yorker*

Alec : 15

One of Loonis's innovative projects for WBTV was a weekly program called *Newcomers,* which aired for thirteen weeks in the early 1960s. It was a musical show featuring local teenagers who, with guidance from Loonis, wrote the scripts and selected and performed the songs. Its purpose, in addition to entertaining the television audience, was to give talented youngsters some experience with television, which was still a relatively new medium. *Newcomers* also created an unplanned opportunity for Loonis to make what would be—with the exception of marrying Nan—the most important connection of his life.

As they neared the end of the thirteen-week schedule, Loonis told his young cast that he would choose the songs for the final program. It was mid-April—a good time, he thought, for young people to perform songs about youth and springtime. And he wanted to do a program of music by Alec Wilder, who had written a lot of songs on those themes, including "Love among the Young," "While We're Young," and "Soft as Spring."

Rehearsals for the final show were going well, and Loonis could sense that, as he described it later, "the kids were really getting into Alec's music." He decided he should let Wilder know about the program. He didn't know Wilder, but he had read that Wilder lived at the Algonquin Hotel in New York City. Using that address, he wrote to Wilder, telling him about the television show on WBTV in Charlotte featuring Wilder's music, and offering to send him a tape of the show after it aired. A few days later Wilder telephoned Loonis to thank him and to ask if the show had been performed yet. It had not, and Wilder said he would like to come to Charlotte and see it.

Loonis was surprised, delighted—and nervous. For more than twenty years, Alec Wilder had been one of his musical heroes—indeed, his most venerated musi-

Loonis introduces Alec Wilder to the Newcomers at Freedom Park in Charlotte during the filming of a television show featuring Wilder's music in the early 1960s.

cal hero. Wilder was not, in large part by his choice, a widely recognized celebrity; but among aficionados of the kind of music Loonis wrote and played, he was a legend, even something of an icon. And suddenly, spontaneously, he was coming to Charlotte, to meet Loonis, to see a program Loonis was producing, to hear some North Carolina teenagers play and sing his music. For Loonis, it was exhilarating —and scary.

Wilder, who spent a lot of time on trains when he wasn't at the Algonquin, came from New York to Charlotte by rail and checked into a hotel. The night before he arrived Loonis was unable to sleep. He met Wilder the next day and took him to Freedom Park, where the *Newcomers* program would be filmed out-of-doors, by a small lake surrounded by woods that were already bright green in the early southern spring.

Wilder was a tall, thin man with a lean, handsome face that, in his midfifties, was already creased and chiseled by age and the erosive effect of heavy smoking. His thick hair was brushed straight back from his face with little apparent regard for where it ended up, and he had dark, deep-set, intimidating eyes under formidable brows. He was usually dressed in a tweed sport coat, flannel trousers, and loafers—well-tailored clothing but worn with a sort of lanky, rumpled insouciance.

To Loonis's great relief and pleasure, Wilder was friendly and gracious and seemed genuinely impressed by the show and charmed by the young performers. And he charmed them, and Loonis, in return. He accepted an invitation to dinner at the McGlohon home, where he obviously enjoyed Nan McGlohon's cooking but otherwise paid little attention to her. The next day he returned to New York.

Wilder was of a generation in which family and friends stayed in touch by mail, and his prolific letter writing displayed a generosity of spirit that, for his friends, was a sort of antidote to his fierce candor. He wrote to Loonis to thank him for the show and to say again how impressed he was with it. They exchanged letters several times, sharing thoughts about music and about songs and people they liked, and those they didn't like. Among the things they didn't like was rock and roll, which both considered crude, obnoxious, and juvenile, a commercial corruption of authentic African American blues and country and western music. They were appalled that a kind of entertainment they had dismissed as a passing fad was increasingly dominating radio station playlists and retail record racks, and displacing traditional American popular music in the process. Their tastes in that and other such matters were rarely in conflict.

At that point Wilder was not aware that Loonis wrote music, but Loonis felt he now knew Wilder well enough to send him some songs and ask his opinion of them. As he put them in the mail, he felt a bit of the same kind of trepidation he had experienced when Wilder first came to visit. A few days later Loonis's telephone rang, and when he answered, he heard Wilder saying:

"Where the hell have you been? I've been looking for you."

In other words, he liked the songs Loonis had sent, and Loonis was the kind of writer he would like as a collaborator.

"Send me a lyric," Wilder said, implying that he would write a melody to go with it.

Loonis obliged, and that was the beginning of a twenty-year personal and working relationship that would take Loonis to a new level in his career as a pianist and composer.

Alec Wilder called again to ask for more lyrics, and then after Loonis had sent several more, Alec said, "I'd like to come and see you." He returned to Charlotte and stayed with the McGlohons for a few days, and he and Loonis wrote a song or two while he was there. It was the first of many such visits. But they also collaborated by phone. Loonis later described the process as "an interesting shorthand for writing. He'd call and give me a tune over the phone and ask me to write a lyric. Or the other way around. 'It's in the key of F,' he would say. 'The first bar has three quarter notes, A, B-flat,' et cetera, and I was writing it down."

They were an unlikely team—a polite, soft-spoken, upper-middle-class southerner raising a family in a leafy suburban neighborhood and directing the choir at his Presbyterian church; and an eccentric, agnostic, sometimes acerbic New York bachelor who lived in a hotel. Loonis had grown up in a rural community as part of a large, loving extended family. Wilder, born into a prominent Rochester, New York, banking family, had no memory of his father, who had died suddenly in 1909 when the son was just two years old. As Loonis would learn later, Wilder's mother had been an alcoholic who never kissed or hugged her son or showed him any affection. That lack of maternal warmth, along with her drunken behavior, had made his childhood miserable.

Both were sentimental men, but while Loonis was openly, even exuberantly sentimental, Wilder hid his sentimentality behind a facade of sometimes biting wit and occasional cynicism. Wilder hated Christmas. He was probably respectful but personally indifferent to its religious significance, and he was offended by its sentimental and secular excesses. Loonis loved Christmas with all his sentimental heart, loved the story of the birth of Jesus, loved the carols and ceremonies and customs, loved giving and receiving gifts, and refused to let the commercial exploitation of the holiday spoil his or his family's enjoyment of it.

But on the subject of music they shared certain core values—an abhorrence of tackiness, an appreciation of the creative tension between tradition and innovation, and most important of all, an aesthetic integrity that eschewed flaccid, superficial sentiment and pretentious rhapsodizing or any other form of musical bombast. His collaboration with Alec Wilder was one of those paradoxes that defined Loonis McGlohon: It was perhaps because of their differences that the values they shared produced such a fertile, complementary relationship.

Maybe because of his own childlike qualities, which he happily made no effort to outgrow, Alec had an affinity for children. He wrote a number of songs for and about children. But the McGlohon children were immune to his charm. Laurie and Fan found him an often grouchy and presumptuous presence who intruded on their space and without apology disrupted the rhythms and routines of their lives. As creative children inevitably will, they found ways to retaliate and reassert themselves. Knowing Alec put sugar in his morning coffee, they once put salt in the sugar bowl when he was a guest in their home. They also dropped one of those artificial ice cubes with a fly embedded in it into his iced tea. Alec predictably detested the music of Lawrence Welk's band, a throwback to the "sweet" bands (as opposed to "hot" bands) of the big band era. When Alec was at the McGlohon's over a weekend and Loonis was playing a Saturday night gig, as he almost always was, Nan and the children would tune in the Lawrence Welk show on television, knowing that would send Alec storming out of the room, leaving them to enjoy the evening without his intrusive influence.

Television was, of course, the ultimate example and showcase of much that Wilder detested in contemporary entertainment and culture. One night he and the McGlohons were watching the Academy Award presentations on television when Barbara Streisand appeared to sing one of the songs nominated that year for an Oscar. Wilder was not impressed by Ms. Streisand's celebrity or popularity, and he detested her singing, which he considered histrionic. As she began to sing, he began to shout: "Sit down! Sit down! The world is not your stage, and we don't want to hear from you!" Fan and Laurie sat there, astonished, their fingers in their ears.

While his visits clearly created some problems for the children, for adults Alec Wilder as a friend and houseguest was at best a mixed blessing. At the McGlohon home he tended to reinforce shared values, and that kind of presence was always welcome. But he also could challenge the patience of his hosts. His biographer, Desmond Stone, wrote:

> He was concerned with the essence of things. In his music, he kept in what was buoyant and true and not rigid, and shut out what was dry and cerebral and shallow and dissonant and too grand. He valued friends no less for the same kinds of qualities: for freedom from cant and hypocrisy and bragga-docio, for integrity and for intellectual honesty, and above all, for their cele-bration of life [qualities he found in abundance in Loonis McGlohon]. Those friends also had to be extraordinarily tolerant. "Alec was witty, erudite, rude, warm, cantankerous, and he was all of those things when he was a house guest," Loonis McGlohon has said.

Wilder's relationship with Nan McGlohon was strangely impersonal, at least on his part. When she first met him, Nan thought he was "very odd," and he never gave her much opportunity to get beyond that perception. "He said hello and that was it," she recalled. "He never talked to me. He never called my name." Perhaps he was so focused on Loonis and their mutual interests that he simply had no time or energy for her. Or maybe, given his bitter feelings toward his mother, and the fact that he had never married, he simply didn't know how to relate to the wife and mother in the McGlohon home. At least, Nan found, "he was easy to feed. He en-joyed food. And he had very nice manners."

Others certainly would challenge the part about manners. But if Nan found Alec cool toward her, she appreciated the warmth of his relationship with Loonis, and she realized how much Loonis enjoyed working with him. And later, when she would have opportunities to talk about her experiences with wives of some of Alec's other friends, she would learn that they had encountered the same indifference.

Eventually, a rather strange request from Alec gave Nan an opportunity to win his gratitude for something other than her cooking. Alec's brother was hospitalized with a serious illness, and Alec was concerned that there was no family, other than himself, to send his brother letters and try to keep his spirits up. He asked Nan if she would write his brother a "get-well" note. Nan had never met the man, but she wrote him a letter, and then another, and another. She wrote him almost daily as long as he remained in the hospital.

The first of the Wilder-McGlohon songs to be recorded was a waltz called "Be a Child." Teddi King recorded it first. The fine British singer Cleo Laine recorded it twice, once on an album that featured the actor Dudley Moore on piano, and then live at Carnegie Hall with a band led by her husband, the top bandleader in England, Johnny Dankworth. It was also recorded by Mabel Mercer, Marlene Ver-Planck, and Eileen Farrell.

"We wrote a lot of songs about being a child, about youth," Loonis recalled. "It was something we both believed in, the innocence of the young."

Sometimes Alec would come up with a phrase or a title that he found intriguing, and he would challenge Loonis to develop it into a song. That was the genesis of one of the two songs they wrote in the late 1970s that were recorded by Frank Sinatra. One title Alec suggested was "South to a Warmer Place."

"How about writing a lyric with that title," he said.

Loonis wasn't sure what the title meant. Should it be about someone being tired of the cold North and deciding to head south? Or should it be a metaphor about lost love, about leaving someone whose heart had turned cold? Before he had a chance to query Alec about those possibilities, Loonis was off to London for a recording session. On the flight back, he took out a yellow legal pad and wrote two sets of lyrics. When he landed at Kennedy Airport, before boarding another plane to Charlotte, he mailed the yellow sheets to Alec at the Algonquin. Alec chose the words about a cold heart and wrote a tune to go with them. Sinatra heard the song, liked it, and recorded it. So did Marlene VerPlanck and Joyce Breach.

When Alec was visiting the McGlohons, his primary interest was writing songs with Loonis. As Loonis later described it, "He thought music constantly." But Loonis had a job at WBTV and had to go to the office every weekday morning. Sometimes Alec would go with him and sit beside Loonis's desk. He usually had a three- by five-inch music manuscript pad with him, and he would jot down musical ideas or even write an entire song while Loonis was working. But his presence was a distraction, and occasionally an embarrassment. Loonis later recalled those occasions when, "if somebody came in to ask something, and Alec was sitting there, he would say, 'Why don't you leave him alone?' or 'Why don't you ask somebody else?'" So most mornings Loonis no longer invited his guest to go to the office with him. During those days Alec would work alone at the piano, or if the weather was good, meander in the yard or around the wooded neighborhood, sometimes with a bottle of liquid soap and a children's "bubble wand," blowing bubbles into the air as he walked.

Often when Loonis was at his office or otherwise not immediately available, Alec would write lyrics and, when Loonis returned, ask him to compose a melody. On other occasions Alec would write a melody, or the beginning of one, and then ask Loonis to finish it, or write words for it.

One example was the day Nan and Loonis were taking their youngest child, Laurie, to Greensboro to begin her freshman year of college. They invited Alec to ride with them, but he declined. When Loonis and Nan returned several hours later, they were feeling very sad because their last child, their baby, was now away in college. Alec met them at the door and, paying no attention to their feelings, asked Loonis to come to the piano. He had written a tune while they were away, one he thought Loonis would like. He wasn't at all an accomplished pianist, but he could play chords and a melody line, and he played his new composition and asked Loonis to write the words.

"I think it's a crazy kind of love song," Alec said. "Maybe a 'list' song, something about a boy trying to impress his sweetheart with a really crazy, loony list, polka dots and balloons and all that."

Loonis said he simply wasn't in the right frame of mind to write, but Alec was so enthusiastic about the tune that Loonis finally sat down and tried to write something. Nothing happened.

"Alec," he said, "it's a lovely song, one of the best I've ever heard, but I can't write about polka dots and balloons and young love right now. If I write anything it's going to be a catharsis for me, and not what you have in mind at all."

Fine, Alec said, do that. So over the next few minutes Loonis wrote about the house feeling empty, about no children playing in the yard, about what they should do with the posters on the wall. It was called "Where's the Child I Used to Hold?" and when he had finished, Alec said, "That's perfect." The song was later recorded by Meredith d'Ambrosio and Dick Haymes.

What was perhaps the best known of their songs came out of a similar process. Loonis returned home one day and Alec said, "I want to play you something." He played and said, "I'm just intrigued by this phrase." It was a wistful melody that included strings of eighth and sixteenth notes. "Are they too repetitive?" he asked.

Loonis said he thought it was a very interesting song—so far. He sat down at the piano and they finished the first sixteen bars of the song. Alec asked him to write a bridge. He said the tune so far was into a pattern, and the bridge needed to break out of the pattern. Loonis quickly composed a bridge that broke the pattern like a velvet hammer and then rose to a crest of barely restrained angst before settling back into the original melody. Like the sixteenth notes Alec had strung like pearls in the opening bars, Loonis's bridge lifted the tune out of the ordinary and made it something very special.

Alec then asked Loonis for a lyric. Out of nowhere, or perhaps because the syllables fit the tune, Loonis thought: *blackberry winter.* Alec had never heard the term, which refers to a southern weather phenomenon—a few days of cool weather that sometimes interrupt spring, usually in late May after the blackberry bushes bloom. Loonis completed the words, and Alec was delighted. So were a lot of musicians and singers who recorded "Blackberry Winter," including Teddi King, Eileen Farrell, Mabel Mercer, Marlene VerPlanck, and pianist Keith Jarrett, and others who have performed it in concert, including singers Mary Mayo and Barbara Lea and trumpeters Joe Wilder and Robert Levy.

Among the few concert pieces for saxophone is one originally credited to Alec Wilder, to his surprise, but written in fact by Loonis and Alec. The saxophone is a prominent instrument in jazz and other popular music, but is rarely used in "serious" music and is not a standard part of classical music ensembles. One of the few and finest players of "serious" saxophone music is James Houlik, who was a great admirer of Alec Wilder's concert pieces. He very much wanted Alec to write something for tenor saxophone that he could play. He didn't know Alec, but asked a mutual friend to make the request. Alec declined, saying he only wrote such pieces for his friends to play. Later the request was routed through Loonis. The next time Alec was visiting in the McGlohon home, Loonis tried his best to persuade Alec to write something for Houlik. Just something short, Loonis said. "It wouldn't take you very long, and it would mean a lot to him." Alec again said no, and his stubborn refusal to do a favor for a fine musician made Loonis a bit angry.

The following morning, a Sunday, Loonis was up early and at the piano, writing a few bars of simple melody. When Alec came into the room and asked what he was working on, Loonis said, "Just a little something. Maybe it could be a concert piece."

Alec said he liked it so far.

"Maybe it could be a piece for flute," Loonis said.

"Wrong pitch," Alec said.

"How about for alto saxophone?" Loonis said, careful not to say tenor saxophone, lest Alec realize what he was up to.

"Yes, that would work," Alec said.

Loonis wrote the title "Air for Alto" across the top of the page. Then he looked at his watch.

"It's time for me to go to church," he said. "I've done eight bars. You finish it."

When Loonis returned from church, Alec showed him the finished piece. That night Loonis transcribed the music for tenor saxophone and sent it to Houlik the next day.

Alec returned to New York and a few days later telephoned Loonis.

"There are some strange people in this world," he said. "I just got a call from some man thanking me for writing a piece of music for him. I never even heard of him. How would he get the idea that I had written something for him?"

"Well, Alec, you did write something for him," Loonis said. "Remember that Sunday morning when you finished the piece I started, for alto saxophone?"

"You son of a bitch," Alec said. "How dare you trick me like that?"

"How long did it take you?" Loonis asked. "Maybe forty-five minutes? And you made the man very happy."

Alec continued to fume, but by his next visit he had cooled off, and he told Loonis he really liked the piece and thought it should be published. When he sent it to his publisher, he insisted that it be credited to Loonis McGlohon and Alec Wilder. It has been played a number of times in concert.

Loonis kept the original manuscript of "Air for Alto" in his files, with the first few bars in his sketchy notation and the rest of it obviously in someone else's (Alec's) musical handwriting.

In addition to individual songs, Loonis and Alec worked together on two major projects. One was a mountaintop musical theme park, conceived by Jack Pentes, a spectacularly creative Charlotte artist and designer.

In the mid-1960s Pentes was invited to Beech Mountain, in the "High Country" of North Carolina, just below the Tennessee border. His hosts were brothers Harry and Grover Robbins, indigenous High Country entrepreneurs who already had developed a popular family-oriented tourist attraction, Tweetsie Railroad, and an upscale, gated golf community, Hound Ears, both a few miles from Boone and Blowing Rock. Their latest venture, along with other investors, was a resort development

Jack Pentes in 1976. (Photo from and courtesy of The Charlotte Observer.)

company called Carolina Caribbean Corporation. Its first project, a ski resort on Beech Mountain, was under construction, and the Robbins brothers wanted something that would make Beech Mountain a year-round tourist destination. They leased an old apple orchard, about eight acres in all, near the top of the mountain, at an elevation of about 5,500 feet, and asked Pentes what they could put there to attract visitors outside of ski season. When Pentes saw the thick, glossy, emerald "bear grass" that covered the ground, the gnarled trees stunted by mountaintop winds, the large outcroppings of rock that begged to be climbed, the answer was immediately obvious. It should be the Land of Oz. Grover Robbins agreed.

Back in Charlotte, Pentes called his friend Loonis to enlist him in the project. Loonis then enlisted Alec Wilder. They obtained permission from Harold Arlen to use his classic song "Over the Rainbow," from the film version of *The Wizard of Oz*. Loonis and Alec wrote the rest of the score. Alec loved the project and the place, which he visited often.

It is an easy place to love, particularly in summer. While daytime temperatures in the Piedmont, little more than an hour's drive away, are hovering around ninety degrees, with humidity to match, and nights without air-conditioning would be sleepless, the temperature on Beech Mountain, more than 5,000 feet above sea level, usually peaks in the midseventies and almost never gets to eighty. Summer days in the sixties are not unusual, and the nights are cool. The mountain is green and shady, and wildflowers blanket the roadsides and meadows. On clear days the vistas in all directions are breathtaking. When a cloud settles over the mountain and silver mist swirls in the trees and limits visibility, there is a different kind of beauty, and an atmosphere haunted by memories of ghost stories and spooky mountain legends. And when the fog lifts and blows away, as it eventually does, the contrast, the sudden revelation of sunshine and the bright colors of the landscape, is dazzling.

Loonis later wrote about the Land of Oz:

When Jack called me to ask if I would collaborate on a project he was calling "Land of Oz," I didn't have to think about it. Working with Jack Pentes has always been exciting and challenging and as much fun as anyone could have.

Jack explained that the top of Beech Mountain would become Oz, with Aunt Em's farm, her farmhouse, a yellow brick road, and an Emerald City, with performances by the Tin Man, the Scarecrow, and the Cowardly Lion. The wizard would appear on a rear screen in the Emerald City theater. And there would be a Dorothy, of course.

Jack suggested we invite Alice Lamar, a wonderful choreographer, to create dances and movements for the characters. I volunteered Alec Wilder to help me with the musical score, and as I would have guessed, Alec said "Yes" when I telephoned him.

Jack, Alice, and I had to get together for a brainstorming session and lay out plans for the production. Alice flew in from Hollywood, and since she could spend only one night on this first visit, we agreed to meet at our house. Nan planned a dinner that could be served on a moment's notice, during a break in our session. We had gathered in the living room when the telephone interrupted. It was a club manager in town. He said, "Loonis, if you were here right now, you'd be ten minutes late." I had forgotten a booking at his club. I had no choice but to go, immediately. I started putting on a tuxedo and finished dressing in the car while I drove downtown.

It was 10:40 when I got home. Jack was asleep on the living room carpet. Ruth, Jack's wife, had gone home. Alice and Nan were talking quietly, sitting on a sofa. We woke Jack. Nan made a pot of coffee, and we began to work. Creativity and energy flowed, and, miraculously, we finished outlining the production by 2:30 that morning.

With Carolina Caribbean financing and the creative genius of Jack Pentes, Alice Lamar, and Alec Wilder, the Land of Oz came to life on Beech Mountain.

The audience, upon arriving at the entrance to Oz, would walk through the farm and would be entertained on Uncle Henry's front porch by musicians and singers. Then Dorothy would appear and invite everyone inside the Kansas farmhouse, circa 1900. As the audience toured the house, a tornado warning would hurry everyone down to the cellar, which was in fact a wind tunnel. The wind blew as the audience saw pictures of buildings and animals flying past (on a movie screen). Then everyone found themselves back inside the farmhouse, which was a replica built down the hill from the house they had entered. It was all askew, with furniture and dishes scattered around by the storm.

The visitors then left the house and found themselves walking along a yellow brick road through lush mountaintop scenery: emerald green grass, waterfalls, ponds, gnarled trees, boulders the size of a house, and long vistas of blue mountains miles away.

The Tin Man suddenly came out of his house (a tin house, of course) and performed a song and dance, "I Lost My Heart . . . and I Don't Know Where to Find it." Further down the road, the Scarecrow greeted the audience in front of his tumbledown house and sang, "I'd Like to Have a Brain." The Cowardly Lion was a big hit with the audience. His cave was inside a boulder about thirty feet tall. When he emerged from it, he danced and sang. The song was called "I'm a Fraidy Cat." When we added the Witch to the cast, I didn't want her to frighten children, so she *became a befuddled and wacky old witch who was having trouble remembering what she put in her "stew." She stirred her black cauldron and sang, "How Do I Brew This Stew?" Behind her, the castle loomed gray and mysterious.*

At the end of the yellow brick road, the audience sat in the Emerald City theater, where Dorothy and the other characters begged the Wizard (appearing on a rear screen) to grant their wishes. When he told Dorothy she could go home, she clicked her red heels three times, and a smoke pot was activated. Hidden by the smoke, Dorothy disappeared (actually she slipped into the wings of the theater). When the smoke cleared, the Lion and the Tin Man point upward, and suddenly we see Dorothy flying overhead in a big colorful balloon basket, with her dog, Toto, safe in her arms. The second Dorothy was a double, of course.

As Dorothy sailed out of sight, the park became alive with the voice of Mary Mayo singing "The Wonderful Land of Oz." A magnificent sound system in the park made it sound as though Mary's voice was coming from all directions, floating in the treetops.

Despite its glorious concept, its brilliant execution and its spectacular site, the Land of Oz may have been cursed from the beginning. Grover Robbins did not live to see his and Pentes's vision fulfilled. Just fifty-one years old, he died of cancer some six months before the park was completed. Oz opened for business in June of 1970, drawing about 4,000 people its first day and about 400,000 in its first year. It was a magical place, and there's probably never been anything else that so successfully blended the natural scenery with the mythical sights and sounds of a classic American fantasy. But it lasted only ten years, and they were ten difficult years. Despite the publicity it received and its popularity with visitors, it was never a financial success for Carolina Caribbean Corporation. Disney World opened in Orlando the following year. It was hundreds of miles away, but a direct competitor for vacation theme park business in the Southeast. A couple of years later another theme park, Carowinds, opened just south of Charlotte. Meanwhile, Americans were waiting in line to buy gasoline for their automobiles, if they could find any. And winter weather on a 5,500-foot mountaintop made the facilities at Oz a major maintenance expense. The company sought to increase revenues by adding vendors with cheap souvenirs, and it balked at the cost of maintaining the quality of the park. Jack Pentes's original pristine vision was quickly compromised. Inflation and soaring gasoline prices took their toll. Before the decade was over, fire and vandalism had ravaged the Land of Oz, and in 1980 it was abandoned.

Loonis did retain something of considerable personal value from the project. Part of his compensation for his work on the Land of Oz was a bit of property on Beech Mountain, whose residents incorporated and survived the demise of Carolina Caribbean Corporation. Loonis and Nan built a house there, which became their favorite getaway and hideaway place, and a happy gathering place for them and their children and grandchildren.

As Loonis and Alec were writing music for the Land of Oz, Alec was working on a much more ambitious, difficult, and ultimately more significant project of his own. In the late 1960s and 1970, he wrote a book called *American Popular Song: The Great Innovators, 1900–1950,* which was published by Oxford University Press in 1972. As his biographer Desmond Stone wrote, "Almost everything Wilder did in the popular music field was prelude and preparation for the book. Nothing like it had ever been attempted before."

In its five-hundred-plus pages, Alec dissected what in his opinion were the best and best-known 800 or so of the more than 300,000 songs submitted for copyright during that fifty-year span. He offered his opinions on each song, just how good it was, and why or why not. The opinions reflected his biases, of course, but they were based on objective technical analyses and established aesthetic principles as well as emotional impact. He devoted entire chapters to the songs of the major composers of that era—including George Gershwin, Jerome Kern, Irving Berlin, Harold Arlen, and Richard Rodgers—and talked about their particular styles, strengths, and weaknesses. It is a monumental book born of an audacious vision. That he was able to complete it at all, given the enormity of the task, his paralyzing periods of self-doubt, and his tendency to go on drinking binges, was amazing. With considerable help from a gifted, inspirational friend and editor, James T. Maher, he not only got it done, he did it with wit, style, and language that was at once precise, efficient, colorful, and evocative.

It was perhaps understandable that in the book Alec did not mention himself or any of the songs he had written, some of which clearly deserved to be included. But he also refused to allow the publisher or editor to include any mention of his songs in an introduction or epilogue or editor's note that could have been written by someone else. They argued the case vigorously, but he would not budge.

The book was almost universally praised, and it inspired Dick Phipps of the South Carolina Educational Radio and Television Network to propose a series of public radio broadcasts based on *American Popular Song* and hosted by Alec Wilder. There was at least a slender thread of previous connection between Phipps and Wilder. Phipps had once produced a television show featuring Mabel Mercer and the great cabaret singer Bobby Short, and Alec had been in the audience.

Everyone with whom Phipps discussed his concept, including Loonis, thought it was a great idea, but no one who knew Alec very well believed he would agree to do it. For all his unsettling candor and unflinching opinions, Alec was essentially very shy, always shunning the spotlight and declining any offer of a platform. When Phipps asked Loonis if he would be interested in working on such a program with Alec, Loonis said, "I'd love it, but Alec ain't gonna to do it. For one thing, he hates microphones."

Phipps was persistent. He called Loonis again and asked what could be done to persuade Alec to do the program. "What does he like?" Phipps asked. Loonis answered that Alec liked nature, the outdoors, the woods. And great singers singing great songs, of course. Of course. Loonis realized that if they could line up some of Alec's favorite singers, who were also his friends, he might agree to host the show.

Phipps had a house on Lake Murray, outside Columbia, South Carolina, about ninety miles south of Charlotte. He described the large living room with a big window overlooking the lake and told Loonis they could tape the show there instead of in a studio. Maybe that would suit Alec better. Fine, said Loonis, but then he again mentioned Alec's dislike of microphones. Phipps said they could hide the microphones in some greenery.

The idea was to have a different singer each week. Each program would feature the songs of a single composer or lyricist, or would be based on some theme that the songs chosen would have in common. Loonis invited Thelma Carpenter to do the first show. "I knew she wasn't a prima donna and would be fun to work with," he said. Loonis would be the cohost and musical director, and his trio, with Terry Lassiter on bass and Jim Lackey on drums, would accompany the singer. With those elements in place, Alec agreed to give it a try, and *American Popular Song with Alec Wilder and Friends* became the second major project on which Loonis and Alec collaborated.

In the late spring of 1976, Thelma Carpenter flew to Charlotte for a brief rehearsal, and then she and Loonis and Alec drove to Columbia. After a night in a motel there, they drove to Phipps's house on Lake Murray to tape the pilot show for the new radio series. Phipps had gone all out—and perhaps overboard—to bring the outdoors inside, as Loonis had suggested. When they walked into his living room, they found a sort of jungle of ficus trees, and Phipps had hidden the microphone in some kind of exotic potted plant. Alec looked around and asked, "Where is Jane?"

"Who?" they all asked. "Jane who?"

"You know, Jane," Alec said. "Tarzan's mate."

He thought the decor was unbelievably tacky but hilariously funny, and he knew it was for his benefit, and the show would go on.

The South Carolina Network secured a grant from the National Endowment

for the Arts to produce the show. National Public Radio liked the pilot and distributed the series to 190 NPR affiliates around the nation. (None of them was in Charlotte, which had no NPR affiliate at the time. WBT-FM later arranged to broadcast the series.)

No improvisation, Alec decreed. He loved jazz and was in awe of musicians who were skilled improvisers. But this show was about songs and songwriters, and he wanted the songs sung as written.

The show featured some of the finest singers in the country. With the age of rock music stretching on indefinitely, and into its full maturity, almost none of the singers Alec and Loonis picked for the show were currently celebrities, or widely known outside a small but devoted group of fans of cabaret singing and classic American popular songs. Some, like Dick Haymes, who had been a singing movie star in the 1940s, and Margaret Whiting, had once been famous. Some, like Tony Bennett, had made hit records and would again. Some, like Bobby Short and Mabel Mercer, were living legends within their niche. Most worked regularly in jazz clubs,

Alec Wilder with Thelma Carpenter, rehearsing the first show in the public radio American Popular Song *series in the spring of 1976.*

supper clubs, and small concert halls in New York City or other major cities, and recorded, if at all, for obscure labels.

One of the great achievements of the show was that it brought such great interpreters of the American popular songbook, such great voices as Mabel Mercer, Barbara Lea, Jackie Cain, David Allyn, and Teddi King, back to public attention, and in some cases generated a revival of interest in recording them and booking them into clubs, concerts, and festivals. It provided valuable exposure for singers deserving of more attention, such as Marlene VerPlanck, whose voice was widely known, but anonymously, because of her work in commercials, and Anita Ellis, who also had done a lot of her singing in anonymity, dubbing vocals for actresses in movie musicals.

National Public Radio announced the new series with a party at the Algonquin Hotel on a Tuesday evening. Loonis arrived for the occasion fresh from playing a free weekend gig at the annual Collard Festival in his hometown of Ayden. The abrupt change in venues from Ayden to Algonquin surely would have been disconcerting to most people, but it was typical of Loonis's priorities and scheduling, not only then, but even as his reputation grew and spread nationally and internationally.

The first program in the series was broadcast during the week of October 3, 1976. After the series began airing, Alec and Loonis began getting calls from singers who hadn't yet been asked to appear, including Haymes, Bennett, Steve Lawrence, and Frank Sinatra. They wanted to know when they could be on the show.

"After that," Loonis recalled, "we could get anybody we wanted. Everybody wanted to be on."

In fact, there were only three singers Loonis and Alec wanted who did not appear on *American Popular Song*. Sinatra, who was Alec's good friend and an advocate for Alec's music, wanted to appear, but they could never overcome scheduling problems. The magnificent Sarah Vaughan was scheduled to tape a show but became ill and had to cancel. The third disappointment was Eileen Farrell, the former diva of the opera and concert stage who had turned to popular music and sang it beautifully. Her husband, who apparently considered himself the guardian of her career and reputation, told her not to do the show. Alec called her several times and pleaded with her, and then asked Loonis to try. Loonis later described the experience.

"I did not know the lady," he said. "Finally, to get Alec off my back, I called her. She answered the phone. The great Eileen Farrell. I was stuttering and stammering, trying to tell her who I was. She said, 'I know who you are. I hear you on that wonderful radio program with Alec.' But she wouldn't do the show without her husband's approval." Although Loonis failed to persuade her, the call marked the beginning of a long friendship, and he and Eileen Farrell would perform together and record together many times over the years.

Of those singers who did participate, most found it one of the great experiences of their professional lives. They were awed by Alec Wilder, charmed by Loonis, and quickly put at ease by the relaxed atmosphere of a comfortable lakeside home in the South Carolina midlands. They were impressed by the reverence with which everyone involved treated the great songs they were singing, by the way the songs and their singing were presented like perfect diamonds in simple, classic Tiffany settings, without the distractions of large orchestral arrangements. No one else was quite as effusive on the quality of the experience as Barbara Lea, who on a Sunday, after taping the program on Saturday, told writer Whitney Balliett of the *New Yorker:* "Yesterday was the best time I've ever spent. I plan to live a lot longer, but I could legitimately and calmly die now, and feel wholly at peace." But clearly everyone had a good time and enjoyed the feeling of being part of something very special.

The songwriters featured on the program were also enthusiastic and appreciative. Hugh Martin probably expressed the feelings of many of them when he sent this message to Alec via Western Union Mailgram: "I just heard your treasured Hugh Martin program. If it had been my only reward after 35 years of work I would consider it well worth it. Please communicate my delight with your artists and their perfect performances."

American Popular Song was a success on many levels. It reminded listeners who were past thirty-something of the names of the composers of those wonderful songs they had heard when they were growing up and had been replaying in their memories ever since. It gave a lot of people who would never know about, much less read, Wilder's book some exposure to Alec Wilder—to his personality, his wit, his deep knowledge and understanding of the music.

The program also brought about at least a small renaissance in cabaret music —usually a singer with a piano accompanist, or maybe a trio, performing in a bar or small café. It once had been a staple of the nightlife scene in New York City and other major cities, but in the age of television and rock music it had all but died. One survivor was the elegant Bobby Short, whose musical kingdom was the Café Carlisle. (His presence there was such that if anyone in the room was conversing during his performance, he would stop playing and singing and stare at the offending party until respectful silence was restored.) Now other cafés and clubs once again were bringing in performers whose distinctive and intimate styles carried on the great tradition of cabaret singing. Teddi King, a singer much admired by Loonis and Alec who had been working in relative obscurity in small rooms in Boston, was brought into the Café Carlisle when Short was taking some time off. Gil Wiest, owner of Michael's Pub, an intimate jazz venue, started booking singers and programs based on the *American Popular Song* series. One featured Loonis accompanying Marlene VerPlanck, and it drew praise from jazz reviewers in the New York press. Several other clubs in New York had live shows using the same format.

Several record companies picked up on the cabaret trend, and a new record label, Audiophile, was born from the influence of the Wilder-McGlohon program on NPR. George Buck, a recording entrepreneur, already had several labels, mostly specializing in traditional New Orleans jazz or swing bands perpetuating the music of the early 1940s. He created Audiophile to record some of the same singers, and the same kind of music, featured on *American Popular Song*—frequently with Loonis and his trio providing the accompaniment.

In short, the NPR series revived the Great American Songbook, revived interest in the great songwriters of the first half of the century, and revived the careers of several talented singers who had been all but forgotten when rock music began to dominate the commercial broadcasting and recording industries.

Most important for Loonis McGlohon, who had chosen to live outside the spotlight, in Charlotte, the program exposed him to a national radio audience, as a talented musician, a charming personality, and part of the inner circle of partisans and practitioners of classic American popular music. It also brought him into musically intimate relationships with some fine singers, many of whom would seek him out to accompany them, in concerts and recordings, in years to come.

One with whom he would not be working in the future was Teddi King, who had been in the first series of thirteen programs. She was in Charlotte rehearsing with Loonis for another taping of *American Popular Song* in 1978 when she got a call from the composer Richard Rodgers. There was some sort of benefit concert in New York that Saturday night, and Rodgers wanted King there to sing a particular song of his. So she flew back to New York for the concert. Before she could return to Charlotte she became ill, was hospitalized, and died. The cause was spinal meningitis. She was fifty-two years old.

Loonis, grieving over her sudden and premature death, was driving to Columbia when his feelings began to take the form of lyrics and melody. He pulled off the highway and, in a few minutes, wrote a song called "Songbird." It is arguably the best song he ever wrote. It immediately announces that it is no ordinary song: It is written in the key of E-flat, but it begins with a suspenseful D^7 chord that then sort of melts into the E-flat^7. The effect is something like a deep sigh, or the sun suddenly slipping above the rim of a dark cloud. From there the song is at once poignant and celebratory, with a lovely melody that ascends a stairway of harmonic changes that are original, unexpected, and yet in retrospect resonate with the same sense of inevitability that characterizes the structure of all great music.

The radio series won the George Foster Peabody Award, broadcasting's "Oscar," and as the weekly shows attracted more attention, promoters began calling and asking Loonis and Alec to present concerts based on the *American Popular Song* format. But Alec said he was not a performer, and with the exception of a Smithsonian Institution request for a concert featuring the music of Richard Rodgers and Lorenz Hart, Alec declined all such invitations.

After they had taped twenty-seven shows, the last featuring Tony Bennett's second appearance, Alec said "enough." He was tired of the exposure, and tired of the weekly responsibility. (The jazz pianist Marian McPartland, who knew Alec quite well, once asked Loonis how he managed to get Alec in one place consistently enough to do a weekly radio show. She thought it was amazing.)

Then one night Loonis and Alec were listening to records, and Loonis played one featuring a singer named Mark Murphy. Alec had never heard him before and thought he was wonderful. Loonis said Murphy was known mainly to jazz audiences. Alec declared that Murphy was one of the best singers he had ever heard, and said, "We have to get him before the public. We'll do another radio show." So Alec and Loonis agreed to tape thirteen more shows in the series, the first with Mark Murphy singing Cy Coleman songs.

One of their lesser-known collaborations, but one that meant a great deal to both of them, was a short musical, or folk opera, called *Mountain Boy*. It grew out of Alec's long friendship with Father Henry Atwell, pastor of St. Agnes Catholic Church in Avon, near Rochester—a pairing perhaps even more unlikely than McGlohon and Wilder. Alec would often talk at length with the priest, and on one such occasion they speculated about the boyhood of Jesus, and how his boyhood might have been if he had been born in a different time or place. That evolved into Alec's idea for a story about a boy with some of the same characteristics as Jesus, growing in the hills of Appalachia, and what the impact would be on his family and community, and how they would react to him. He mentioned it to Loonis, who wrote a libretto based on the concept. Alec wrote the music, and dedicated the work to the memory of his friend Father Henry Atwell, who had since died.

Mountain Boy premiered October 4 and 5, 1980, at the Downtown United Presbyterian Church in Rochester. In a review of the performance for the *Rochester Democrat and Chronicle,* Desmond Stone wrote: "A moving mini-musical, *Mountain Boy* . . . transported several hundred people from Rochester to the October hills of Appalachia. There, with the winesap apples ripening in the sun and with the corn in the crib, they witnessed the brief unfolding and flowering of a boy of unusual goodness, and in so many ways different from other boys." Stone called the play "tender and touching."

Just two months and twenty days after that performance, Alec Wilder died of lung cancer in Gainesville, Florida, on the day before Christmas. He had insisted that there be no funeral, no religious memorial service, no gravestone beyond whatever minimal marker might be required by law or regulation. His friends were torn between the desire to honor his dying wishes and the need they felt for some way to express their sorrow and to take note of his burial. The interment, which was to be in a cemetery near Rochester, had to be delayed until the ground in upstate New York had thawed. After it was scheduled for May 10, his friend and executor, Thomas Hampson, wrote to Alec's closest friends and invited them to a simple graveside ceremony on that date.

Desmond Stone described the ceremony in the prologue to his biography of Wilder:

> On May 10, 1981, a quiet, overcast spring afternoon, a score or more of the friends and admirers of American composer Alec Wilder gathered in Saint Agnes Cemetery. . . . They had come to honor a man with a song in his heart, a maverick who valued nothing so much as his independence, an old-fashioned knight who lived and died with his lance leveled against the tumultuous modern world. . . .
>
> One by one the mourners stepped forward to say a personal goodbye. . . . Loonis McGlohon, musical partner for many of the later years, spoke directly to Wilder and thanked him for the way he had given of himself: "Letters from strangers never went unanswered, even when they came from, in your own words, people who lived in old soldiers' homes who thought you were Thornton's brother. . . . You were a soft touch, Alec. As long as people believed in something, you could not say 'no.' . . . "
>
> A soft, sensitive trumpet floated the notes of one of Wilder's songs . . . , "It's So Peaceful in the Country." . . .
>
> Then boyhood friend Louis Ouzer did something the irrepressible Wilder had often done himself: he stepped forward and blew a string of bubbles. They sailed over the grave and captured for one last, shining moment the magic of the man and his music.
>
> The grave diggers looked on in astonishment.

McGlohon on Wilder : 16

From time to time during the 1990s, Loonis set out to write recollections and profiles of some of the people he had known and admired. Here is some of what he wrote about Alec Wilder.

When I was still a teenager I heard a recording of octets written by Alec Wilder. That music changed my life! If I had been asked then or even today to describe it, I would probably say it was classical music played behind a jazz rhythm section. Whatever it was, it was new, never heard before.

Mitch Miller, the finest oboist in New York and a young executive with Columbia Records, had waved the banner for Wilder's unorthodox compositions and persuaded Columbia to provide a few hours of recording time. He gathered eight of New York's best musicians into a studio to record the pieces. The compositions were short, none over three minutes long, and they were not expected to sell very well, despite such provocative titles as "His First Long Pants," "The Children Met the Train," and "Bull Fiddles in a China Shop."

After I heard the octets, I became an Alec Wilder fanatic. I would look for the name on record labels, and I found a few of his pieces: "Soft as Spring," recorded by Benny Goodman, "It's So Peaceful in the Country," written for Mildred Bailey, and "I'll Be Around," recorded by the Mills Brothers, a group I would not have listened to otherwise.

By the time I was thirty-five or forty years old, I knew almost everything Alec Wilder had written. Frank Sinatra once conducted a chamber orchestra recording some of Alec's wonderful concert pieces, including "Air for Oboe," "Air for Flute," and "Slow Dance." Alec's popular songs, always full of surprises, were recorded by

Sinatra, Tony Bennett, Rosemary Clooney, Peggy Lee, and many other great singers. Then there were Wilder pieces for solo piano and virtually every instrument in the orchestra, even a work called "Child's Introduction to the Orchestra," in which instruments were given names, such as "Tubby, the Tuba." He wrote suites for Grandma Moses, Albert Schweitzer, and other people he admired.

After I got to know Alec, we wrote songs together—probably fifty or more. We also wrote an opera, a musical score for the Land of Oz, a Las Vegas revue, and many art songs.

As a frequent visitor in our home, he did complicate our lives. I wonder now how Nan and our children tolerated the man, who didn't just come for dinner but sometimes seemed to take over our lives and home. I suppose they put up with him because they knew he was my hero and I thought he was America's greatest composer. (I still think that.) And they must have known what a thrill it was for me to write music with him.

I have been asked a few times to describe Alec. He was erudite, witty, ill-mannered, well-mannered, rude, caring, Edwardian, hostile, loving, insulting, well-read, childish, intolerant, protective, eccentric, ill-kempt, critical—and one of the most fascinating people I have ever known.

A lovely piece of music could move Alec to tears. A trite and sophomoric piece of music would make him scream and yell. He espoused good manners, but he would stir his coffee with a fountain pen, then wipe the pen on his napkin or his coat lapel before returning it to his pocket.

Alec became indignant when he was called "eccentric." Yet he always took a plastic "bobble-bird" everywhere he went. The bird would be fastened on the rim of a water tumbler, and he would watch as it appeared to drink water from the glass.

His tweed coat (he owned just one at the time) bulged with an assortment of things in the pockets: a small pad of manuscript paper, a package of cigarettes, a silver pillbox Sinatra had given him, packages of saccharin, several scraps of paper on which were written telephone numbers, appointments, notes to himself, train or airline tickets, a bottle of glycol solution and a plastic wand used to blow bubbles. On any clear sunny day you would find Alec walking about outside, blowing bubbles, oblivious to any stares he may have attracted. When asked why he blew bubbles, he would say, "Soap bubbles are among the most beautiful things man can create. So why not?"

He also carried plastic bags filled with small pieces of chocolate candy he bought from Schwartz, an elegant candy shop on Seventy-fifth Street on the east side of New York, which is now out of business. They were the small imperfect pieces that the store otherwise would not have sold, but bagged for Alec to buy at a discount. Alec called them "trash." The problem was that Alec never offered his hosts any of the "trash." Instead, he ate it at night after going to bed. He smeared chocolate candy all over the sheets, and finally, Nan confronted him: "Alec, if you eat any more chocolate in bed, you will wash the sheets yourself. And I'll show you how."

Although he slept in the bedroom usually occupied by our youngest daughter, he assumed the room became his own the minute he dropped his suitcase there. Laurie was gracious about giving up her room, but she would sneak into the room sometimes to make one of those telephone calls that teenagers seem to have been born to make. Often, Alec would start to walk into "his" room, then turn and stomp into the den where we were sitting and shout, "Laurie's on the phone in *my* room."

But Alec could also be an entertaining guest. At dinner, he and the family frequently made up games. For instance, one night he asked each of us to name the person we would most like to meet or take to lunch. Alec had met many fascinating people—Albert Schweitzer, Grandma Moses, Maurice Ravel, for example. When Fan asked him whom he would most like to meet, he said, "Montaigne, but of course he is dead. I would like to spend some time with Pablo Casals, because I think he may be the greatest living person today."

When it came my turn, I said, "Harry Truman. He is one of my heroes."

"Have you told Mr. Truman that he is your hero?" Alec asked.

I laughed and said I didn't think Mr. Truman would be very impressed if I did. Alec switched to his "Now Hear This" voice:

"But he does want to know," he roared. "He needs to know that he is admired, and no one is too busy to stop and hear someone telling him that he is a hero. You must write Mr. Truman tonight and tell him how much you admire him!"

Later that night he asked me three or four times if I had written to Mr. Truman. He continued to ask over the next couple of days. Finally, to get him off my back, I wrote a note to former president Truman, telling him about our discussion and "to let you know you are my hero."

I received a prompt reply from Mr. Truman, thanking me and agreeing with Alec, that we should always let people know when we admire them.

A few years later Alec called me one night and told me I should call Harold Arlen, who wasn't feeling well and needed cheering up. I said I didn't know Harold Arlen and didn't want to intrude on his privacy. Alec gave me Arlen's number and insisted that I call. At that point the operator at the Algonquin, where Alec lived, cut in to tell Alec she was ready with his call to Africa. Before he hung up, Alec again said I must call Harold Arlen. When I dialed Arlen's number, I got no answer, which was just as well. Later Alec called again to ask if I had talked to Harold Arlen. I told him there was no answer, and then I asked whom he was calling in Africa.

Alec said he had called Robert Ardrey, the author of *The Territorial Imperative* and *African Genesis.* He said he had recently read that Ardrey said he was not going to write any more. "I told him he must not stop writing," Alec said, "that we need him, that we need the books he writes."

Alec had a lot of unlovely habits, but he also had the lovely habit of always telling people when he loved and admired and appreciated them.

When we had other guests while Alec was visiting, he was often rude to them. He refused, most of the time, to accompany us to have dinner with friends. On the few occasions he decided to join us, he was usually gracious and polite, even complimenting the hostess on her dinner. But not always, unfortunately.

Once when he was here, our friend Charleen Whisnant, a poet and teacher (now Charleen Swansea) invited us to bring him to a party at her house, which she said was in Alec's honor. Alec declined, and I explained to Charleen that he never went to parties when he was here. The night of the party, while we were eating dinner, Charleen called again and said she had invited a lot of musicians, and the famous jazz promoter George Wein was in town and would be there, and that Alec simply had to come. She had told Wein that Alec would be there, and it would be embarrassing if Alec didn't show up.

"Well," I said, "tell him that Alec is in bed with syphilis."

I told Alec of Charleen's call, and reminded him that the party was in his honor, and given the kind of friends Charleen had and the kind of parties she usually threw, he probably would enjoy it.

"Who is this woman?" he grumbled.

"She is a daring and creative and fearless woman," I said. "For example, Charleen had always admired Ezra Pound, and when he was committed to a hospital in Washington, even though she was just a teenager, Charleen rented a uniform and went to the hospital and passed herself off as Mr. Pound's private nurse. That way she got into his room, got to meet him, and in time they became good friends. Before he died, Pound wrote her hundreds of letters, which are, in effect, his memoirs. Charleen won't allow them to be published until she feels the time is right.

"Also, Dylan Thomas named one of her children, and—"

Alec interrupted to ask more about her friendship with Ezra Pound.

"Remarkable," he said, "that she became a repository for his letters and that she still keeps them private."

A few minutes later he said, "Perhaps we should at least put in an appearance."

We were among the first guests to arrive. Charleen and her husband, Murray Whisnant, ushered us into the living room, where there was a contemporary abstract painting hanging over the mantel. Alec glanced at the painting and said loudly, "My God, what is that?"

Charleen bristled and asked, "What do you think it is?"

"A dartboard?" Alec replied.

The evening went downhill from there, but at least it didn't last long. Alec soon said he was ready to leave, and I knew if we didn't he probably would create a scene and cause us even more embarrassment. Charleen escorted us to the door and said, "Mr. Wilder, you may be a talented composer, but you are a very rude man. A dirty, rude old man."

Alec said, "And, madam, you are one of those creatures who scratches and opens little windows to look inside of people."

He unbuttoned his coat and held it open and said, loudly, "Scratch! Open a window! Take a look, madam. Scratch!"

I grabbed his arm and led him out to the car. On the way home I told him how embarrassed I was by his rude behavior in front of my friends. He didn't say anything. Just pouted.

About a month later Charleen called and said she had received a long letter from Alec. It was more than just an apology, she said. It was strangely personal. Within a few days she received another letter in which Alec talked about himself, his childhood, his fears, his contempt for today's society. Then came another long, revealing letter.

Suddenly I realized what was happening. The next time Charleen called to report a letter from Alec, I said:

"I told Alec about your friendship with Ezra Pound. It was after that when he decided he should go to your party. He wanted to meet you, to find out more about you. Now he has decided that you are a safe repository for his letters, his memoirs. I suspect you'll be hearing from Mr. Wilder very often."

Over the next two years, Alec wrote many more long letters to Charleen, who kept them all. She took them with her, of course, after she divorced and moved away. Eventually she moved into a great old house on Sullivan's Island, near Charleston, and one day in 1985, when she was away, the house caught fire and burned to the ground. Everything there was destroyed, including the letters of Ezra Pound and the letters of Alec Wilder.

In the late 1970s, after Alec and I had done the National Public Radio series called *American Popular Song*, the Smithsonian Institution asked us to present a program of Rodgers and Hart music there. Alec didn't like to be on stage, on display, so I was surprised that he agreed to do the program at the Smithsonian. It was scheduled for the Sunday after Thanksgiving, and Alec arrived at the hotel in Washington on Saturday, along with Barbara Lea, who would sing at the concert. That afternoon as the stage was being set up for a sound check, Alec told the stage manager he would not walk out on the stage. Instead, he informed the crew, he would sit on stage at a table and talk from there. They procured a table and a chair. Then he asked them to put something over the table to reach to the floor. He said he didn't want anyone to see his feet and legs. So they draped something—a bedsheet, maybe—over the table. They placed a microphone on the table for Alec, and suddenly he moved the chair, so that instead of facing the audience, he would be looking stage left. That meant the audience would see him only in profile, unless he were to turn around and look at them, which I knew would not happen.

At the concert, he faced stage left, never turning his face to the audience, even when he was supposedly talking to them. No doubt the audience thought his behavior was strange, and it was. Alec later said I had made him appear and look like a fool, and he never fully forgave me. In fact, neither I nor anyone else could make Alec do anything. But until his death he complained to anyone who would listen that I had made him go to the Smithsonian and perform "like an organ grinder's monkey."

Alec was the subject of a lot of fascinating stories, many probably exaggerated and some perhaps not true. Here are a few that I know, or am reasonably convinced, are true.

During the depression years, Frances Alexander, Mitch Miller, and Alec became good friends while they were studying at Eastman School of Music in Rochester. Frances was to become Mitch Miller's wife. Mitch was to become an icon in American popular music. And Alec was to become a great and underrated composer.

One afternoon Alec ran into Fran on campus and asked her if she would go with him to visit a new friend of his. It seemed that Alec had met a very nice black man, now unemployed, with two children. Alec explained that he was so impressed with the family that he had wanted to do something for them. "So I bought them a grocery store," he told Fran.

Alec had lots of money he had inherited from his late mother and father. He could afford to be extravagant with friends, so Fran was not surprised, and she was pleased that Alec would have thought of buying his new friend a business.

"So he is going to run the grocery store?" she asked.

"Oh, no," Alec told her. "I don't know that he has any experience in operating a store. No, I just bought the store and had all the contents delivered to his house. That is where you and I are going now, to see if everything has been unloaded there."

"Why didn't you give him the keys to the store, Alec, and let him operate the business?" she asked.

But she already knew the answer. Alec would never have thought of that. He probably had never been in a grocery store in his life. His mind didn't work that way. He figured that this family could use the contents of a grocery store. He had told the owner to go ahead and dispose of the store building after the contents were delivered to his new black friends.

Later Fran said that she would have known the location of the house long before they arrived at the address. "Rotted meat, chickens, and I can still smell the rotten cabbage that was piled behind the house and on the street, waiting to be picked up by the garbage people," she said.

When they entered the family's small rented house they found bags of flour, sugar, and bread stacked to the ceiling in the hallway. Canned goods filled the parlor and the kitchen. Perishables had to be discarded. Alec seemed pleased at his generosity. He told Fran, "They will have enough to eat for a good while, I think."

"Yes," she said. "And so will all the buzzards in Rochester."

The Algonquin Hotel is not and never has been glitzy and opulent like some of the Helmsley palaces or the Plaza. It is on West Forty-fourth Street and looks much the same as it did in the 1920s—a small lobby with vintage upholstered chairs scattered about, a newsstand in one corner, and an adjoining dining room. There used to be two. That the owners of the hotel have kept the hotel lobby looking the same is one of the Algonquin's charms. The guest rooms are small, but lots of icons and legends have slept here. The hotel's longest-staying guest was Alec Wilder, who lived there more than sixty years. He and his brother, George, moved into the hotel after their parents died when they were young boys. Alec remembered this parents always stayed at the Algonquin when they went to New York on business.

Alec lived at the hotel during that fabled time when the Round Table was flourishing—a group of writers and personalities who were supposedly shaping the thinking of the literary world. Alec disliked most of them. He dismissed Dorothy Parker as a bitter and poison-mouthed old maid. He disliked James Thurber to the point that he would sometimes move a footstool or a chair so that Thurber, nearly blind, would stumble over them as he tried to cross the lobby.

The talented actor Zero Mostel and Alec were very close friends, and they enjoyed playing pranks in public. One night while they were dining together, Zero ordered a bowl of whipped cream with which he proceeded to lather Alec's face.

Then picking up his dinner knife, Zero began to "shave" Alec while singing in full voice "The Barber of Seville."

Alec was friendly with actor John Carradine and told me a funny story about him. Carradine was staying at the Algonquin and had telephoned for a bellman to come to his room. When the bellman opened the door, he saw that the bed was on fire, with flames a foot high. Carradine, a tall and spindly man, was standing at the foot of the bed, weaving slightly (he drank a lot) with an unlighted cigarette in his hand. With the calm demeanor typical of an Algonquin employee, the bellman said quietly, "You rang, sir?" "Yes, my good man," Carradine said, trying hard to steady himself. "Do you have a match?"

Alec always liked the hotel employees more than he liked the guests. The telephone operator, the bellmen, the wait staff, the maître d' all were friends who called Alec by his first name. They spent a lot of time talking with him and exchanging gossip about some of the famous guests. But Alec also could be brusque and impatient with them at times. One morning I was having breakfast there with him. He ordered cereal with a banana. He scowled and muttered all the time he was eating his cereal, and finally he called the maître d' over. "I will not pay for this banana," he announced. "It was plopped down on the table, still in its skin. It should have been sliced and served to me on a silver salver. It is not my place to peel a banana or to slice it. You will please remove the banana from my check." The maître d' obligingly removed the charge from the ticket.

But most of the time Alec and the employees were like a family. Jeannette, the telephone operator for many years, would call Alec's room and warn him that somebody she didn't think Alec would want to see was in the lobby asking for him. And Alec might tell Jeannette to explain to the unwanted guest that he had died.

One night she called to tell him that a radio station had just announced that he was dead. "Great," Alec roared. "Get me a ticket to Montreal, train or plane, and I'll be down in a minute to get a taxi." He threw some clothes into a bag and hurried down to the first floor, where Jeannette told him, "You can go back and unpack, Alec. They just made a correction." Alec told her that was too bad, because he wanted to go to Montreal and hide out and see what the critics had to say about him now that he was dead.

One of the saddest stories about Alec—one that some people might find hard to believe, but I, sadly, do not—was told by a fan of his from Chattanooga, Tennessee, who was in New York and called to invite Alec to lunch. Alec asked if he would mind driving him up to see his mother's grave. She was buried along the Hudson River about an hour's drive from Manhattan. The man said he would be glad to, and so one morning they drove up to the cemetery where Mrs. Wilder was buried. When they arrived, the man told Alec to go into the cemetery by himself and have as much time as he wanted visiting his mother's grave. He felt this was a very private moment for Alec, and he waited in the car. But Alec returned in just a few minutes with a great smile on his face.

"Is everything all right, Alec?" his friend asked.

"Splendid!" Alec said. "I had planted some poison ivy on my mother's grave, and it is growing like wildfire—just splendidly."

Alec was also fond of Douglas Colby, grandson of the Bodners, who owned the Algonquin during the sixties and seventies. Mr. Bodner, a retired businessman from Savannah, Georgia, had bought the Algonquin as an anniversary gift to his wife. As long as the couple stayed at the hotel, Mrs. Bodner could usually be found sitting in the lobby in a special chair that gave her a view of all the celebrities who came into the hotel to meet other celebrities. The Bodners told Alec that they would reduce his room rate if he would write a book about the Algonquin. But they were disappointed when he finished the manuscript and gave it to them. Instead of a name-dropping book, which the Bodners wanted, Alec's book was all about the employees and the superb way in which they ran the hotel. The Bodners threw the manuscript away, and Alec's room rate went back to the normal fee. (I must confess that after reading the manuscript at Alec's request, I was as disappointed as the Bodners. Reading about incidents such as a bellman looking for lost luggage or the news vendor going out to buy another copy of the *Daily News* for a guest quickly became tedious. Alec was a brilliant writer, and if he had worked with a good editor and included some amusing anecdotes about guests who came and went at the Alongquin, the book would have been entertaining and would have had historical significance.)

As recently as 1997, singer Weslia Whitfield and her husband stayed at the Algonquin, and we sat in the lobby and talked about Alec. No one working there had been around when Alec lived there. The employees we talked with had only heard about him. I have always thought the hotel should have mounted a plaque on the door of his second-floor room announcing that "Composer Alec Wilder lived in this room for sixty years."

Bill Ploss of Gainesville, Florida, was Alec's personal physician. When Alec knew he was dying of lung cancer, he called Bill and told him he was coming down to Gainesville, and that he was ready for Bill to give him "the big pill." Alec and Fran Miller, his lifelong friend, flew to Gainesville, but Bill didn't give his friend and patient the "big pill." He did, however, look after Alec in the hospital until he died about ten days later.

Later I asked Bill, since his practice was in Florida, how he met Alec, and how he became Alec's doctor. His answer was another one of those bizarre Alec Wilder stories:

"I was practicing medicine in Key West," Bill said.

On a Sunday evening, my wife had just said that since we had enjoyed a big lunch, she hoped I wouldn't mind if we had the leftovers for dinner. About that time our doorbell rang. I went to open the door, and two people were standing there—no, I should say weaving there, because they were both drunk. I recognized the lady. She was Tallulah Bankhead, the great actress. The man was a stranger. But he said to me, "We thought we might have dinner with you." They stood there, waiting for me to invite them in. I opened the door, and they sort of staggered in, and the man introduced himself as Alec Wilder. The name meant nothing to me. They came into the living room and sat down. I ran to tell my wife that two strangers had come, uninvited, for dinner. I told her the woman was Tallulah Bankhead. She panicked, but somehow my wife managed to put something together, and the four of us sat at the dining room table, rather speechless, as I remember.

Tallulah and Alec babbled about things, and they managed to pick up bits of food on their forks, but all of it fell off before they could get the forks to their mouths. They laughed a lot, and my wife and I laughed, only because it seemed to be the thing to do. It was a very tedious and upsetting evening. Tallulah and Alec were both rather vulgar but in a strange way, very foreign to us, and interesting. Very interesting!

It was the next Sunday night, a week later, when Alec rang our door bell. He was alone. I had learned from Tallulah's drunken comments the week before that Alec was a composer—that he was a kind of musician's composer, highly respected by his peers. Now, he was standing at my door again, sober this time. I asked him to come in. Alec said, "You must be wondering why I came to see you last week. Well, you see, I have been told that I should have a doctor. That everyone will need, at some time or other, a physician. I had checked on you before I came to see you last week. And now I have decided that I want you to be my doctor. That's why I came back, to let you know. I suppose you will want to see me at your hospital sometime. Yes?"

That was the beginning of long, long relationship between Alec and Dr. Bill Ploss, a friendship of more than thirty-five years. It was Bill who told Alec in the 1970s that he had lung cancer and needed an operation. Alec always fussed because Bill, he said, had directed the invasion of his body. But it was also Bill to whom Alec turned in his last few weeks. He knew he would be in good hands.

I always thought that Fran Alexander, who married Mitch Miller, was the love of Alec's life. He never told her after the marriage that he loved her. He would never have done that. But he talked about her all of his life, and when he was dying he wanted her to come to the hospital in Florida and see him one last time.

Twenty years after his death, we learned that Alec had a daughter, living in London. It was a complete surprise to all of us when Margot suddenly wrote to Lou Ouzer, Alec's boyhood friend in Rochester, telling Helen and Lou Ouzer that she had discovered a birth certificate and other evidence that her mother had a brief affair with Alec, and that he was her father. Margot's mother has been dead for some time, and Margot kept quiet about her discovery until the year 2000. Then she flew to America, stayed at the Algonquin, and visited the Hampsons and the Ouzers in Rochester.

As Zena Hampson, the writer and Tom's wife, has said: "There is no doubt about it. Margot looks exactly like Alec without the mustache."

Margot's daughter is a pianist, and for no reason that can be explained, one of the first pieces she learned was "While We're Young."

She is to singers what Niagara is to waterfalls.

—Alfred Frankenstein in the *San Francisco Chronicle,*
writing about Eileen Farrell

Eileen : 17

Even though Alec Wilder had died, Dick Phipps of South Carolina Public Broadcasting knew the success of *American Popular Song* begged for a sequel. He and Loonis came up with a variation on the original theme for a new series. This time it would be *American Popular Singers,* and both agreed that a fine choice to host it would be the woman many considered the finest of all American singers, Eileen Farrell, indisputably one of the great voices of all time.

Eileen Farrell was unique, in that she was at once regarded as the finest operatic soprano of her time and one of the best interpreters of popular songs. Most of the great popular singers don't have the vocal power to sing opera. And even the most sincere efforts by opera singers to sing popular songs—except for those popular songs that are truly art songs, or have art-song pretensions—sound stiff and overstuffed. Eileen Farrell had all the volume and range necessary for opera, but she could lighten it, distill it, and focus it for a popular melody. Her popular music voice was conversational and supple, and even into her sixties, it had an almost girlish quality.

Eileen was barely out of her teens when she began singing on CBS Radio in 1940, and she soon had her own musical show on the network. She began her concert career in 1947, and her opera career in 1956, with the San Francisco Opera. She began singing with the Metropolitan Opera in 1960. But she loved the great popular songs she had grown up hearing, and she was a great admirer of the people who sang them well, particularly Mabel Mercer. Perhaps it was her genuine, lifelong affection for that music that made it possible for her to sing it with such sensitivity, understanding, and respect. By the time she began singing at the Metropolitan Opera, she was also gaining a reputation as a fine popular singer.

When Alec and Loonis were making a list of singers they wanted for *American*

Popular Song, Eileen Farrell was an obvious choice. Both were fans of hers, and Alec was a good friend. At her husband's insistence, however, she had declined their invitations to be a guest on the show. But now the reputation of that series and of the people who were part of it was securely established. Whatever the reasons, she and her husband no longer had any reservations about such a project, and she agreed to host the new show with Loonis.

In 1981 they began taping a series of thirteen shows, mostly in New York City and a few in Columbia. The first show aired in January of 1982. Guests on the series included Bobby Short, Julius LaRosa, Mabel Mercer, Joe Williams, David Allyn, Barbara Cook, Maxine Sullivan, and Marlene VerPlanck. The theme music for the series was Loonis's "Songbird."

The project cemented the friendship between Loonis and Eileen, and before they had finished taping the series, Bob Reagan, Eileen's husband, called Loonis to ask if he would like to be Eileen's accompanist and musical director for a concert tour she was planning. Nothing could have pleased Loonis more. The tour included the San Francisco Opera House, Lincoln Center and Carnegie Hall in New York, and many points in between.

Jazz impresario George Wein asked Loonis to produce two concerts for his 1982 Kool Jazz Festival in New York City. The first, on Sunday, June 27, at Carnegie Hall, was a tribute to Alec Wilder. Performing Wilder's songs were Eileen Far-

Eileen Farrell and Loonis. (Photo courtesy of Anita and Steve Shevett.)

rell and Mabel Mercer (then eighty-seven years old), the singing duo of Jackie Cain and Roy Kral, pianists Marian McPartland and Ellis Larkins, trombonist Bob Brookmeyer, Gerry Mulligan on baritone sax, Stan Getz on tenor sax, and trumpeter Joe Wilder. A brass ensemble conducted by Gunther Schuller played some of Wilder's concert pieces. Loonis and his trio, with Bill Stowe on drums and Jay Leonhart on bass, were on hand to accompany some of the singers. It was a great night for Wilder fans and jazz fans—and for Loonis, of course—and was greeted with almost universal praise by the critics.

The next night, Monday, June 28, Loonis and his trio and Eileen and Mabel Mercer moved to Alice Tully Hall at Lincoln Center to perform a concert called *Listen to the Words*—a program of songs with great lyrics. It, too, got very favorable reviews in the New York press.

Loonis continued to work with Eileen from time to time, and in the late 1980s they began a series of recordings, first for the Audiophile label and later for Reference Recordings in San Francisco. Most of the sessions were recorded at Reflection Sound Studios in Charlotte, with Eileen accompanied by Loonis and his trio, with Bill Stowe on drums and Terry Peoples or Doug Burns on bass, and a group of other musicians that varied from session to session. Joe Wilder came down to play trumpet and flügelhorn on some of the recordings, but most of the supporting cast consisted of Charlotte-area musicians—most prominently, Jim Stack on vibes, Phil Thompson and Doug Henry on reeds, and Greg Hyslop on guitar. Loonis prepared most of the arrangements, and Manny Albam contributed a few.

Most of the recordings featured the work of a particular composer, including *Eileen Farrell Sings Rodgers and Hart; Eileen Farrell Sings Harold Arlen; Eileen Farrell Sings Johnny Mercer;* and *Eileen Farrell Sings Alec Wilder.* Another was a theme album, *Eileen Farrell Sings Torch Songs.*

Although there obviously are many, many great songs and many composers not included, in that series of recordings Loonis and Eileen probably came as close as anyone has to creating a definitive collection of classic American popular music.

During that same period Loonis worked with Eileen on several recordings made in London with a large orchestra arranged and conducted by Robert Farnon. Loonis had gotten to know the highly regarded London-based conductor a few years earlier, and Farnon previously had prepared several orchestral arrangements of songs written by Loonis, including a chart of "Songbird" for a recording by the pianist George Shearing. Loonis considered Farnon the best arranger in the world in that genre, and it was always a thrill for him to hear a Farnon arrangement of one of his songs. André Previn, the jazz pianist and Hollywood film composer turned symphony conductor, had said at the time that Farnon was the best writer of string arrangements in the business. Farnon's lush, elegant orchestral settings seemed to bring out a bit more of Eileen's dramatic power than the small-group accompaniments.

One of the recordings Eileen made with Farnon, *This Time It's Love*, released on the Reference label in 1991, included a new song by Loonis. The liner notes for the CD describe it as a "song written especially for this project by Miss Farrell's renowned accompanist, who also plays keyboards on the album." The song, "Everything I Love," never seems to come up in writings or conversations about Loonis's best compositions, but it is a beautiful example of the contemporary songwriter's art. At first impression it may seem to be one of those somewhat familiar, easily hummable tunes, but after only a couple of hearings the listener would be hard-pressed to hum it. The deceptively simple melody maneuvers through a harmonic structure that provides a bit of a surprise at almost every turn and then ends rather abruptly, but perfectly. Farnon's arrangement brought out all the emotional potential of the song. The lyrics have a powerful simplicity, and Eileen gave them a reading that suggested that the song was very special to her, perhaps because Loonis was so special to her. "Everything I Love" is a little gem that deserves to be in the repertoire of many more good singers and musicians.

The Farnon recordings were among the last Eileen made. She was then into her seventies, and her intonation was not as precise as it used to be. Loonis was concerned that on some of the songs she had been slightly off pitch on a few notes, and he wanted Farnon to let her do additional takes. Farnon said he thought what they had was fine.

"But I don't want Eileen to be embarrassed," Loonis said.

Farnon refused to redo any of it.

"It doesn't have to be technically perfect," he said. "It's the emotion she puts into it. I've never heard such emotion."

That was what mattered most, he said, and he didn't want to lose that.

Eileen had been a victim of stage fright during concert appearances all her life, and that anxiety eventually led her, in the mid-1990s, to stop performing. But during the Charlotte recording sessions she was relaxed, happy, and enthusiastic, and in great voice. She liked Reflection's facilities and personnel, she enjoyed working with the musicians Loonis brought in, and she enjoyed being a guest in the McGlohon home during those periods. Nan loved having her, and Eileen loved being there.

All of that relaxed ambience and affection flowed into the recordings made during those times in Charlotte, when Eileen was in her late sixties and early sev-

enties but sounding fresh as ever. They represent some of her best work—at ease, down-to-earth, warm, and loving.

In that same period, Eileen performed at Spirit Square in Charlotte with Loonis and his trio, and she sang briefly at one other Charlotte venue—the room at Carmel Presbyterian Church where Loonis rehearsed the choir. Eileen sometimes went with Loonis to choir practice. On one of those occasions, Loonis recalled,

> We got there early, and I was distracted for some reason, and Janet Bean, one of the sopranos in the choir, who had never met Eileen and didn't recognize her, said, "I hope you sing." And Eileen said, "Well, a little." I'm sure they introduced themselves, but Eileen often introduced herself as Eileen Reagan, which was her married name.
>
> The rest of the choir arrived, and as I was rehearsing them from the piano, I could see Janet sitting next to Eileen in the soprano section, and I could see Janet's eyes rolling over toward Eileen and getting bigger and bigger.
>
> When we took a break Janet went over to her husband, Rick, and said, "Did you hear that new woman in the soprano section? She can really sing!"
>
> "Well," Rick said, "I should think so. Loonis says she's been called the world's greatest dramatic soprano."

McGlohon on Farrell : 18

Eileen Farrell died on March 23, 2002, less than two months after Loonis died.
Here's a profile, with personal anecdotes, that Loonis wrote about her.

When Eileen Farrell was presented the Living Legend Award in New York on November 12, 1995, the Singer's Forum founder, Andrew Anselmo, said, "Her career spanning over fifty years in classical and popular singing is absolutely unique in the history of music."

To which accolades, Eileen would probably say, "Oh, hell, it don't mean nothing!" Which is exactly what the sweet-faced Irish lady said when I asked her once how she shouldered the responsibility of having been called the greatest dramatic soprano in the world.

Eileen doesn't regale you with stories of her Metropolitan Opera triumphs, her world tours with the Bach Oratorio Singers, her dozens of appearances at Carnegie Hall with practically every famous conductor of this century. Instead she talks about her children, her friends, the best way to cook lobster, how to fix an Irish stew, and she asks about you, what you have been doing. If pressed, she will tell you about the jokes she and Richard Tucker played onstage, and she may tell you which were her favorite roles in opera. But don't think you're going to sit down in the presence of a temperamental, arrogant diva. You'll be in the presence of one of the loveliest ladies you ever met.

The voice is glorious, of course. She just opens her mouth, and the full round sound, which could soar above a hundred-piece orchestra without a microphone, comes out. It will give you chill bumps. For a long time during her career as an operatic soprano, no one outside a small circle of friends knew that she also sang pop music.

She had always been a fan of jazz and pop music, and even when she was performing opera, she would wipe off the makeup, take off the costume, and hurry to Tony's or some other small club to listen to Mabel Mercer. Eileen has said many times that Mabel was her teacher.

The public first heard the pop voice of Eileen Farrell in the 1950s. Louis Armstrong was slated to appear on the Ed Sullivan show, but he became ill. Someone remembered having heard Eileen sing jazz at a private party one night, and when asked, she agreed to sub for Louis on the television show. It was the beginning of a new career. Eileen recorded several pop- and jazz-tinged albums, infuriating some opera purists but delighting a new coterie of Eileen Farrell fans. People were amazed that she could convincingly sing Jerome Kern and Harold Arlen and Alec Wilder with as much style as Judy Garland or Frank Sinatra.

From that time on, Eileen Farrell moved comfortably between two worlds that had always been far apart—singing *Maria Stuarti* with Beverly Sills, recording a monumentally successful *Medea,* recording the Grammy-winning *Messiah* with Leonard Bernstein, and at the same time singing pop and jazz with André Previn, and later with the Loonis McGlohon Trio.

I couldn't believe my good luck the day Eileen's husband, Bob Reagan, called to ask if I would be interested in going on the road as Eileen's musical director. He said the first date would probably be in New York. I said, "I could start walking tomorrow!" We had already appeared together on the National Public Radio series *American Popular Singers,* so I knew she was no moody prima donna. Those were some of the happiest days of my life, rehearsing, traveling, and performing with the world's greatest opera singer now turned world's greatest popular singer.

Going overboard in praise for this unique lady is easy to do. There is simply no one else quite like her. Stories about her "sailor's mouth," as Beverly Sills referred to it in her autobiography, are common among musicians and promoters. Many are exaggerations, but not all. Even though an expletive may slip out of her mouth, Eileen is always considerate, sympathetic, and endearing, without the fat ego attributed especially to opera singers.

One day we were in New York rehearsing for a television show. When we broke for lunch, Eileen and I and a couple of other people found a small Italian restaurant nearby on Forty-seventh Street. It was a hole-in-the-wall kind of place, but as we walked in the young Italian at the front counter recognized Eileen and shouted loudly, "The great diva is here! *Cara diva!*" He came out from behind the cash register and bowed low to Eileen, who was immediately applauded by two or three other waiters (all Italian—and all into opera, I would guess), who also exclaimed how thrilling it was to have her here. As we were threading our way down a narrow aisle to a back table, one of our group said to Eileen, "It must make you feel good, Miss Farrell, to walk into a place and be given such a royal welcome."

Eileen whispered, "Oh, hell, they think I'm Kate Smith."

Eileen always seemed rather surprised when a fan approached her while she was shopping, or dining in a restaurant. After she let her hair grow silver-white, she never expected fans from her opera career to recognize her. It made her uncomfortable when a fan stopped her and said, "I recognize you, Miss Farrell, because you are just as lovely today as when you were in *Gioconda.*"

One of the highlights of Eileen's career was the night in June 1982 when she and Mabel Mercer performed a historic concert together at Lincoln Center. Unfortunately, the union would not allow a recording to be made of the program, so there is no way to revisit or pass along what was, indeed, a once-in-a-lifetime performance. Eileen, in the early part of her career, had received thirty-two curtain calls at a concert one night in San Francisco. I don't remember how many times Eileen and Mabel had to return to the stage that night in 1982, but I do remember that the trio and I got tired of playing for their bows.

"Why don't these people shut up and go home?" I asked Jay Leonhart, the bassist. The drummer, Bill Stowe, complained of wrist cramps when we finally left the stage.

Looking back now, I know that the audience was seeing together on stage, for the first (and only) time, two of the greatest performers in the world of popular music. None of us who were there will ever forget it.

Bill Stowe, bassist Jim Ferguson, and I traveled the continent with Eileen. Every date was memorable: Los Angeles, San Francisco, Milwaukee, New York, Washington, St. Paul. I learned something about Eileen on each date. There was the night in Los Angeles when the theater manager came to Eileen's dressing room and nervously told her that he wanted to apologize for the two or three hundred seats that would be empty that night. (Two or three hundred out of five thousand isn't that bad, is it?) Eileen told the manager, "Please don't worry about empty seats. If there are only five people out there, I will sing for them just the same as if we had standing room only." That was a good lesson. Since that night, I have never fretted over having a small audience. At least not as much.

Once during a rehearsal with a symphony orchestra, the orchestra manager had failed to set up the orchestra on stage as clearly set out in a package from the New York office. Instead of having our trio close to the conductor and just behind Eileen, we were strung out across the stage with the drum set almost in the wings. It didn't work, and when the first number was rehearsed, it sounded like a train wreck. Eileen was trying to vent her anger by changing the words to "S'Wonderful." She was singing, "Horrible! Terrible! What a catastrophe." Nobody could hear her but me, and I decided to tell the conductor we would have to reset the orchestra. He agreed, and it was necessary to take a long break while chairs and music stands were moved.

Eileen and I sat out in the audience. The orchestra manager, a dour lady, approached Eileen and asked, "Is everything all right, Miss Farrell?" I kicked Eileen, meaning, "Be nice." Eileen smiled and said, "Everything's lovely."

As the manager started walking away, Eileen said, "Wait a minute. Everything is not lovely. You received a diagram from my manager telling you how to set the stage and orchestra. For some reason you decided not to follow instructions. Now, personally, I don't mind sitting here for forty-five minutes while the stage is reset, but I hate that the musicians in your orchestra have to hang around all this time. May I ask why you chose to ignore my manager's instructions?"

In a haughty manner, the manager said, "It was because the maestro said he could not see the orchestra from that position."

Eileen didn't take a breath. She said, "Then why don't you get him a [censored] seeing-eye dog?"

While we were on the road, there were a few other instances of Eileen showing her Irish temper—but only when it was deserved. She never asked for "perks," like many of the big stars—dressing rooms painted lavender, bottles of Château Rothschild 1970, bowls of beluga caviar, and green M&Ms (all other colors discarded). She was, in fact, indignant about performers who asked for the moon and put in their contracts, as some reportedly did, that no one backstage was to look at them or make eye contact.

"Hell," she said, "there have been times when I had to dress in the ladies room with the customers. And I could never ask stagehands to look at the floor every time I pass by."

Eileen and another famous soprano were in St. Louis once to perform at the opening of a renovated opera house, and they were staying at one of the best hotels there. Eileen was in the lobby, waiting for the limo to take them to rehearsal, when the elevator door opened and the other soprano stepped out, followed by bellhops carrying all her luggage. Eileen asked her where she was going. She said she was moving to another hotel. Eileen wanted to know why. The other soprano said she didn't like that hotel because they had terrible orange juice, the worst she had ever tasted. She told Eileen to go ahead to rehearsal and she would catch up with her there, as soon as she checked into another hotel. As she walked away toward the door, with her entourage, Eileen said, in her outdoor voice, in that lobby full of people, "Oh, don't be so [censored] grand."

But in my fifteen years with Eileen, I never heard her say anything rude to a fan. She always complimented the stage crew, and she loved to have a vodka and tonic with them backstage. She was thoughtful and generous. She insisted that Nan accompany us on many trips, all expenses on her. She was appreciative for every gesture made to her by fans, strangers, and friends. She is, in fact, one of the most unselfish and caring people I have ever met.

She was a wonderful houseguest. She would stay with us when we were rehearsing or recording together in Charlotte. I can remember only one occasion when she said a cross word to anyone while she was there. That was to Gladys, and it was not exactly gratuitous. To understand what happened, you have to know a little about Gladys.

Gladys Albritten was born in 1900 and spent her childhood in an orphanage. When she was eighteen years old she went to work and live in the Lovelace home. The Lovelaces were expecting their sixth child, who was Nan. Gladys never married or had children, and to her, Nan was her one child, and would remain so the rest of her life.

After Nan and I were married and living in Charlotte, Gladys visited us often. Our children loved her as they would a grandmother. Everyone accepted Gladys as a member of the family, but Gladys could be blunt and outspoken about her opinions, and her lack of tact could try your patience. One night, for example, she was having dinner for the first time with our son Reeves and his wife Debbie, who had worked hard to prepare the meal. Debbie had put a lot of effort into an exotic soup she served for the first course, and she made the mistake of asking Gladys how she liked it.

"I've had better," Gladys replied.

On more than one occasion Gladys was staying with us during one of Eileen's visits. Gladys wasn't into the arts and didn't know anything about Eileen's career. To her, Eileen was just a nice family friend from out of town. One day when Eileen and I were in my studio, just behind the house, talking about a format for an upcoming concert, Gladys walked in and said, "Eileen, I didn't know you were a singer."

Eileen laughed and asked, "How did you find out?"

Gladys, who was then ninety-one years old, explained that she had been watching an interview with Carol Burnett on television, and Carol had mentioned Eileen as a great singer and one of her favorite guests on the *Carol Burnett Show*. Eileen said yes, she had been on the *Carol Burnett Show* several times, and yes, she was a singer.

Gladys sat down in a chair near the piano. "Well," she said, "sing something."

"What would you like for me to sing?" Eileen asked.

"Oh, I don't know. Something I like."

"What about a song Loonis wrote?"

Gladys said that would be all right. Eileen sang "Songbird." When she was finished, Gladys said, "I don't really like that kind of music, even if Loonis did write it."

Patiently, Eileen kept trying to come up with something Gladys would enjoy. "Did you like Judy Garland?" Eileen asked.

Gladys said she had seen Judy Garland in *The Wizard of Oz.* Eileen asked me to accompany her on "Over the Rainbow." It was a song that belonged to Judy Garland, of course, but Eileen had also put her stamp on it. When she sang the final words, "Why can't I?" she would hit the last note in a very soft, almost tearful tone, and then she would hold the note and let her voice swell, finally bringing the note to a soft pianissimo that seemed suspended forever. That's the way she did it that day for Gladys. In concerts, that finish always left the audience hushed and silent for a few seconds before the thunderous applause followed. In the studio that morning, Gladys said quickly, "Well, I never liked that song. It's not my kind of music."

Eileen, great lady and devoted friend that she was, didn't give up. She was determined to find something that would please our beloved Gladys.

"Well, you must have some favorite songs, Gladys," she said. "Or a favorite singer. Who's your favorite singer?"

Gladys said she did have a favorite singer. "But I can't think of her name," she said. "I can't remember, but she's a fat lady, like you."

Now Eileen spoke very slowly. "That would be . . . Kate Smith?"

"Yes," said Gladys, delighted. "That's who it is."

"And the song," said Eileen, still very slowly, "is 'When the Moon Comes over the Mountain'?"

"Yes, yes, that's it," said Gladys.

"Well," said Eileen, "that's a piece of shit and I won't sing it."

Gladys didn't say anything else. She was giggling softly as she got up and left the studio. She went back into the house and told Nan, "You won't believe what Eileen just said to me."

I love Eileen Farrell's sense of humor. And I love that glorious voice. There has never been another voice like it. She was called a mezzo, but once when she recorded a film track she also sang as a lyric soprano. When she did popular music and jazz, she sang in the range of a low contralto.

She never recorded anything in a pure jazz idiom, but in the privacy of my studio, she sang wonderful improvisations. She was so fearful that her jazz style did not compare favorably with Sarah Vaughan, one of her favorites, that she would never try to do jazz improvisations in public.

In fact, Eileen had terrible stage fright. She admitted the reason she performed more easily in opera was that she could hide behind the costume, that she was "being someone else." In concert, she had to be Eileen Farrell. She had a case of nerves before every performance. Sometimes she had nausea. When she wore a chiffon gown, I could see it shaking visibly on stage. I think the reason she finally said "I quit" was because of the stage fright.

"Why do I do this to myself?" she would ask.

But we are so glad that she did.

Marlene VerPlanck has had a large, almost-cult audience for some
years now. . . . She has an absolutely straight-ahead approach to singing,
tender but never maudlin, and a wonderful ear for the right song.
—Peter Reilly in *Stereo Review*

Other Voices : 19

Except for Eileen Farrell, no singer was more closely associated with Loonis Mc-Glohon on recordings and in clubs and concert halls than Marlene VerPlanck. She also has the distinction of having been heard by more people who never heard of her than any other singer, ever, anywhere. Her audiences have numbered in the millions, but her fame is limited to the relative handful of people who love cabaret singing and the repertoire of classic popular songs. The millions have heard her anonymous voice on radio and television commercials: the "mmm, mmm, good" ditty for Campbell's soup was one, and another was "Winston tastes good, like a cigarette should," a ubiquitous jingle that drove English teachers and other grammatical purists crazy before cigarette advertising was banned from radio and television in the early 1970s.

She had a promising start as a singer with bands headed by Charlie Spivak and Tex Beneke and then with the last Dorsey Brothers band, where she met Billy VerPlanck, an arranger and trombone player who would become her husband. As rock music pushed other forms of popular music out of the commercial mainstream and big bands became all but obsolete, she found she could make a much better living singing advertising jingles. She also sang with backup vocal groups behind other singers, including Frank Sinatra, and even on some rock records. Billy found he could stay busy with studio work.

Despite a voice of extraordinary clarity, flawless pitch, and perfect enunciation, Marlene VerPlanck had all but vanished into the anonymity of singing commercials by the mid-1970s. Then Alec Wilder tapped her for the *American Popular Song* series he and Loonis were taping for National Public Radio. Alec had heard her in person, probably at Michael's Pub in New York City, where she occasionally

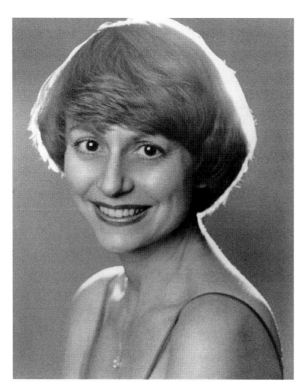

Marlene VerPlanck. (Photo from Marlene VerPlanck, courtesy of The Charlotte Observer.)

appeared, and on a couple of recordings on Mounted Records, a label established by Marlene and Billy to record music they really cared about.

So, at Wilder's summons, Marlene showed up at Columbia, South Carolina, in the spring of 1976. There she met Loonis and was immediately impressed by his musicianship and taste and charmed by his personality. Loonis, in turn, realized she was an extraordinary talent.

(In later years Loonis occasionally would describe her as "the best singer in the world." He used the same description for Eileen Farrell and probably a few others over the years. There was nothing disingenuous about the hyperbole, just a sort of rhetorical generosity reflecting Loonis's capacity for enthusiasm. In fact, they were very different kinds of singers, even working in the same genre and with the same material. Eileen's voice, even in its "pop" phase, could express layers of emotion the way a fine wine contains layers of flavor. Marlene's was more like bubbly champagne, or a crisp, ice-cold martini. Each was about as good at what she set out to do musically as any singer ever has been.)

Marlene taped a program primarily of songs by Hugh Martin. She also taped one on "one-shot wonders," composers credited with one truly outstanding song who had never reached that level of excellence again. Both were well received, and Marlene became one of a number of singers whose careers were revived by their appearances on the series with Alec and Loonis. In her case, the revival was largely accompanied by Loonis McGlohon, as she acknowledged in an interview years later: "When I met Loonis I was a studio singer in New York, and he was the one that got me back into performing and into recording and all those nice things. My whole life has just evolved now into performing and recording and doing his songs and Billy's songs."

She and Loonis recorded a number of LPs and later CDs for Audiophile. Because it remained a little-known label without serious marketing and distribution capacity, the recordings were generally ignored by the music and entertainment press. But they received favorable reviews from critics in the *New York Times, Stereo Review,* and other writers and publications sophisticated enough to recognize the quality and significance of work being done outside the commercial mainstream. She was also booked for clubs and concerts with Loonis and his trio. Billy VerPlanck provided arrangements for some of their collaborations, and he and Loonis wrote a number of songs together.

Another fine singer rescued from oblivion by the NPR series was Dick Haymes, although the revival was sadly brief and aborted. Haymes was, as Peter Reilly wrote in *Stereo Review* in 1978, "probably the only serious competition Frank Sinatra had during the Forties." Sinatra was more versatile. He not only was a great ballad singer; he could swing an up-tempo number like a great jazz horn player. But the *Charlotte Observer* columnist Kays Gary, who came of age with big band music and the great vocalists of that era, did not exaggerate at all when he wrote that Dick Haymes "may have been the greatest ballad singer of all time."

Haymes was born in Argentina, into a family that a few years later would have been described as part of the "jet set." He grew up in expensive boarding schools but with little or no attention from parents. At some point he discovered that he had a special voice, and a special affection and appreciation for good songs. Like Sinatra, he got his start with big bands when they were big not only in numbers of musicians but also in popularity. By the late 1940s his voice and good looks had gotten him into motion pictures, musicals in which he was leading man to some of the most glamorous female stars of the time. One was Betty Grable, the most popular pinup of American GIs in World War II. The movies were pretty silly, but the music was wonderful. In one memorable scene, a quintessential Hollywood moment from that era, he sang "The More I See You" to a luscious, pink and blonde Grable, over a picnic lunch.

Haymes went through a succession of highly publicized marriages and even more publicized divorces and had a serious drinking problem. Long after his fame and popularity had passed, he continued to display the arrogance of stardom. But Alec Wilder and Loonis remembered the voice and recruited him for their NPR series. As did most of the singers on that show, he found a true friend in Loonis.

Haymes's voice had somehow survived the excesses of his lifestyle. His appearance on NPR served to remind fans of classic popular music that he was one of the great interpreters of ballads. He recorded an album called *For You, for Me, Forevermore,* accompanied by Loonis and his trio, for Audiophile, and followed it with *As Time Goes By,* also with Loonis and his trio, recorded at Reflection Sound Studios in Charlotte. The second album was for an even more obscure label, Ballad Records, and financed by a Dick Haymes fan club in England. Both recordings were greeted with praise by critics in *Stereo Review* and *Radio Free Jazz.* One critic called it the best work of Haymes's career. He seemed poised for even more of a comeback, with a television special about his career in the works, when he died of lung cancer at age sixty-one. His primary legacy to American popular music is on those Audiophile recordings he made with Loonis, and they are unexcelled examples of the art of singing ballads.

There were two other singers who worked with Loonis late in his career and were very special to him. One was Mike Campbell, a Californian who, fresh out of college in the late 1960s, was part of that youthful choral group called the Doodletown Pipers. Trying to establish himself as a jazz singer, at a time when the greatest and best-known jazz singers in the world were sinking into obscurity, was a frustrating experience that yielded only some Las Vegas lounge gigs, and club and restaurant work as a single, accompanying himself on guitar. Finally he put his fine voice to the service of commercial jingles to make a living for his family. He did manage to record an LP of good songs, called *Secret Fantasy,* in the early 1980s. It attracted little attention, but someone sent Loonis a copy, and he was impressed with the quality of the voice, the almost conversational style, and the musical taste reflected in the choice of songs and the way Campbell handled them.

Loonis reacted to this discovery as he often did: He tracked down Campbell and told him how much he liked the record. Meanwhile, coincidentally, Campbell had recorded a second album that featured "Blackberry Winter" as the title track. As a practitioner of great American songbook, he knew Loonis by reputation and by his compositions. So he was thrilled and encouraged to hear from Loonis, and another great Loonis friendship was born. He and Loonis worked together in several venues, including Spirit Square in Charlotte. In 1994 they recorded an album called *Loving Friends,* for Audiophile, and then *My Romance* and *Let's Get Away from It All,* with Loonis on piano and Charlotte's Ron Brendle on bass.

More than once, Loonis declared that Mike Campbell was his favorite male singer. Certainly Loonis was Campbell's favorite accompanist and one of his favorite songwriters, as well as one of his best friends.

In a 1998 interview for an article in *Jazzbeat* magazine, Campbell told writer James Gavin: "Loonis is like my second father. This guy has given me so much in my life, I can't even tell you. It's not only him, it's his whole family. They just welcomed me into their home. Loonis has done this for so many other people."

Campbell teaches singing and coaches singers in California.

Because of her talent and her proximity, singer Maddy Winer was an important colleague for Loonis during the last decade of his life. Maddy had moved from

Florida to Asheville, in the western mountains of North Carolina, just over a hundred miles from Charlotte. In addition to performing, she became director of music and special weekend packages, including an annual midwinter jazz weekend, at Asheville's historic Grove Park Inn.

Loonis and Maddy got in touch with each other and began to work together from time to time. They recorded together, and Maddy made numerous trips to Charlotte and elsewhere to sing with Loonis and his trio. In return, Loonis was a regular at the Grove Park Inn's annual jazz weekends and helped Maddy line up outstanding regional and international talent for the occasion. One of the most memorable of those weekends was in 1999, when Loonis brought in two friends, the great George Shearing and the esteemed guitarist Gene Bertoncini.

Loonis's favorite local singer probably was Daryle Rice, a young woman whose voice has a rich, round tone. He was a mentor to her and accompanied her in a number of concerts, and they recorded several CDs together, bringing her to the attention of a larger audience, which her talent certainly merited. "He taught me a lot about phrasing," she said, "and told me the right people to listen to. He introduced a whole new world to me."

Oh, who can ever count the lovely songs you've sung
Or know about the many old hearts you have made young?
—"Songbird," words and music by Loonis McGlohon

Songbirds : 20

Loonis knew and accompanied some of the finest singers in the world, and over the years he wrote profiles of some of them. These are his words, and his titles for each of the profiles.

Miss Whiting

She has led a charmed life: the daughter of songwriter Richard Whiting, the close friend of Johnny Mercer, star of her own television series, recording artist with three all-time hits, appearances in half a dozen movies, author of her autobiography, international singing star. Margaret Whiting is bigger than life. Ask her friends and fans about her, and they will tell you, first of all, she is helpful to all aspiring singers and caring about her friends.

Miss Whiting is not, however, the girl next door, or a neighbor who brings you homemade fudge or a casserole. Margaret Whiting is a star, and the room belongs to her when she walks in. Yet all of us who have been admitted to her circle love her dearly.

A few years ago Eileen Farrell was booked to do a concert in Charlotte. Eileen became ill three weeks before the performance date and had to cancel. The theater manager was not happy when I informed him. In fact, his voice was just a notch down from screaming when he told me that one of the important patrons had bought a hundred tickets for his friends and was giving a dinner for them before they came to see Eileen. His parting comment was, "Get Barbra Streisand or Margaret Whiting to replace Miss Farrell. This man is a fan of both Streisand and Whiting."

Miss Streisand would not know me from Li'l Abner, and even if she were avail-

Margaret Whiting.

able for the date, she would want five times what Ei-leen was going to be paid for the concert. It was a fee based on our friendship, and considerably lower than almost anyone in the star realm would consider.

But I did call Margaret Whiting. After we said our hellos, Margaret began to tell me how excited she was about a performance she was going to do in Hollywood. It would be the kickoff for a concert to raise money for down-and-out singers who were unable to pay their bills. The concert would be a tribute to Ella Fitzgerald, who would perform and present an award to be called the "Ella" to an up-and-coming singing artist. Margaret told me that everybody was going to perform on the show, including Barbra Streisand. Then she told me the date, which was the same date I was going to ask her to perform in Charlotte. Well, I thought, there go both ladies, Streisand and Whiting. My heart sank.

Margaret continued to tell me about the upcoming concert and also a little bit of current news about herself and a few of our mutual friends. Suddenly, she said, "Darling, I've been running off about what I'm doing. But I want to know how you are."

I tried to laugh when I said, "Well, not so good at the moment."

She asked why, and I told her my predicament. There was only a short pause, before she said, "Of course, I will be there to help you out."

"No," I told her. I said I could never expect that and wouldn't allow it.

"But, darling, they will never miss me at the Hollywood concert," she said. "There are a dozen great singers on that show. Besides, you are my friend, and you need my help. And that is what we are all about."

The lovely lady bowed out of the "Ella" concert, came to Charlotte at a very low fee, and performed beautifully. Never once did she complain about missing a great night in Hollywood. That was just one of several such instances I know about, when Margaret has put friendship in front of money and good reviews.

After her autobiography, *It Might as Well Be Spring,* was released, Margaret called Nan one day and said she would like to come down for a short visit, and would I be willing to drive her to Winston-Salem for a book signing. As we drove to that city, Margaret asked how I liked the book. I had read it. The truth is always safe between friends. I blurted out, "I don't like it."

"Well, I said nice things about you," she said.

"And I thank you, too, Margaret. But what I don't like about your book is that nowhere do I read how loving and considerate and caring you are. You tell us too much about the men you've slept with, that sort of thing. The Margaret we love is not in the book."

I think that stunned her, but it was the way I felt.

Margaret and Johnny Mercer were very close, like brother and sister. Johnny always called Margaret when he had finished writing a new song, played it for her, and asked her opinion. This he did after he and Henry Mancini wrote "Moon River." Margaret gave him her opinion: "It's lovely, Johnny, but there's one line you must change. I don't like it. That's the line about 'my huckleberry friend.'" Johnny and Margaret had a short argument about the phrase, and Johnny told her he would certainly take her advice under consideration.

It was about six weeks later when Margaret's mother asked her if she had heard Johnny's most recent song.

"I don't know, Mother. What's it called?"

Mrs. Whiting said, "I think it is called 'Huckleberry Friend.'"

Benny Goodman called me one day and said, "I just heard a record you made with Margaret Whiting. Is she really singing that good now?"

What was I supposed to say? "She is singing just like you heard on the album, Benny," I told him. "She sounds wonderful."

"You have her telephone number? I want to ask her to do a Town Hall concert with me," he said.

Margaret called me a couple of days later to thank me for recommending her. "I've never worked with Benny before," she said. "I look forward to it."

She sounded delighted. I saw no need to warn her that Benny could be very strange. After all, Margaret was a big girl.

The day after the concert she called me and said, "Don't ever give Benny Goodman my telephone number again!"

I realized at once that she'd had one of those Benny Goodman experiences. She said rehearsals had been fine. She had rehearsed five or six tunes with the band, and they played her music very well. At the concert, she was standing in the wings, waiting for Benny to introduce her. At that point an overeager stage manager, standing just behind her, said, "You're on, Miss Whiting." And he gave her a little push that propelled her, a little off balance, onto the stage. She continued to walk out to the mike. The audience recognized her and applauded, even though she had not been introduced.

When she reached stage center, Benny looked at her quizzically and asked, "Margaret, what are you doing out here?"

Margaret is a pro, so she smiled and said, "Oh, Benny, I thought I would love to sing with you and the band."

He smiled and asked her what she would like to sing. Even that didn't throw her. She shrugged and said, "Oh, whatever"—meaning, of course, the music they had rehearsed.

Benny said, "OK," turned to the band, and said softly, " 'Lady Be Good' in F." The band began to play the song, which was not in Margaret's repertoire. She might have tried to fake it, but it was in the wrong key for her voice. The only thing she could do was stand there while the band played several choruses of "Lady Be Good."

After the band stopped playing, Margaret suggested one of the numbers they had rehearsed, which they played and she sang. But that did not relieve the embarrassment Benny had caused her. And, although he certainly deserved it, Margaret was too much of a lady to kick the King of Swing where it would sting.

The Man Who Sang the Blues

His hair was beginning to get white when I first met Joe Williams. I had followed his career from the time he sang with Count Basie through his on-his-own stardom. His voice was immediately familiar when he sang his signature number, "Every Day I Have the Blues."

So it was understandable that I was a little nervous when I walked into a studio to record a show with Joe Williams. He had spent a lot of years with the best of pianists, all the way from Count Basie to Norman Simmons, each different in his approach to accompanying a great vocalist like Joe. When I asked him to tell me what he would like in the way of accompaniment, Joe laughed and said, "It ain't easy being white, is it?"

Joe suffered my work patiently, and it must have passed with a D-minus or something, because I had the pleasure of working with him many times, even after his hair became snow white. He was a tall, robust man, and his teeth and hair seemed even brighter and whiter against his dark skin. He must have worn a size 14 shoe.

He was a gentle soul with a marvelous sense of humor. He could imitate a snobbish British accent beautifully—perhaps in part because he was married to a British lady. They lived in Las Vegas.

While Joe Williams was always called a "blues singer," he confessed to me once that he had a preference for singing standard tunes by Harold Arlen, Cole Porter, George Gershwin, Jerome Kern, and Alec Wilder. He had a very intellectual approach to show tunes, and I have never heard "Nobody's Heart," a little-known gem by Rodgers and Hart, sung as well as Joe sang it on a show we did in San Francisco.

His voice was still robust and flawless until his untimely death. He was in a hospital in Las Vegas for congestive heart problems, and he decided to check himself out and go home. Unfortunately, he got disoriented as he started walking toward his neighborhood. He was found dead on a street that led in the wrong direction.

I still hear his voice as he said to me, every time we met, "It ain't easy being white, is it, Loonis?"

From stories he told me about the indignities he and other band members suffered, the racism they encountered, while touring with Count Basie in the early days, I knew it wasn't easy being black, either.

The Other British Queen

When Mabel Mercer returned to her home country in 1977 to perform, the staid *Times* of London carried this headline: *Two Queens in Residence in London for the First Time: Elizabeth at Buckingham Palace, Mabel Mercer at the Savoy.*

Mabel, the singer's singer, was in London to perform at a new room at the Playboy Club. It was a triumphant return for a lady who had been the toast of London, Paris, and Rome in the 1930s. It was her first trip back to London since then, and she also went over to Paris, which she had not seen since 1938, when the Duke of Windsor told her she must get out of France before the Nazis arrived. "The Paris I knew and loved was gone," Mabel said sadly when she got back to New York.

She was born February 3, 1900, in Staffordshire, England. She never knew or saw her father, a black musician. Her mother, also a rather shadowy figure in Mabel's life, came from a British family of bohemian people. If Mabel thought of herself as looking different from other English children, she became painfully aware of the difference when she went off to boarding school. When she asked a teacher why the children called her a "golliwog," the teacher had to explain that this was a vulgarism for a child born of racially mixed parentage. In America at that time Mabel might have been called a "nigger." Someone has described her skin as looking like cream with a little coffee added. Her eyes were a bluish-green, but her hair was black and kinky. In her later years, Mabel often wore an "invisible" hair net to control the wiry curls.

As a young girl, Mabel was devastated to learn that others considered her a "freak." Seeking people who did not view her as different, she wound up joining a "minstrel" group when she was a teenager. She danced and sang, and soon she was good enough to join a larger traveling troupe, also African.

Eventually, Mabel Mercer became a singer whom the rich and the royals came to see. In Paris, she was an international star, holding court at Bricktop's club in Montmartre.

Mabel tells a story about performing Cole Porter's "Just One of Those Things" one night in the early 1930s. Out of the corner of her eye, she was aware that a man in the audience had gotten up, walked over to her pianist, shoved him to the end of the piano bench and sat down. He began to accompany her himself. Later the man introduced himself to Mabel and apologized for his behavior.

"I'm sorry," he said, "but your accompanist was playing the wrong chords. I know, because I wrote the song."

Throughout her life, Mabel Mercer sang the songs of Cole Porter, and those of a handful of other composers, including Harold Arlen, Richard Rodgers and Lorenz Hart, Bart Howard, and Alec Wilder. And it was a high point in my life when Mabel sang my song, "Grow Tall, My Son," which I wrote when our son, Reeves, was born.

When Hitler's Germany began invading its neighbors, the Duke of Windsor arranged for Mabel to leave Paris and stay at his home in the British West Indies until a visa could be obtained for her to come to America.

"I left my apartment in Paris with only my clothes. I never saw the apartment again," Mabel told me. "I don't know what became of my personal belongings."

For the next forty years, Mabel Mercer performed at only a handful of clubs, most of them in New York. She made rare visits to a few other cities, including opening the Hungry I in San Francisco. It didn't matter where Mabel performed. Those who wanted to see her would have gone anywhere. The word got around that this short, plump lady had a way with songs that no one else had ever matched.

She sat in a thronelike chair, sometimes playing with a brightly colored shawl across her lap, leaning forward into the audience and interpreting the best of American popular songs in a totally unique way. Those who came to see and worship her included Frank Sinatra (he called her "the best teacher in the world"), Barbra Streisand, Lena Horne, Eileen Farrell, Julius LaRosa, Steve Lawrence, Madeline Kahn, Judy Holiday, and most of the best songwriters of her time. If she had a mind to, Mabel could lift a song out of obscurity and make it a standard. Even though "Little Girl Blue" and "Wait Till You See Her" had been dropped from the Broadway shows for which they were written, Mabel rescued them, sang them over and over until they caught on. And they always remained her songs.

Her voice was a rather thin soprano that in later years became cracked and wavery. On the recordings that have survived her, she is not an impressive singer, maybe not even a very good singer. You had to see her in person to understand why she was so revered. Her hands performed. The fingers touched, barely, her lower lip when the song expressed surprise or a childlike wonder. The eyes became very sad, and the face showed pain when she sang about unrequited love. Mabel called every good song "a one-act play," and she was the actress who could explain the play to you in three minutes.

But there was something else, and that is what I remember most. There was an aura of goodness about Mabel Mercer. There was a presence that made you sit in awe. I have never seen more goodness radiate from a face. It was no wonder that, at her farm in upstate New York, wild birds and other creatures would eat out of her hand.

Mabel was a devout Catholic, and when she visited us, we had to make sure we got her to mass every Sunday. She never used profanity, and a certain look from her whenever anyone told an off-color joke was a clear signal that the act had to be cleaned up. In fact, Mabel enjoyed a risqué story, but only with a close friend or two.

She was happiest when she was puttering around her cluttered and always-in-need-of-repair farmhouse in the Berkshires. She kept an apartment in Manhattan, but it finally became so piled up with gifts she had received it was practically unlivable. Mabel would unwrap gifts, ooh and ah over them, then rewrap them (complete with ribbon bow) and stack them on the floor. Eventually, people had to move single file through the hallways and rooms. Material things were not an important part of Mabel's life.

In the daytime, Mabel was an ordinary-looking woman in her shapeless dress and comfortable shoes. It was at night when she became a queen, royal, elegant in brocades and silk, sitting enthroned before

Mabel Mercer enjoying a Carolina spring day in the McGlohon's yard.

her subjects. It was then, as Mabel sang, "I put on me pumps." As she grew older, songs like "When the World Was Young" and "Once upon a Summertime" became less sung than spoken. It didn't matter. The communication was just as powerful.

Mabel never understood the effect she had on her audience. "Perhaps one of my songs touches them, reminds them of another time, some moment in their life," she would say shyly. Then she would shrug, "I really don't know."

It was a great privilege for me to work with Mabel Mercer for about six years. She knew what she wanted from an accompanist and was quick to let him know. She never sang a song until she had first memorized the lyrics, gone over every word, line by line, shifting emphasis here, sometimes moving a comma around, but never changing a syllable. She had too much respect for the song and its writer to change a word. When she was through examining every note and every word, she would perform the song with more understanding and more clarity than any other singer in the world. It was no wonder that so many of the great singers and actors in the world came to listen to the Queen and learn from her. And it was from her, as Frank Sinatra said, "We all learned the most."

[When Mabel Mercer died in April of 1984, Loonis was one of the pallbearers at her funeral in Chatham, New York.]

I Loved Thelma in Spite of Herself

When Thelma Carpenter joined the Count Basie Orchestra as a vocalist in the late 1940s, she had already been a star in New York and Europe. Segregation was still the rule in a lot of places, but she was surprised, and then indignant, when the Basie band bus pulled up in front of a run-down hotel in St. Louis.

"Whatcha stopping here for?" Thelma asked Basie.

"This is where we have to stay when we play St. Louis," Basie said.

"Not me." Thelma said. "I'm staying at the Chase."

"Nah, you ain't," Basie said, laughing at her.

"Let me off this damn bus, and give me my suitcase," Thelma commanded. She told Basie, "I'll call you later."

Thelma got a taxi and told the driver to stop by a fabric store, where she bought several yards of silk material. Another stop was at a hardware store, where she bought a small roll of black tape. With her manicure scissors, Thelma cut a round dot from the tape and pasted it in the middle of her forehead, and by the time the taxi pulled up in front of the first-class, whites-only Chase Hotel, Thelma was swathed in silk from head to toe. She demanded that the driver take her bag into the hotel, where beautiful tan-skinned Thelma registered as a princess from India.

From her room, she called Basie. "What time is the gig?" she asked the Count.
"Nine o'clock," he grumbled.

"Well, when you come by to pick me up, don't you drive that bus in front of my hotel," she ordered.

"Where are you, Carp?" he asked.

When she told him she was staying at the Chase, he said, "Nah, you ain't."

"Yes, I is," she cooed. "And like I said, I don't want to see that busload of niggers in front of my hotel. You call me before you leave that dump you're in, and I will meet you around the corner from the hotel. And when you call, don't ask for Miss Carpenter. Ask for Her Serene Highness, Princess Yasmin Shafir."

Thelma Carpenter was one of the most beautiful women in music and theater. She was only five feet two inches tall, but she had the poise of a tall model. She was part Native American, and she had beautiful milk chocolate skin and lovely features, with a sprinkling of freckles across her nose.

For her brief biography, Thelma herself is the best source. One day on a Manhattan street she ran into Arthur Godfrey, the popular radio and television host of the 1950s and 1960s.

"When did you get back from Europe, Carp?" Godfrey asked. "Didn't know

Thelma Carpenter.

you were back. I want you to call my producer, Peter deSalle, and tell him to book you on my show as soon as possible."

Thelma called deSalle, and after telling him her name and that Mr. Godfrey had asked her to call, he asked, brusquely, "What do you do, Miss Carpenter?"

"I sing," Thelma said politely, but she was getting ready for battle.

"Where have you sung?" he asked, impatiently.

"I sang on the streets for nickels and pennies when I was eight or nine years old. Then one day I auditioned for the Major Bowles radio show. Now, I don't think he was a real major. Probably just a stage name, but I got on the show, many times, in fact. Then I went to the Apollo Theater. That is a theater up in Harlem, Mr. deSalle. I won a talent show there. And you know, when I was about sixteen, I sang with a band on the road. And I sang for several years on Fifty-second Street at the major jazz clubs, and then I went on Broadway, where I played in many shows, like *Inside USA,* and a major revival of *Show Boat.* I toured with a band called Count Basie. Now, he is not a real count. Just a stage name. And then I went to Europe, where I have been living for many years, and I might add, as the toast of the Continent . . . "

At this point, deSalle interrupted to ask, "My god, how old are you?"

"I'm a hundred and three, but there are other things about me that are unique. I'm just four feet tall, and I got two mothaf——— heads. And I'll see you later, baby."

Not exactly the way to get on the good side of Godfrey's producer. But I loved her. I first met Thelma in the 1950s, when she was touring with *Show Boat,* playing the role of Magnolia. Her phonograph records were already familiar to me, and Nan and I had seen her in 1946 in the New York production of *Inside USA.* She was a wonderful singer and a fine actress. Unfortunately, Thelma could not keep her foot out of her mouth.

She had been a major star in Europe, and she never adjusted to being just another good black performer in America. If Thelma liked a person, a lifetime friendship developed. If she didn't like you, watch out. She had the talent and the looks to become one of the top stars in America. Every time she came close, she jinxed herself.

In the 1950s, Pearl Bailey asked Thelma to join her and husband Louis on a long-running tour of a musical show. Thelma passed out a Hugo Winterhalter arrangement written for her of "Someone to Watch over Me" at the first New York rehearsal. It was obvious that the musicians in the orchestra were enjoying the Winterhalter arrangement and Thelma's treatment of the song. Pearl Bailey, listening from the wings, decided she didn't like it. She ran on stage declaring, "I don't like that arrangement. Too slow. It's gotta go. Take it out."

Thelma and Pearl didn't get along. Thelma managed to curb her temper and stay with the show until they got to Washington, D.C. There, Thelma decided it was time to leave. The show opened with a procession of the cast from the rear of the theater, down the aisle, up onto the stage, with everybody singing. Miss Bailey, as a part of her shtick, dragged a mink coat behind her down the aisle. Thelma went to a costume shop, had the seamstress take a ratty fake mink coat, cut the fur into two-inch squares, and tack the pieces very lightly back onto the lining. She subbed that coat for the usual fake fur Pearl used. During Pearl's entrance, the movement of the coat caused the pieces of fur to come loose and fall to the floor. Thelma, who was directly behind the star during the procession, helped matters along, so that when Miss Bailey arrived on stage, there was very little fur left on the coat. The audience loved it. Miss Bailey did not. Thelma was fired.

It would not be the last time. When Thelma played the role of the Good Witch in the musical *The Wiz,* she never got along with the star. And she didn't want to prerecord her song, as the director insisted. "Lip sync is for the birds," she told him. "I've always sung live, and I've been singing for forty years." When you see the film, you will notice there are no tight close-ups of Thelma. She never got the hang of lip synchronization. She thought it was unrealistic.

In the film *Cotton Club* she does the unthinkable. She ad-libs part of her lines. But the director liked it and left it in.

When she starred in the television series *Barefoot in the Park,* she didn't like the other stars. The show was canceled after thirteen weeks. I suspect the producer had had enough of Miss Carpenter.

Late one night, Thelma called from Boston. She had just finished the third night of a two-week engagement at the Copley Plaza.

"Honey," she began in her sugarcoated ladylike voice, "Can you come up to Boston tomorrow and play for me? I got seven more nights here, and I need you."

I knew she had booked a very well known jazz pianist for the gig in Boston, so I asked her what had happened.

"This piano player has been putting me in the wrong keys and playing introductions for me that sounded like Ben Hur was going to come on stage driving his chariot," she said. "It's been awful. This man has played everything wrong, hoping I would just give up and leave the stage."

I knew better than that. I asked, "What did you say to him, Thelma? You must have said something to make him do that."

"Well, the first night, I did say, 'You know, I paid twelve hundred dollars for that arrangement. I sure would love to hear it played correctly.'"

"You said this over the mike?" I found it hard to believe that even Thelma would toss this insult to the band and the audience.

She admitted maybe she had not been too tactful. I told her that I could not come up to help her out, and that she should apologize to the pianist and try to make up with him.

"All right, baby, I'll try. But if that son of a bitch don't play no better tomorrow night, I am gonna slam the shit out of his fingers."

Thelma was her own worst enemy. Nan and I loved her dearly, in spite of her dirty street mouth. She hexed her own career time after time. We were always amazed when we would learn that she was going to star in another movie or on Broadway or play in a television series. We knew it would be a short-lived run for her, because sooner or later she would create a scene that would sabotage the production.

But she was witty, brilliant (she spoke five languages), caring, and beautiful. Even in her last years, she stopped a show whenever she appeared. Her last television appearances were in the role of Bill Cosby's mother in his hit series.

A television station in Richmond, Virginia, was doing a March of Dimes telethon on the same weekend that we were having a similar fund-raising show on WBTV in Charlotte. The Richmond producer called to ask me what I thought of the lineup he had booked for his show. It was always strategic to book three or four celebrities, not only for entertaining, but also to make hard pitches to the audience to raise money. The Richmond cast was fine, but I thought it lacked a black personality, and I recommended he consider Thelma Carpenter, who had Richmond ties and had spent some time there. He liked the idea and asked if I would call Thelma.

It turned out she was available for the weekend of the show, and the money, although not great, was sufficient. But she didn't say "Yes" until after she asked who else was going to be on the show in Richmond. When I mentioned the name Betty Johnson, she asked, "Isn't that the girl who used to wear blue gingham dresses and pigtails and claim she was a farm girl from somewhere in the South?"

"That's the girl," I told Thelma. "In fact, she is from Charlotte, although her publicity claims she was born in Possum Walk."

Thelma said, "Yes, I'll do the show. I need to settle a score with that woman."

I don't know anything about the score she wanted to settle, but I remembered some corny pictures that were made about the time Betty Johnson, who was a member of a gospel-singing family, went to New York in the late 1950s to appear on national television and to record what turned out to be hit songs. The publicity photographs were the idea of some public relations guy in New York. Since Betty claimed to have been raised on a farm in Possum Walk (as far as I know, there is no such town), the photographer came down and located a small log cabin room (probably a small storehouse for crops) in the country. There he set the stage for the publicity photographs for Betty Johnson. My favorite showed the family, Ma and Pa Johnson, the twin sons, and Betty (who looked to be about seventeen), sitting around a kitchen table, placed in the middle of the dirt-floor cabin. There was a bowl of pork and beans in the middle of the table, and just before the Johnson family served themselves, they had lowered their heads in prayer. Ma wore a sunbonnet, the men all wore bib overalls, and Betty, complete with pigtails, wore a blue gingham dress with a white apron.

I sent the photograph to Thelma Carpenter.

Between the time the publicity shots were made and the year of the telethon in Richmond, Betty had been a successful recording star and appeared at such glamorous places as the Waldorf. She had also become something of a great lady and had tried to put her past as a tobacco farm girl far behind her. She was married to a successful man, and between performing and being the lady who lived on Park Avenue, she restored historic houses in Connecticut and Massachusetts. In fact, on one of her return trips to Charlotte, her hometown, she couldn't even remember the name of our downtown main street. So you know she had long since forgotten about Possum Walk.

But Thelma reminded her of her "humble beginnings" when she passed the photograph down along the table where the cast sat after the show in Richmond and asked Betty to autograph it for her. Betty was a little peeved when she saw the photograph.

"Where did you get this?"

"Well, I have some friends down in North Carolina, and when I was visiting them recently, they took me out to your birthplace shrine. And I bought this at the souvenir stand."

Thelma Carpenter called us every week during the last several years of her life. She called me her "white cousin," and during my first several years of enduring cancer, Thelma would send money to a convent in upper New York state, asking the sisters to light candles for me. When the nuns would ask about me, Thelma would say, "Cousin Loonis is feeling better. Fact is he had Madame Walker come over to his house and fix his hair. She did a good job with the front, but I think she rode a bicycle on the back."

The last call we had from her was on a Sunday night in 1997. She was found dead in her Central Park East apartment the following Thursday.

Woman of the Ghetto

Marlena Shaw was about twenty-two the first time I saw her. She had agreed to do a television show for TRAV, the audiovisual arm of the Presbyterian Church in America. The show would try to explain the relationship between jazz music and the church. Many early spirituals had been important vehicles for jazz musicians, and a lot of contemporary black composers had written new music inspired by the church.

Marlena Shaw was a perfect choice to sing both spirituals and contemporary church works. She had grown up in New Rochelle, New York, singing in a church choir. When she accompanied herself on piano in later years, she played gospel piano.

Marlena Shaw.

I was not prepared to see such a beautiful young woman when I met Marlena at the airport. She is tall, and her skin is a flawless milk chocolate color. Her dark brown eyes are almond shaped, and they, along with her perfect nose, give her a kind of oriental look. Some forty years later, she is still lovely, and we have become close friends.

I think Marlena Shaw is the best female jazz singer in the country today. She swings effortlessly, and her improvisational skills would intimidate many a jazz musician. It may also be her great sense of humor that makes her singing unique. She is a very funny lady, and the humor creeps into many of her songs. One night, for instance, we were performing at an outdoor concert, and while she was singing "Our Love Is Here to Stay," a big cloud rolled over the park and dropped a major rain shower. Marlena, without changing the harmony of the Gershwin song she was singing, injected quotes from another song, "Pennies from Heaven," assuring the audience that there was no need to run under a tree. The crowd listened, took her advice, and stayed. The rain moved out.

In the past several decades, Marlena has had several hit records. "Woman of the Ghetto" was probably the first, and she still gets requests for that one. Other hits have included "Go Away, Little Boy" (and when she begins this, she tells the audience they ain't gonna get no Donny Osmond version) and "Street Walkin' Woman."

Marlena is one of those very loyal friends who constantly preaches, "Don't ever let a friend down. Your enemies? Well, whatever you come up with!" She practices what she preaches. I had booked her for a concert in Charlotte, and then, on the same date, she had an offer to sing at the Monterey Jazz Festival with Count Basie. She turned down the festival and honored a promise to come to Charlotte.

"Oh, I'll do Monterey later," she shrugged. And she did, many times.

She cut her teeth on the Basie band, traveling with them for four years as a guest star. She was a friend to all the sidemen, and they depended on her to make red beans and rice in her hotel room for all of them.

The first time our two daughters saw Marlena, they became her groupies. Not that they understood the subtleties of her art (they were very young teenagers), but she was wearing miniskirts before miniskirts became in vogue. She wore a pair of fire truck–red hip-length boots, and our daughter, Fan, thought those boots— not Nancy Sinatra's—were made for walking. Twenty-five years later—in fact, very recently—Marlena mailed those red boots to Fan, just to say, "Fan, I know you always liked 'em."

Marlena could have become a great actress or a comedienne had she chosen to take either path. Her wit is lightning quick. A few years ago, she gained a few unwanted pounds, and one night while walking from her dressing room to the stage, she caught a glimpse of herself in a full-length mirror in the wings. She was wearing a black top and a long, full white skirt. When she got to the microphone, instead of cuing her pianist for the opening song, she said to the audience, "Ladies and gentlemen, you are looking at a small table for one."

Recently, at the Blue Note in New York, where she is often a headliner, she spotted the great singer Marlene VerPlanck in the audience. At the end of her show, Marlena told the audience, "If you liked me, ladies and gentlemen, my name is Marlena Shaw. If you didn't like me, my name is Marlene VerPlanck."

She has lost those unwanted pounds she claims come from too much ham hock with the greens, but she is still likely to tell her audience, "What you see is what you get!"

I have always believed that Marlena has never become a superstar because she won't compromise—either her morals or her taste. She gives thanks to her Creator every day for her gifts, her family, her friends. And everybody in my family, thank the Lord, is on her list of friends.

When I was in New York recording in the early sixties, Marlena came by the studio when we were finishing the session. It was about six o'clock in the afternoon, and she wanted me to go to her house and have some pork chops, southern style, she said. But I had promised to have dinner with Thelma Carpenter, and I asked Marlena to come with me to meet Thelma. We were going to have dinner at Pete's Tavern in Greenwich Village.

Marlena, wearing blue jeans and a sweater, said, "I couldn't go looking like this. Miss Carpenter will be wearing a pretty caftan and a turban and dripping with jewelry."

I laughed and told her that Thelma would be wearing blue jeans and cowboy boots.

"Nah," Marlena said. "She'll be dressed to kill."

"Well, come on and I'll show you," I insisted. Besides, the great British cabaret singer, Elizabeth, was going to be performing.

Marlena finally agreed to join me, and we took a subway down to the village. She was still uncomfortable about meeting Thelma Carpenter.

"She's a big star," Marlena kept telling me.

She was excited about meeting one of the great icons for black entertainers. Thelma had replaced Pearl Bailey in *Hello, Dolly,* but this was her night off, and she thought I would enjoy hearing Elizabeth.

When we arrived at Pete's Tavern, I asked for a table. Thelma was habitually late for appointments, so we had time to order drinks before Carp, the Star, arrived. I nearly spilled my drink when the lady swept through the door.

Marlena said under her breath, "I told you!"

I had never seen Thelma dressed this way before. She was wearing an oriental caftan with a beautiful turban on her head. Five minutes later it was making no difference. Marlena felt at home with Thelma, and Duke Ellington came over and joined us. When he saw Marlena, he asked Thelma, "Who is this beautiful child?"

Thelma said, "Would you believe she is a love child Loonis and I had a few years—what, about twenty years ago? Ain't it a blessing she looks more like me?"

Wee Bonnie Maxine

Maxine Sullivan looked tall and regal on stage. If another singer or performer joined her on stage, then it was obvious the lady did not reach five feet, even with high heels.

She used to say, "I weigh eighty-five pounds soaking wet. A little less after I've dried myself."

Maxine stood very tall, however, among the world's great jazz singers. She had a relaxed and effortless way of singing around a tune, and this easy style made her popular with musicians and fans. She was also one of the most prolific recording stars of all time. Fortunately, she left a great legacy of recorded material when she passed away in 1987.

Maxine Sullivan.

In the 1940s when Maxine was getting started in the business, there was a strike, brought on by music licensing companies, that forced singers and musicians to limit performing and recording to public-domain material—meaning that every song had to be more than fifty-six years old and no longer protected by copyright. A lot of folk songs got brought out of the attic, dusted off, and given new life by recording artists.

Some wise soul suggested that Maxine record the Scottish folk song "Loch Lomond." It seemed a little strange for a black girl from Pittsburgh to sing about missing her true love on a lake in Scotland, but the swing arrangement for Maxine became an instant hit all over America.

The record was played on juke boxes all over the country, and one evening in a Boston bar, a Scotsman boasted loudly: "We are very proud of our wee bonnie lass, Maxine Sullivan."

An Irishman, sitting nearby, slammed his beer down on the bar and shouted: "Begorrah, you're daffy! She's an Irish lass, and her name is Maxine O'Sullivan."

The Scot insisted she was a Highlander. The Irishman doubled his fists, insisted, "She is Irish, you bloody fool."

One thing led to another, and soon the two men were on the floor fighting. A black bartender stepped from behind his bar, bent down, and told his two customers, "Sorry, gents, you're both wrong. She's one of us."

At least that's the story Maxine told me, with her deep, throaty laugh. She added that for a long time many fans did not realize she was black, because she also followed that hit recording with another Scottish folk song. Eventually, the strike was settled, and Maxine, after leaving the John Kirby Orchestra, began to record the best of Tin Pan Alley songs with her unique jazz style. Songs like "A Hundred Years from Today," "I Thought about You," and "Fools Rush In" became her property.

Recording with Maxine was, in the musicians' vernacular, a blast. For one thing, she was always prepared, and she seldom did more than one take on a recording date. She usually nailed the song right off the bat, so she and the band could be in and out of a studio in half the time most artists required for a session.

While recording, Maxine stood, feet apart (and she usually wore bedroom slippers or tennis shoes), with hands on top of her head, which was covered with a baseball cap. She moved very little, closed her eyes and let the swinging sound inspire everybody around her. There was no temperament, no showing off, no fingers pointed toward anybody who might have made a mistake. When the song ended, she waited for two breaths, then said, "All right! Whew, yes, sir." That meant she was pleased with the take.

I was very fortunate to be able to make four records with Maxine. One has never been released, as far as I know. Maybe I played some wrong notes. I know Maxine was letter-perfect.

Maxine was a musician, too—a trombone player. "But the horn was too big and heavy for me to carry around," she said, "so I gave it away."

While she never really retired from music, in her later years she formed a ladies' dance line, using all retired women who needed, Maxine said, some exercise. The group even performed two or three times.

She smoked too much, and eventually lung cancer began to rob her of her ability to hold notes. She refused to give up cigarettes, and finally cancer took her life.

Some musicians said her voice and style reminded them of Billie Holiday. That could be taken only as a compliment, of course, but little Miss Sullivan was her own lady. Everybody who ever heard her perform a song like "Miss Otis Regrets" will remember the unique sound of Maxine Sullivan.

The Man with a Heart

Someone wrote that Johnny Hartman had a voice like melted chocolate—a good analogy for a black man who sang white men's songs and did it better than most white singers.

Johnny passed away from lung cancer, but his voice is still heard wherever classic popular music is appreciated. At least one of his albums is a classic—the one he recorded with John Coltrane. Clint Eastwood used four uninterrupted Hartman recordings in his movie *The Bridges of Madison County*. And not everybody who loved Johnny is dead yet.

A slender, good-looking man, Johnny never built his career on singing the blues or black gospel-tinged material. From the beginning he was addicted to the songs of Cole Porter, Harold Arlen, George Gershwin, and Richard Rodgers. Per-

haps it was his exquisite taste in songs that kept him from being a household name in America.

His taste was also discerning when it came to choosing a mother for his children. Tedi, Johnny's wife, is one of the loveliest women in New York. She is still his biggest supporter, and although he has been gone for many years, she has never remarried. "I belonged to Johnny," she says.

Much of Hartman's early career was spent in New York, Chicago, Detroit, and Los Angeles. His audience was both black and white, and club owners liked to present Johnny, because he was suave and personable on stage. It was not until the late 1970s that Johnny Hartman was booked for an engagement in the South. I remember his nervousness and discomfort one night when we went to a country barbecue shack fifty miles south of Columbia, South Carolina. It did not occur to me that he had never before been in an all-white redneck restaurant.

"They won't lynch me, will they?" he whispered to me, as we went through a buffet line.

"They couldn't find the right kind of tree," I assured him. "Ain't nothing around here but loblolly pines. No branches strong enough on them."

Johnny Hartman was like a brother to Nan and me. Whenever he went to Japan, where he was a superstar, he always brought us special gifts. When Nan and I were in New York, we spent lovely evenings with Johnny and Tedi. He had a wonderful sense of humor. He never talked about himself. He had a long list of people he admired, and he saw them often.

Johnny Hartman had no faults that I ever saw, except that he could not give up cigarettes. They robbed music lovers of many fine singers, and in Johnny's case, at a young age, when he had much more singing to do.

A State of Grace : IV

No matter where I am in the world . . . people just know his name. They say his name wrong, but they know who I'm talking about. "Oh, yes, we heard him on National Public Radio. He wrote this or that song." . . . Everywhere you go, all you do is say Loonis. *"Oh, yeah, that guy from North Carolina." He's really become a household name.*

—Marlene VerPlanck

Fruition : 21

When Loonis McGlohon reached his fiftieth birthday, in 1971, he had much to celebrate. He had a fine family and a good home. Reeves had graduated from Lenoir-Rhyne College in Hickory, North Carolina, and was in graduate school at the University of North Carolina at Chapel Hill, preparing for a career in education. Fan was beginning her college education at Lenoir-Rhyne. Laurie was in junior high school. Home, presided over by Nan, was a place of comfort, refuge, and joy. He and his family were financially comfortable. He had a good job that he loved, despite some dismay at what was happening to the radio business. He was highly respected locally and regionally as a musician, and although rock music was taking over the commercial musical mainstream, he found steady after-hours work as a pianist and bandleader. Many of his songs had been published, and a few had been recorded. His boyhood musical hero, Alec Wilder, was now a close personal friend and songwriting collaborator. In his city of Charlotte it was unlikely that anyone else, outside of politics, was as popular, or as respected and loved by as many people, or that anyone else of any consequence had fewer enemies.

If he contemplated his life to date, as many people do on their fiftieth birthdays, he surely found little to regret and much cause for gratitude. It might even have occurred to him that life couldn't get any better. But it could, and did. Had he been able to see the future, he could have said what few people at age fifty can say: that the best was yet to come. He couldn't see the future, of course, but Loonis was the kind of person who seemed always to feel that the best was yet to come. And it was. Within the decade his plans and dreams, cultivated through years of hard work and late nights and tireless good cheer, blessed with more than a fair share of good luck, were blossoming into remarkable achievements and ever wider recognition that generated more and more opportunity.

In a 1978 interview with Bob Wisehart of the *Charlotte News,* Loonis declared that the last two years had been the best of his life, creatively and professionally. He had been selling everything he had written, he said, and the radio series with Wilder had brought him a lot of national attention.

His collaboration with Wilder had exposed his talent as a composer and lyricist to the upper echelons of the music world. Through their National Public Radio series, his playing and personality had reached a national audience, and he had achieved some measure of renown among aficionados of his kind of music. Some of the best pop singers in the world had learned firsthand, and were telling others, that he was a splendid accompanist. His recordings, as accompanist with Barbara Lea, Marlene VerPlanck, Julius LaRosa, and Dick Haymes, among others, were being reviewed in the *New York Times,* the *International Herald Tribune,* and other newspapers, and in *Stereo Review, Billboard,* and lesser-known but respected music periodicals in the United States and abroad. Knowledgeable critics not only applauded the music and the talent, but also were excited by the reemergence of some of those great singers and happy to be reminded how good they really were. *Stereo Review* named *Lovers and Losers,* which Loonis recorded with Teddi King shortly before her death, its 1978 Record of the Year. Loonis's name also appeared in the entertainment pages of the *New York Times* in usually favorable reviews of concerts and club appearances with outstanding singers and jazz horn players.

Whitney Balliett traveled to Columbia to watch and hear an *American Popular Song* taping session featuring Barbara Lea in the spring of 1976. Balliett's long article in the *New Yorker* included this description of the pianist and cohost of the program:

> Loonis McGlohon is a quiet, funny, sandy-colored man with a cornerless tidewater accent. He is a remarkable and deceptive accompanist. At first, his chords and occasional arpeggios had a stiff, Sunday-school sound, but he was invariably in the right place at the right time, and on Richard Rodgers' "A Ship Without a Sail" he developed a series of rolling aqueous chords that suggested a barcarolle. He is a man of consummate patience and tact. His only reaction was a blink if Barbara Lea decided on still another take when the last one had been perfect.

Balliett then continued with a brief interview in which Loonis told a bit about his background, including this explanation of why he lived in Charlotte: "We talked about going to New York to join Ralph Flanagan's band, but we decided they wouldn't have grits in New York and probably wouldn't take too kindly to bib overalls."

Meanwhile, back at home, the Charlotte Junior Woman's Club "roasted" Loonis at a dinner in 1977 celebrating his twenty-two years as music director and later producer of the club's annual *Serenade to Autumn* fashion show and fund-raiser. In February of the following year, NCNB, the state's largest bank, sponsored "A Tribute to Loonis McGlohon" as a benefit show for the Arts and Science Council. George Shearing, the great singing team of Jackie and Roy, Mary Mayo, and Eddie Montiero (rarest of rarities, a jazz accordion player) were on hand to perform and to honor their friend Loonis. It was a glittering evening at the Civic Center and one of the major civic and social occasions of the year in Charlotte.

Despite his growing national and international fame, Loonis was still the same person who as a high school student in Ayden and a college student at East Carolina would play any piano anywhere for any audience, just for the love of it. He was still eager to donate his talent for good causes in his hometown and state, and he acted as if hometown gigs, even the wedding receptions and cocktail parties, were just as important to him as appearances in New York or San Francisco. He continued to rehearse the choir at Carmel Presbyterian every week and direct it every Sunday morning, unless he was out of town. The only difference was that his growing renown was taking him out of town more often, and sometimes out of the country.

In January of 1979 Loonis and Nan flew to Japan, where Loonis and singer Mary Mayo were booked for a month-long engagement at the Tokyo-American Club. The McGlohons were sophisticated travelers, but there were moments during their stay in Japan that tested their savoir faire.

"A musician friend and his wife invited us to Japan's most famous epicure of fish delicacies," Loonis told *Charlotte Observer* columnist Kays Gary.

It was a truly elegant place. When the appetizers came, they turned out to be white bait worms, and Nan said to me, "Don't put on your glasses because they've got black, beady little eyes."

I had looked around and hadn't seen anything hot, no sign of a stove, and I might have known. Everything would be with sauces, but raw. Nan forced a smile and said, "I can do it. I must." But when the squid was served, it was bloody and still moving, and she finally apologized to the host, saying, "I'm sorry, but I can't eat a live animal."

The chef came out with a cleaver and a board, and when he got through chopping it wasn't moving anymore, so we didn't have any excuse. We didn't chew anything. We swallowed some things whole, like sea urchins and bits of abalone, because chewing didn't do a thing to it. It just stayed the same. The chef was pleased at our efforts and said, "The Americans are very courageous."

Despite the raw seafood, Loonis called the time in Japan "the most exciting, most memorable month Nan and I have ever known." He said they were treated like royalty. Their room was at one of the world's fine hotels, the Okura, where each morning they were greeted with fresh flowers and kimonos, new disposable razors and toothbrushes, and an American newspaper. They were invited to some kind of banquet or fine dinner almost every night before the set at the Tokyo-American Club began. Loonis and Mary Mayo, working with a Japanese bass player, drew enthusiastic crowds to the club. Many nights after the set they would go to a jazz club and jam with other musicians.

Loonis found that the ambience of a Tokyo jazz club was different from what he was accustomed to in one very obvious way. "Drinking isn't allowed in those places," he told Gary. "No drugs. Nobody high. Nobody stoned. Music is the whole thing. I finally managed to explain what 'stoned' means, and one of the guys said, grinning, 'Stoned is for day off.'"

The release of an Audiophile album taken from Marlene VerPlanck's appearance on *American Popular Song* brought Loonis once again to the attention of New Yorker jazz writer Whitney Balliett. Balliett commented favorably on the album and noted that "McGlohon, who played for the whole series of radio programs, is a subtle, funny and adept accompanist."

Back in Charlotte, Loonis remained loyal to his commitments. He had been involved with the annual Fine Arts Festival at Rockingham Junior High School in Rockingham, North Carolina, a town some seventy miles east of Charlotte, since its inception some years earlier. He continued to help plan programs, recruit artists, and perform for the festival. In 1982, he brought a legend to Rockingham—eighty-two-year-old Mabel Mercer, arguably the most revered "cabaret singer" in the world. She talked with the students and sang for them, in a voice squeezed and cracked by age, but still able to tell stories and evoke emotions. Surely there has never been any comparable performance at any other junior high school, anywhere.

Loonis also continued to create new ways to showcase talent—his own, and the talents of his fellow musicians and artists. He had composed and performed special music for gallery showings of the work of the North Carolina artist Bob Timberlake, renowned for his realistic Piedmont landscapes with weathered buildings and other images of rural and small-town life. In early 1980 Loonis recuited Rosemary Clooney and Johnny Hartman to join him in a musical celebration of Timberlake's art. The show, called "Sketches in Jazz," featured Loonis and his trio, with David Powell on bass and Bill Stowe on drums, improvising in response to a series of Timberlake paintings. Clooney and Hartman sang some new and old McGlohon songs, also matched to Timberlake paintings. With a grant from Erskine College, in Due West, South Carolina, the program was produced in February at the studios of WNSC in Rock Hill, part of the South Carolina Educational Television Network. It aired on the network in September.

In 1981 the Salvation Army in Charlotte honored Loonis with its "Others Award" for unselfish contributions to community and church. That year he also performed for the Beaufort County (North Carolina) Arts Council and the Museum of York County (South Carolina) and was appointed by Governor Jim Hunt to the Historic Bath Commission, dedicated to the preservation and promotion of the oldest town in North Carolina.

The following year, in January, as *American Popular Singers*, which he co-hosted with Eileen Farrell, began its run on National Public Radio, Loonis and his trio—this time with Jim Ferguson on bass joining drummer Bill Stowe—appeared with Mabel Mercer on the CBS *Sunday Morning* show with Charles Kuralt.

Through the first half of the 1980s Loonis continued his duties as director of special projects at WBTV while maintaining a demanding schedule of appearances in Charlotte and beyond. His energy, as well as his versatility and creativity, was astonishing, and the satisfactions were substantial. A note from a friend in Atlanta, Frederick Barber Jr., general manager of WSB Television, in the early summer of 1983, provided a brief but meaningful summary:

> Dear Loonis:
>
> Our youngest, Eric, graduated from high school two weeks ago. When we attended the graduation exercise, I was pleased to see that the chorus was performing a McGlohon piece.
>
> And a few months ago, I was in Las Vegas and heard Frank Sinatra perform at one of the hotels. During the concert, Ol' Blue Eyes took a sip from his glass and said, "Now I'm going to sing a song written by Loonis McGlohon. . . ."
>
> Obviously, things are going well for you.
>
> Best,
Fred

Loonis had been involved from time to time in the Charlotte Choral Society's annual *Singing Christmas Tree,* one of the most beloved traditions of the city's holiday season, and in 1984 he brought in Marlene VerPlanck to be part of the program. That same year he was featured in the Chamber Music Series at Coastal Carolina Community College in South Carolina. In November of that year he provided the concept and composed and arranged special music for the Charlotte District's celebration of the bicentennial of the United Methodist Church. Performed at 3 P.M. and 7 P.M. on Sunday, November 11, at First United Methodist Church in downtown Charlotte, the program featured Loonis and his trio—Terry Peoples on bass and Bill Stowe on drums—with a brass ensemble and the church organist and choir.

Some of Loonis's songs had been on recordings nominated for the music industry's Grammy Awards several times. In 1984, he was finally part of a Grammy winner. *All in Good Time,* by Rob McConnell's Canadian ensemble, which won the award for best big band recording, included Loonis's "Songbird." That year "Songbird" and "Blackberry Winter" were included in an anthology of music called *The 100 Most Beautiful Songs.* Also that year, a solo album, a rare undertaking for Loonis, called *Loonis in London,* received *Stereo Review*'s Award of Special Merit.

In those years Loonis was frequently in New York for concerts in memory of Alec Wilder, some of which he helped organize. He and his trio performed in Singapore, Rome, Germany, and Tokyo.

Over the years Loonis had worked with several drummers and bass players, but in his last ten or fifteen years as an active performer, the Loonis McGlohon Trio usually meant Bill Stowe on drums and Terry Peoples on bass. Stowe and Peoples were considerably younger than Loonis, but they loved him as a mentor, and he appreciated their youthful energy and talent—and their loyalty. Playing with Loonis meant playing with some of the finest musicians in the world and all the great singers they accompanied. On trips abroad he appreciated being included in some of their after-hours activities—"It's been fun for me to see the world through their eyes," he once said—and they appreciated his determination to see, and show them, the places they were visiting. Loonis always seemed to know some "in" places to go, and to know about the people and the traditions, wherever they went.

When they were in Rome, he insisted one day on taking them to Florence for lunch. They took the train to Florence and to a restaurant Loonis knew about, for one of the best meals they had ever eaten. In Singapore, Loonis suggested they spend a day in Malaysia. He booked a tour on a minibus, and they experienced an exotic place and culture and ate some "delicacies" they probably had never realized were edible.

In 1986 Loonis turned sixty-five and retired from WBTV. He would have more time for his garden, more time to write music, more time to travel. But he would also have plenty of work to keep him busy. One reason was a place called Spirit Square, one of the more significant developments in the history of entertainment and the arts in Charlotte. It set the stage, literally, for what amounted to a second career, and a second wind, for Loonis as a performer in his hometown.

In 1975, in one of those rare moments when a few visionaries manage to ignite the imaginations of otherwise pedestrian public officials (for a conservative southern city, Charlotte seems to have had more than its share of such moments), the

The Loonis McGlohon Trio, with Terry Peoples and Bill Stowe.

Mecklenburg County Board of Commissioners voted to buy the historic building in downtown Charlotte being vacated by the First Baptist Church. The idea was to convert the building into an arts center, to be named Spirit Square, with classrooms for instruction, gallery areas, and a small theater in what had been the church sanctuary. Alex McMillan, a county commissioner with strong ties to the arts community, who would later serve several terms in Congress, was a significant influence in the county's decision. He and Loonis served on the first Spirit Square board, which was chaired by stockbroker and arts patron William H. Williamson III. A private fund drive raised $350,000 for the first phase of the renovation. The voters of the city of Charlotte approved a $2.5 million bond issue to finance the completion of the project.

The centerpiece of Spirit Square was the conversion of the old sanctuary into a theater. NCNB had been a major corporate contributor to the renovation, and the theater opened in April of 1980 as NCNB Performance Place. The opening celebration on April 16 featured the Oscar-winning singer and dancer Joel Grey, accompanied by the Loonis McGlohon Trio, with David Powell and Bill Stowe. It was the first of many memorable nights there for Loonis. The schedule for the first season at NCNB Performance Place demonstrated the significance of the new venue. It included the great folk singer Odetta, ragtime pianist Max Morath, actor William Windom in a solo performance as James Thurber, blues duo Sonny Terry and Brownie McGhee, guitarist Carlos Montoya, jazz trumpeter Dizzy Gillespie, George Shearing, the Preservation Hall Jazz Band, and a number of plays, including some cutting-edge contemporary dramas.

The renovation of the old sanctuary created as fine a venue for small-group jazz as any in the world. It could accommodate almost eight hundred people, but the rows of seats were curved and tiered, with a balcony. It had the intimacy of a good jazz club and the acoustics and sight lines of a well-designed small concert hall. When the house lights went down and the performance began, the lights went on behind the original stained glass of the sanctuary. The effect was quietly dramatic. Some people even found it, appropriately, spiritual. Musicians loved the intimacy and the ambience, and that was reflected in their playing. Over the next few years, Spirit Square would host some of the finest jazz talent in the nation, including Stan Getz, Ahmad Jamal, Dave Brubeck, Marian McPartland, and McCoy Tyner and, courtesy of Loonis, a host of great singers.

It was Loonis who made the place even more special and made it his own. He immediately realized it was the perfect setting for live versions of the *American Popular Song* and *American Popular Singers* format. Through the 1980s and well into the 1990s he brought in some of the best singers in America to sing the great American songbook at Spirit Square. They included Margaret Whiting, Marlene

VerPlanck, Carol Fredette, Maxine Sullivan, Julius LaRosa, Carol Woods, Johnny Hartman, Mike Campbell, Marlena Shaw, Maddy Winer, Eileen Farrell, and local favorite Daryle Rice.

There were nights at Spirit Square when the last scheduled song ended and a standing, cheering audience brought the performers back for an encore that turned into an extended jam session. If you were in the audience on one of those nights and if you loved that kind of music, there was no better place in the world that you could have been.

In retirement Loonis also found more time to enjoy the getaway house at Beech Mountain, and having grandchildren made the house an even more special place. Loonis taught them to fish and loved to take them fishing in the two trout lakes on the mountain. He spent a lot more time putting bait on hooks than taking fish off hooks, but that was pretty much beside the point. What mattered was being together in the fresh mountain air in such a beautiful place. At Beech Mountain, they were only a few miles from Grandfather Mountain and its celebrated natural wildlife habitats, where Loonis could introduce his grandchildren, up close and personal, to bears, deer, eagles, cougars, and river otters, and to the man who owned the mountain, his friend Hugh Morton.

Tar on my heels feels good to me
Here in my state of grace.
—"North Carolina Is My Home,"
words by Charles Kuralt,
music by Loonis McGlohon

North Carolina Is My Home : 22

Here is Charles Kuralt's description of the beginning of what would become North Carolina:

> On a morning in July of the year 1584, two English gentlemen in armor, accompanied by soldiers, well armed, stepped into a small boat from the great ship in which they had crossed the Atlantic. They had come from England . . . sent hither by Sir Walter Raleigh, favorite of the Queen. Sunlight flashed from their helmets as their boat was rowed toward shore.
>
> A single Indian stood on the sandy beach awaiting the men from the ship. He was silent, unarmed and alone, " . . . never making," one of the Englishmen said, "any show of fear or doubt." After they had stepped ashore, this lone man spoke to them gravely for several minutes. They knew it was a speech of welcome. At length, the Indian went to his own canoe, paddled out into the water and began fishing. When he had filled his boat with fish, he returned to the shore, piled his catch on the beach and indicated by gestures that the fish were for the Englishmen. Then he vanished. . . .
>
> The Englishmen took his fish, and claimed his continent.
>
> English America began there, on a North Carolina beach. The next summer, and the next, English ships returned, bringing soldiers and scientists and surveyors, and finally, settlers.

He wrote that bit of history for a recording, show, and book called *North Carolina Is My Home,* created to mark the four-hundredth anniversary of the arrival of those armored Englishmen—North Carolina's four-hundredth birthday. In 1983, Governor Jim Hunt called a number of talented North Carolinians, within and outside

Charles Kuralt and Loonis, on the road with North Carolina Is My Home.

the state, to ask them to do or create something for the celebration the following year. This, again in Kuralt's words, is what happened next:

> Loonis McGlohon is our state's most versatile and accomplished composer and pianist, and this whole thing was his idea. . . .
>
> I called Loonis in Charlotte.
>
> "I just got a phone call from Gov. Hunt," I said.
>
> "I know. So did I," Loonis said.
>
> "You got any ideas?" I asked.
>
> "Sure," Loonis said, "we'll make a record. We'll give it to all the schools and libraries."
>
> "I can't sing," I said.
>
> "Right," said Loonis (who had heard me sing), "but you can type. Start typing."
>
> "What'll I type about?" I asked him.
>
> "The mountains," Loonis said, "the shore. Barbecue, moonshine, pine trees, Thomas Wolfe, wild swans, tobacco barns, textile mills, all that stuff. You know."
>
> I sat down at my typewriter and did as I was told. Loonis sat down at his piano and started writing music. We put the words and music together by letter and telephone.

At one point in the next few weeks Loonis realized that what he and Kuralt were doing provided the opportunity to propose a new official song for the state. The official state song at the time was perhaps the most anachronistic set of music and lyrics in existence. If ever it had been memorable, singable, and lovable, as a state song is supposed to be, that time had long ago passed. Loonis set out to write something more appropriate for the twentieth century. When he got the tune down, he called Kuralt and played it for him over the telephone. Then he gave Kuralt a title that fit the first eight notes of the melody—"North Carolina Is My Home" —and asked him to write the rest of the words. That became the title song of what they created. It was a sort of revue, with words and music ranging from comical to lyrical to elegiac, describing, celebrating, laughing at, and expressing their love for their native state and its people and places.

Kuralt at the time was traveling all over the country taping his *On the Road* segments for the *CBS Evening News,* so the collaboration did not operate under the best possible circumstances. But over the following year they got it done.

Kuralt's lament for a North Carolinian trying to find something fit to eat in a fancy New York restaurant is hilarious. He turned a long list of some of the state's more unusual town and place-names into a humorous ditty that began "Hickory,

Dickerson, Dockery, Dunn, Peckerwood Ridge, and Poorhouse Run" and wandered on through Devil's Gut, Turkey Den, Tally Ho, Lizard Lick, Licklog Gap, Shoofly, Granny Green Mountain, and many, many others. There were spoken passages about the mysterious disappearance of the settlers of the Lost Colony, about the Wright brothers making the world's first powered flight at Kitty Hawk.

Citing lines from "The Old North State"—"where the weak grow strong and the strong grow great"—Kuralt strung together sketches of some North Carolinians who had grown from humble circumstances to great achievements, among them William Sidney Porter (O. Henry), Thomas Wolfe, Daniel Boone, Ava Gardner, Kay Kyser, Andy Griffith, Edward R. Murrow, David Brinkley, Tom Wicker, Frank Porter Graham, Washington Duke, Sam Ervin, the three presidents, Andrew Jackson, Andrew Johnson, and James K. Polk, and one first lady, Dolley Madison.

For a section about North Carolina churches, Loonis recycled one of his earliest compositions, "Dinner on the Grounds," and it was a perfect fit. There were word and music portraits of the mountains and the coast and the urbanizing Piedmont.

The North Carolina Department of Travel and Tourism obtained a grant from Winston-Salem–based Piedmont Airlines to pay for the production and distribution of a recording. Loonis put together a cast and support staff: two of his favorite female singers, Marlene VerPlanck and Mary Mayo; singer Jim Campbell, no relation to Mike, but brother of country-pop star Glen Campbell; guitar and banjo player Eric Weissberg; arranger Billy VerPlanck. They gathered in a New York City studio in July of 1985 with some string, brass, and woodwind players from the New York Philharmonic, Loonis and his trio, and Kuralt, to record *North Carolina Is My Home.*

The large orchestra took Loonis's melodies and harmonies and created shifting layers of mood—mellow, lively, poignant, joyful. Campbell's almost boisterous, country-flavored style was perfect for some of the score's rural imagery. The clear, true voices of VerPlanck and Mayo made Kuralt's lyrics shine. But the spoken passages, against background music that was often perfectly calibrated to the mood of the words, were as moving as the songs, and sometimes even more so. Kuralt was a writer of deceptively simple eloquence. His plainspoken style was a perfect match for his speaking voice, which was a magnificent instrument, deep, rich and resonant, yet totally natural and unaffected. Few singers could match the emotional nuances and range and power of Charles Kuralt just talking. During the recording session, when Kuralt began reciting the piece called "The Farmer," his prose poem about his grandfather and boyhood memories of summer days on the farm, everyone reached for a handkerchief.

Then over the next few years they took the show on the road, across North

Carolina and beyond, but, sadly, without Mary Mayo. The North Carolina singer died in December, some five months after the recording session in New York.

(One North Carolina stop for a performance was at granddaughter Laurie's school in Hickory.)

Kuralt's script was published as a book by East Woods Press of Charlotte in 1986, edited by Patty Davis and illustrated with gorgeous color photographs of North Carolina scenery, many by William Bake and Hugh Morton. Finally, a live presentation of the show was videotaped in the early 1990s and shown a number of times on the state's public television network.

When accompanying scenes were shot for the video, Loonis quietly arranged roles for all of his grandchildren. Max and Laurie are in the segment about Tar Heel heroes; Graham is the boy—perhaps the young Charles Kuralt—hunting rabbits with a slingshot; Brooke got to sample the food from the "Dinner on the Grounds" segment at Rountree Church; Allan sports a Sneads Ferry T-shirt in the song about unusual town and place names, and Edward is seen at the beginning of the video pushing a toy lawn mower across the grass. Loonis wanted all of them to be part of a project in which he took great pride, and no doubt he also was looking ahead to the time they might show the video to their children and point out the cameo appearances.

North Carolinians naturally loved *North Carolina Is My Home*.

But the show's unique concept and musical and literary quality earned it wider recognition. McGlohon, Kuralt, and company took their show far beyond the state's borders. It was a hit at Arizona State University's Sundome Center for the Performing Arts, and in Vancouver, British Columbia. In London, the American Embassy theater had to schedule a second performance because of the demand for tickets.

North Carolina Is My Home widened and deepened Loonis's reputation in his home state, where throughout the following decade he was the recipient of numerous awards and honors.

People in Charlotte who enjoyed music had long been fans of Loonis McGlohon. But in the late 1970s and 1980s, Charlotteans began to appreciate the fact that he was in demand in New York, in London, in Europe and Japan, but that he chose to make Charlotte home, and to share his talent and his influence there more than anywhere else. That was when they began to realize what a treasure they had in their midst, and how grateful they should be to have him as a neighbor.

Through it all, Loonis retained a reasonable measure of his soft-spoken, self-effacing modesty, but it couldn't have been easy. Nan helped keep him down to earth, of course. And the choir surely helped.

The members of the Carmel Presbyterian Church choir knew that Loonis was special, that he was performing all around the world, that he wrote songs that were sung by famous singers. They knew, and said, that it was a privilege to know him and to work with him. And they appreciated the special music and arrangements he wrote for them, and the trips he planned for them, to perform in Israel and in Germany. But with them, he was, as one choir member said, "like an old shoe that you're always comfortable with. He is just—he's just Loonis." They laughed together, cried together, had fun, and together they sang sweet, sacred music that was special to all of them, and maybe to Loonis most of all.

The two Loonis McGlohons—the increasingly honored cosmopolitan celebrity, and "just Loonis," never too proud or too busy for a local gig or one for a good cause in some small town in his home state—continued to coexist comfortably.

In October of 1989 he received the North Carolina Award, the highest honor his state can bestow, from Governor Jim Martin. The award was established by the North Carolina General Assembly in 1961 to recognize "notable accomplishments by North Carolina citizens in the fields of scholarship, research, the fine arts and public leadership."

In December of that year the Charlotte Symphony and the Oratorio Singers of Charlotte presented "A Christmas Jubilee Concert: A Tribute to Loonis McGlohon."

A short while later he was honored with the President's Award from the North Carolina Association of Arts Councils.

In May of 1990 he and Kuralt were the commencement speakers at East Carolina University, and each received an honorary Doctor of Letters degree from the institution where Loonis had graduated forty-eight years earlier.

But he wasn't resting in retirement, or on his honors. In 1990 three new albums with Eileen Farrell and the trio were released: *Eileen Farrell Sings Torch Songs, Eileen Farrell Sings Rodgers and Hart,* and *Eileen Farrell Sings Alec Wilder.* In May of that year Loonis and Eileen recorded an album with the London Philharmonic Orchestra, which was released the following February. December of 1990 brought another CD with another of Loonis's favorite singers, Dardanelle, and a new Christmas CD featuring Eileen, Dardanelle, Margaret Whiting, and others. His 1990 appearances with the trio included a concert to kick off the Anson County Arts Council membership campaign, a concert for the Ashe County Arts Council at the Beaver Creek High School gymnasium, one at the Lexington, North Carolina, Civic Center, one for the Transylvania County Arts Council in Brevard, one at Northern Granville Middle School for the Granville County Arts Council, one at the Tryon Fine Arts Center. They were featured in the Moore County Choral Society's Pops Concert and played for the Nutcracker Ball in Wadesboro, a benefit for the Anson Children's Theater.

As 1991 began, the schedule for Loonis and the trio included a January 11 concert with Eileen at Spirit Square, and later that month another recording session with Eileen at Charlotte's Reflection Sound Studios, this time a collection of Johnny Mercer songs. In February the trio was set for a concert at Theatre Charlotte, then a trip to Rochester, New York, for a concert at the Eastman School of Music celebrating the life and music of Alec Wilder. The night after that concert they would appear at East Carolina University, then head back to New York for the annual Alec Wilder memorial concert. Back in the Carolinas there would be concerts at Pembroke and in the South Carolina towns of Lake City and Bennettsville.

It was a busy month, a busy schedule for a man nearing his seventieth birthday. But it was not atypical for Loonis, for whom retirement obviously meant being able to do work he loved all the time instead of part-time.

Like many other people past retirement age, Loonis in the early 1990s was not exactly quick to embrace the latest fads, whether in music or in technology. But he recognized the advantages of using a computer as word processor, compared to a typewriter, and of putting songs on paper using an electronic keyboard and a computer, compared to the way he had done it all his life, with pen and ink. So he set out to learn how to use the new technology. With the help of son-in-law Larry Shouse, he set up a personal computer in his study, adding a printer, a fax machine, and an electronic keyboard. Larry put it all together and then began to teach Loonis how to use it. It was not an easy task, but both Larry and Loonis persevered, and much to the surprise of the rest of the family, Loonis mastered the new equipment. He had always been a conscientious correspondent, and now the letters to friends and associates began to pour out of the printer. His new skill also came in handy as he began writing profiles of some of his favorite musicians and singers and some of his most treasured friends. And when he wrote music, the notes flowed from the keyboard into print almost as quickly as they flowed from his imagination to his fingers.

In June of 1993, Fan, Laurie, and Reeves told their parents to pack for a trip—both comfortable and dressy clothes, enough for a weekend away. The destination was a secret, but perhaps Nan and Loonis had some idea where it might be. The departure date was their anniversary.

Fifty years ago they had departed from Crisp and traveled by train to Richmond, for a honeymoon at the Jefferson Hotel. This time they were again going by train. Fifty of their friends were at the Charlotte Amtrak station that morning to have coffee and juice and wish the McGlohons a happy anniversary. This time there were no soldiers crowding the train, and Nan and Loonis had their own seats all the way. This time they were accompanied by a son and two daughters and a daughter-in-law and two sons-in-law and several grandchildren—people who had existed only in vague hopes and dreams that were only beginning to take shape fifty years earlier. This time a limousine would meet them at the end of the train ride, but the destination was the same as it had been fifty years ago: Richmond, and the Jefferson Hotel—for a fiftieth-anniversary "second honeymoon."

When you make a list of all the most important things in life,
You may include some treasures which you own.
But if you're like me, at the top of the list will be
The very special people you have known.
—From "Good Old Friends" (for Wade),
words and music by Loonis McGlohon

Friends and Heroes : 23

One of Loonis's projects in his so-called retirement was to write profiles, not only of some of the singers he had worked with, but also of some of his other friends and acquaintances—people he called his "heroes." They are a diverse group. Some are wealthy. Some are not. Some are famous. Some are not. Some have traveled the world, some have mostly stayed home but, like Thoreau, "have traveled a good deal in Concord." Some, but not all, are artists of one sort or another. But for all their diversity, they have certain characteristics in common: intelligence, creativity, a generosity of spirit, a sense of humor, a lack of pretension. Each of them is certainly worth writing about, and worth reading about.

He did not live to finish the project. Anyone who knew Loonis at all well could name a number of other people who surely were on his list to write about. But here, with his titles, are the profiles he wrote before he became too sick to write.

Loonis had a way of making every friend feel he or she was Loonis's best friend. If he had been forced—and it surely would have to have been against his will—to name his one true best friend, other than Nan, he probably would have said Wade St. Clair. St. Clair was a West Virginia native who was a young executive at WBT and also did some on-air work. He had a zany sense of humor and a great talent for mimicking voices. Along with WBT radio personalities, particularly morning drive-time announcer Ty Boyd in the 1960s, he created several hilarious characters and scenarios that brightened the station's programming.

In the 1960s St. Clair left WBT to do public relations work for the National Aeronautics and Space Administration during the heady early years of space exploration, but he stayed in close touch with Loonis and Nan and was a frequent visitor in their home.

Appropriately, then, the subject of the first profile is Wade St. Clair.

Around the World with Wade

Wade St. Clair.

Back in the seventies when Neil Armstrong, Buzz Aldren, and Mike Collins were traveling all over this planet to meet their fans and admirers, it was Wade St. Clair who would decide whether they would have dinner at Buckingham with Elizabeth or attend a reception with Mitterand in Paris. Wade St. Clair was with NASA during its golden era, and after the moon landing, he accompanied the astronauts on many, many trips as their "agent."

I have nagged Wade, urging him to write a book about his experiences with NASA, especially his world trips with the Apollo 13 crew. So far he has refused, saying no one cares about hearing personal stories about these American heroes and a guy named Wade St. Clair. Since he won't tell you the stories, I will. At least I'll try to recall a few of the experiences Wade shared with me.

One story is from the exciting mission of Apollo 14, when the world watched the space rocket blast off from the launch pad in Florida.

Wade had arranged for me and another Charlotte friend, Van Weatherspoon, to attend the Apollo mission as VIPs. This meant that we would be rubbing elbows with people like Vice President Agnew, King Juan Carlos, and Queen Beatrice of Spain, entertainment icons like Robert Goulet and Dyan Cannon, about twenty U.S. senators—well, you get the picture. Another North Carolinian, Hugh Morton of Grandfather Mountain, was also there. On the day of the launch, many of us were in a big holding room that became too noisy, and full of too much ego posturing, for me. I slipped into an office where Wade was working on last-minute details.

I sat quietly in a chair near an elderly lady who must have gone shopping earlier that morning for shoes. There were about four Kinney shoeboxes around her feet. On her feet at the time were blue canvas tennis shoes. She wore a simple cotton print dress, and it seemed a good choice with her well-scrubbed face and her not-too-tidy gray hair, worn in a bun. As I glanced at her, I thought maybe she was the mother of one of the NASA personnel working in the office. Lucky mother, I thought, to be invited to watch the rocket shoot skyward into space. In a few minutes, the woman rose from her chair, and suddenly most of the men in the office stood, too.

"Can we get something for you, madam?" one of them asked.

She smiled. "No, thank you. I am just going to stick my nose outside for a breath of that fresh air."

She walked outside, leaving her boxes of shoes around her chair. Wade walked over to where I sat and told me the lady was the Baroness Maria Von Trapp, the subject of the Broadway and motion picture musical *The Sound of Music.* And she was my seat partner on the bus trip to the VIP viewing stand. I told her what a thrill it was to meet her.

"I hope you are not too disappointed that I don't look anything like Julie Andrews," she said.

I was thinking how lucky Miss Andrews would have been to have lived the experiences the baroness had known in her life. Of course I asked her how she liked *The Sound of Music.*

"Oh, it was lovely," she said, in a soft voice that still had a trace of a European accent. "Maybe not all of it was true, but I suppose the producers had to make all of us a bit more like they thought the audience would want us to be. And of course the baron and I were much older than the very attractive couple you saw on the screen."

The baroness laughed and talked about her life in Stowe, Vermont. And while Maria Von Trapp was a plain-looking lady, I thought she had an inner beauty that Julie Andews could never have captured.

At the launch site, Wade and Julian Scheer, another friend and former Charlottean who was an official with NASA, stayed busy, and we didn't see them after we were deposited at the viewing stand. It was an exciting day, and I will never forget the earth-shaking vibration and the flash of heat across my face as that beautiful and blindingly white rocket lifted into the air. And it was a successful mission.

For Wade and the Apollo 13 astronauts, there were the glorious trips across America after the crew returned from the moon. And then the world tour began.

Wade was especially fond of Mike Collins and his wife, Pat. He liked Neil Armstrong, the first man on the moon, but Armstrong was a private person who tried to accept his celebrity with good grace. Buzz Aldren loved the spotlight and was still a bit unhappy that he was not the first man to step outside the capsule when it landed on the moon.

Early on the day the group was to ride in a big parade in Berlin, Wade remembered that the prince of Luxembourg was to present a medal to the astronauts later that morning. Wade found Mike Collins and asked if he would take a quick trip to Luxembourg to receive the medal. A helicopter was standing by to take him and bring him back in time for the parade. Wade knew he could count on Mike to make the inconvenient trip. And fortunately, everything worked, and Mike got back to Berlin in time to join the parade just as the motorcade was beginning to drive down the wide avenue called Kurfurstendamm.

Thousands of people lined the street, called the Ku-Damm by Berliners. The mayor had proclaimed a holiday for the event, and Wade has said he thought every person in Berlin must have been standing to honor the astronauts. As the motorcade was moving slowly down the Ku-Damm, the mayor was pointing out different sites to his guests. Mike Collins leaned over to Wade, who was sitting in the front seat, and said he had to go to the bathroom. Wade whispered to him that everything was closed because of the holiday.

"I don't care," Collins said. "I gotta go, Wade. Listen, I haven't been since you put me on that helicopter this morning. This is critical."

Wade looked up and down the avenue trying to spot a building that was open. He suddenly noticed people waving from the upper floors of a building a couple of blocks away. If people were inside, that meant the doors must be open. He radioed the lead car in the parade and told the official that a stop must be made, and to gauge the spot where the astronauts' car could stop directly in front of the five-story building coming up. Wade then used the radio to advise everyone in the motorcade that a brief stop would be made for astronaut Mike Collins. When the car was exactly on location, Collins leapt from the car and dashed inside. A few minutes later he was back in the car, and the motorcade proceeded.

The next morning a Berlin newspaper carried a front-page story about the astronauts' visit. The story included this paragraph: "One of the most touching moments came when Astronaut Mike Collins noticed people who had not been allowed to leave their jobs and were waving from upper floors, and suddenly dashed from his auto and ran inside to greet people in the building."

In South America, Wade and Mike Collins were taking an early morning walk near the hotel where they had spent the night. Collins noticed some cinders on an empty lot where a building had burned sometime earlier. The coal-black cinders resembled the moon rocks the astronauts had been carrying on the trip to display. Collins told Wade he would like to play a joke on Neil and Buzz, and he and Wade picked up several pieces of the burnt material. When they returned to the hotel, they removed the authentic moon rocks from a wooden box in which they were transported, replacing them with the black cinders. The real moon rocks were carefully placed in another container.

As the limo in which they traveled sped down a wide highway in Brazil, Collins asked the driver if he would slow down for a bit. He had been saying: "I don't know about you guys, but I am tired of lugging these moon rocks everywhere. It's ridiculous."

As the limo slowed to forty miles an hour, Collins continued: "I've had it with these rocks. I'm gonna give 'em to South America." With that he emptied the box out the window, and the rocks were scattered in the grass outside.

"No, no!" Armstrong and Aldren cried. "My god, you have thrown away the moon rocks."

They screamed for the driver to stop, to turn around and go back.

"We have to get those rocks!" Aldren cried.

The driver crossed the median and headed back. When they reached what they thought was the location where Collins had emptied the box, the car stopped, and everyone jumped out to start searching for the moon rocks. In a few seconds, Collins admitted to have played a joke. The moon rocks, he assured them, were safe in another container in the limo.

While the astronauts were in Japan for appearances, three crates were delivered to Wade at their hotel. He knew the crates contained bust sculptures, commissioned by NASA, of each of the astronauts. Someone at NASA, without realizing the contents of the crates, had them sent by air freight to Wade in Tokyo. Mike Collins was with Wade when the crates were delivered, and as Wade began to make arrangements for the crates to be sent to Washington, Collins said, "Let's open my crate. Let's see what the thing looks like."

When they pulled the bust from the box, they were both surprised to see the likeness was perfect. A grayish stone had been used for sculpting the head. Again, Mike Collins had a joke in mind. He and Wade took the sculpture to Mike's hotel room, where Pat Collins helped them place the carving in bed, pulling the covers up to the neck. Later that evening, Pat placed a frantic call to the physician who traveled everywhere with the astronauts, monitoring them constantly.

"Doctor, come quick," she said. "Something's wrong with Mike! Hurry, please!"

Mike barely had time to hide in the bathroom before the doctor was at their door. Pat let him in, and the doctor rushed over to the bed where the sculpture was bedded. With hardly a glance, he put his hand on the forehead of the sculpture, and when he felt its cold hardness, the doctor yelled, "My god. He's dead!"

Wade St. Clair has led a charmed life. He has been program director for a major radio station. He has been executive director for RIF, a wonderful reading program for children. Best of all, he saw the magic development of the space program, up close, and he traveled the world twice with the famous threesome who first flew from Earth to the moon. I still wonder why he never wrote about it.

The Man Who Owns a Mountain

Hugh Morton could walk eight hours a day for many weeks and still not cover all the ground he owns. Grandfather Mountain belongs to him, but he benevolently shares some of the 25,000 acres with people who admire what the mountain owner has done with his property.

Grandfather Mountain is one of North Carolina's most popular tourist attractions, and the part of the mountain the public sees is pristine and manicured and beautifully developed. There is a mile-high (above sea level, literally) swinging bridge between two peaks on top. At a slightly lower altitude visitors can watch bears, deer, cougars, river otters, and other creatures in their natural habitats. From there it's a few yards to a state-of-the art museum with wonderful exhibits on the flora and fauna, geology, geography, ecology, and climate of western North Carolina, including some rare specimens of Carolina gems. In the same building is a theater showing nature movies, some of which Hugh Morton himself has shot, and an attractive restaurant that offers, among other things, real North Carolina barbecue and steaming homemade soups.

You can read all about Grandfather Mountain in the tourist booklets. It is the man, Hugh Morton, I like to talk about. I was a fan of Hugh before I ever met him. He is a superb photographer. Any time you see a great photograph of some beautiful North Carolina scenery, or of a great moment in a University of North Carolina football or basketball game from anytime in the past sixty years, there's a good chance Hugh Morton took it. He will wait patiently for months to get the right picture. He has a photograph he shot of the Charlotte skyline eighty miles away, taken from the top of Grandfather Mountain on a rare clear morning, and the office towers in Charlotte are easily recognizable. I had admired his photographs for years, and when I finally met him, I was pleased to meet a modest, humble man who loves his home state, its people, and its important institutions. For his support of the nearby Lees McRae College, that institution recently awarded both Hugh and his beautiful wife, Julia, honorary doctorates.

Although he lives and works in the High Country, his influence is statewide. He was born on the coast, in Wilmington, and as a young man he helped organize that city's famous Azalea Festival, and he led the effort to bring the USS *North*

Carolina to its present location at Wilmington, where it is one of the coast's premier tourist attractions.

I have never met a man who is more interested in saving the natural resources of this country. He has documented the ravages of pollution on the state of North Carolina. He will accept a speaking engagement—always without a fee—to go anywhere with his slide presentation, which clearly shows the connection between acid rain and other pollutants and the widespread death of evergreens on the highest peaks of the Blue Ridge Mountains and the Great Smokies.

Hugh is nearing his eightieth birthday, but he still has the energy of a much younger man. So I feel sure that he has a lot of time left to preach to those who may appear to turn their backs on the damage being done to the environment. Hugh is not one of those radicals who march and scream and wave flags. He is soft-spoken and gentle, but he carries a big stick. Well, now that he has recovered from knee surgery, he has thrown away the stick!

There is no more pleasant way to spend a late afternoon than with Hugh and Julia Morton, skimming across their beautiful lake and throwing in a line to catch a couple of rainbow trout. If Julia is not too busy, she may clean and cook those trout for your dinner. That's what she has done for Bob Hope, Charles Kuralt, former governor and former U.S. secretary of commerce Luther Hodges, and Coach Dean Smith. Did I mention that Hugh rarely misses a University of North Carolina basketball game, whether in Chapel Hill or at the King Dome in Seattle?

When Charles Kuralt and I were videotaping *North Carolina Is My Home,* I accepted Hugh's offer to help any way he could. I gave him a list of four things we needed to shoot on an October day. He found all four: Possum hides drying on the back of a barn, a weathered kindly-faced mountain man about seventy years old, a whiskey still which was still operational, and a not-overly-photographed view of Grandfather Mountain. Not only did he locate the things we asked for, but he got down on his hands and knees to break off weeds and brush that partially hid the liquor still, so we could get a better shot. Fortunately for us, Hugh especially, the owner was not at home.

Hugh has protected the wildlife on his mountain. He adopted Mildred, a black bear, who became his friend. Mildred's children, even grandchildren, now roam the habitat Hugh has provided for them. He has developed a sanctuary for eagles, deer, otters, cougars, wild turkeys, even hummingbirds. The visitors to Grandfather see these animals up close, but there are no cages and no concrete floors. One look at these animals, and it is obvious they are well cared for.

The eagles, bears, and deer and, yes, the hummingbirds have been lucky to have a friend like Hugh Morton. And so are we folks.

The Voice of America

When he ambled out on stage, Charles Kuralt looked much like a balding overweight little boy. There was a shy, awkward smile that wiped the years away, and it was obvious that every person in the audience loved this man, symbol of everything apple-pie good in America. Charles was America. He could have won a seat in the Senate had he wanted it. I think he could have been governor of his beloved state, North Carolina.

People have asked me, "What is he really like?" Usually I say, "Well, I have never heard Charles say anything unkind about any person." Which doesn't mean, of course, that he didn't have opinions.

Charles Kuralt always saw the silver lining in any situation. That may have been a part of the greatness of the man. He was always learning, too. He had the ability to walk away from the most banal encounters always having learned something. I saw it happen many times. I was there when someone's Aunt Lucy buttonholed Kuralt and told more than anyone would want to know about how she raised squash in her garden. Twenty minutes later when she released him to go to his appointment, Charles said, "You know, I never knew that about acorn squash."

Charles's world was limited to small towns and cities of North Carolina when he was growing up, and I don't think he ever got the tar off his heels. His father was an administrator in social work, and his mother was a teacher and, as Charles said,

Loonis and Charles Kuralt. (Photo by and courtesy of Hugh Morton.)

"a lover of books." The family moved a few times, but always within North Carolina, and Charles's photographic memory stored fascinating pictures of what rural life was like in the 1930s. His word portrait of his grandfather, written for *North Carolina Is My Home,* is, I think, a great piece of English literature.

Charles was sixteen when I first met him, and I certainly don't claim to be clairvoyant, but I knew even then that we would hear a lot from Charles Kuralt. He was, in many ways, the typical teenage boy, interested in girls, sports, making money on a part-time job, and running with the gang on weekends.

In those days, Charles's part-time job was reading the news on WBT radio. Later he worked as a reporter for the *Charlotte News.* He was also interested in music, and Charles hung around the new television station in town where I was playing jazz on a late-night show.

Charles and I would go to an in-house sandwich shop in the Wilder Building, where we would get coffee and talk music. He had that wonderful bass drum voice even in those days, and I told him he should become a radio announcer. Little did I dream that the Kuralt voice would become one of the most recognizable in the world. We would talk about jazz until I was usually late for the final rehearsal before showtime.

That was all in 1949, and Charles Kuralt and I remained good friends until his death in 1997.

From Charlotte, Charles went to New York. I stayed in Charlotte, but we saw each other frequently. When he began his remarkable *On the Road* series, he asked me to write the theme music. I persuaded him to write the words. Later we collaborated on many projects, a patriotic cantata, a National Public Radio series, and best known perhaps, our gift to our state, a musical portrait called *North Carolina Is My Home.*

But I want to talk about Charles Kuralt, not the projects we worked on, even though we would both admit those contributed to some of the best times in our lives.

He was never quite comfortable with his celebrity. When told how much he was admired, he would shuffle his feet and giggle with embarrassment. One of the last stories he told me had to do with his astonishment that morning when a young girl recognized him in a pharmacy. She told him that she had recently won a Charles Kuralt scholarship of some kind. He told me the story twice, and repeating himself was something Charles never did.

Charles was a great listener. He also remembered everything he heard. There was no subject that did not fascinate him. And he was also a great storyteller, of course. One of my favorite evenings spent with Charles was in our home on the night his "Forty-eight Hours in the Vatican" was aired. We asked him to tell us some anecdotes that were not used on the program. Charles must have remembered every experience, no matter how small. He gave us a description of Pope John Paul that was so personal that it was like being in the room with the Holy Father. The Pope clomped around in worn, scuffed loafers, we were told. His private quarters were spartan. Down the hall from his primitive bedroom, the Pope entertained heads of state in a small chapel decorated in gilt and red.

Charles told us about his visit to the Vatican Library, where he was hosted by the archivist, a red-haired Irishman. "I would never have enough time to see half the treasures in this library," Charles said to the archivist, "but would you be kind enough to show me two or three things that you feel are unique?" One of the treasures the Irishman brought out was a letter from Michelangelo to Pope Julius. Charles, with a limited knowledge of Italian, was trying to read the letter. Very poorly, he admitted. The archivist said to Charles, "Let me paraphrase what Michelangelo was writing. He had been commissioned to produce a great work of art at St. Peter's and now he had spent six weeks working on the ceiling of the Sistine Chapel. Without any pay for himself or the men helping him. So the letter says: 'Dear Pope, for Pete's sake, pay up.'"

The archivist also let Charles hold a letter from Genghis Khan to the Pope. The archivist paraphrased the letter: "Dear Pope, as you must know, I am now king of the world. So you need to come visit me and pay homage. On your way here, pick up all the other kings and queens you run into."

While Charles had access to Pope John Paul during the few days he was taping segments for the show, his conversation with the Pope was confined to seeking information for the program. So he was delighted to learn that on his last day at the Vatican, he, along with five other people, would be granted a personal audience with His Holiness. The six people would stand in line in a corridor near the Pope's chamber, and each person would be allowed to ask the Holy Father one question. Charles told us that he agonized over what question to ask. He realized it should be something significant, something perhaps about what the Pope felt we must do to save the world, or something that would produce from the Pope comments that would be repeated around the world. Yes, even on CBS in New York. Charles had his question framed, and he waited eagerly for the Pope to speak to the five people ahead of him, and then he, Charles Kuralt, would share a moment of history making.

Suddenly the Pope was moving toward him, and the cardinal, walking beside John Paul, was saying, "Your Holiness, this is Mr. Charles Kuralt of New York." The Pope shook his head up and down a few times. "Yes, Charles Kuralt, I know. Yes, Charles Kuralt from New York. I know Mr. Kuralt." By that time, the Pope had already passed Charles, and with a quick smile he moved on. The audience was over. Charles never had the opportunity to ask his question.

I remember that evening and many other quiet evenings spent with my hero, Charles Kuralt. He was the best of company. He was impulsive, and many times when whatever plans we had for the afternoon or the evening were not going to be memorable, Charles would say, "Let's go to that fish camp on the river." Or when we were in London, he would say, "Lloyd Weber has a new show. Opened last night. Let's go to see it tonight." He managed to get four orchestra seats, and he refused to tell me how much they cost him. We got dressed and went to see the second performance of *Phantom of the Opera.*

He thought I would be pleased to get an autograph from Vladimir Horowitz, so he badgered the aged pianist while they were in Russia together until Horowitz finally gave in and autographed an LP to me. In a note inside, Charles wrote, "But the old son of a bitch would not write what I told him to write. So to make up for it, I made him sign a program to you, too."

It would be impossible for me to tell you all the wonderful things Charles Kuralt did for his friends, his family, his country. He was certainly the greatest ambassador North Carolina ever had. He accepted all the tributes he received graciously, gratefully, and always with a little embarrassment. He never liked special treatment. He was intimidated in the presence of people he admired greatly. And the list of people he admired was a very long list: Edward R. Murrow, Walter Cronkite, Lou Gehrig, Sam Ragan, Bill Friday, Mabel Mercer, Billy Taylor, Dean Smith, Eileen Farrell, Hugh Morton, Andy Rooney, Charlie Justice—to name a few of the more prominent.

After Charles died, a lady in Montana sued the Kuralt estate to claim some land in Montana that she said Charles had intended to leave her. She had a letter from Charles saying as much. When the story about the "Montana mistress" was printed, Charles's wife, Petie, who was dying from bone cancer, called us to say: "Let's not worry about this story. We know Charles will survive it."

Her Welchness

She has had three husbands, but she has kept her married name. Her ancestors came from Wales, from a town called Swansea, and that is Charleen's last name.

After she appeared in an art movie, *Sherman's March,* produced by Ross McElwee, the *Los Angeles Times* called her "a new Mae West." Charleen was indignant. "I don't want to be a new Mae West," she said. "I want to be a new Raquel Welch."

She could be anything she wants to be. She has been a poet, an editor, a lecturer, a writer, a wife, mother and one of the loveliest and most entertaining women in the South. Or anywhere, I suppose, but God knows, she is southern. She has the honeyed voice of a debutante from Savannah or a social worker in New Orleans. She has a lovely face that you can't look away from when she's talking to you. If she is overweight, it's probably genetic, not the result of eating too many croissants or chocolates.

When she was eighteen, she wanted to meet Ezra Pound. She bought a nurse's uniform, showed up at the Washington hospital where Pound was confined, and announced that she was the poet's private nurse. She fooled the staff, at least long enough to become Pound's lifelong friend. He wrote her more than two hundred letters.

Charleen has always been happily unpredictable. I was playing piano once at a reception at the Mint Museum for the opening of an Andy Warhol exhibit. The state's most prominent arts patrons were crowded into a small gallery, sipping champagne punch and looking at each other and at Warhol's paintings with obvious puzzlement. They didn't seem to be having a very good time. The party became livelier, however, when Charleen appeared at the top of a staircase leading into the gallery. She looked at me as I was playing and said, in a loud voice, "Oh, Loonis, that's so beautiful! I feel like somebody has just poured molasses all over my boobs!"

When Hubert Humphrey was vice president, he visited Charlotte on one occasion and was the special guest at a talent show. Performers had been asked to volunteer, and way too many had responded. Charleen was on the program, and she decided to stage a very brief version of one of those jazz-and-poetry events that were popular in those days.

She had recruited a young actor named Skip Burns to read a short poem by one of the Beat Generation writers. I think it was called "The Murder of Two Old Men by a Kid Wearing Lemon-Colored Gloves," and it consisted of two words: The first was *wait,* repeated over and over, each time with more intensity, and then, just once, the word *now!* My trio was supposed to play something appropriate during the reading.

After the vice president had sat graciously through more than an hour of soprano solos, bell choirs, and tap dancers, Charleen stepped onto the stage to announce the poem. We began to play a frenetic, repetitious riff. Instead of introducing the poem, Charleen, suddenly overcome with stage fright, looked down at the vice president and said, "Oh, Mr. Humphrey, I am so scared. You can't believe how frightened I am . . . " Before she could say another word, Mr. Humphrey got out of his seat and started toward the stage, apparently intending to try to calm her fears. As the vice president started up the stairs to the stage, Skip Burns, thinking

Charleen had introduced the poem, came rushing out onto the stage. Exactly as he had rehearsed, he went to the microphone at stage left and with hands pointing toward the rear of the auditorium began screaming, "Wait! Wait! Wait! . . . "

Mr. Humphrey had reached the top of the stairs at that point, and suddenly six secret service men appeared as if out of nowhere and tackled the vice president. They rolled him back down the stairs to the floor of the auditorium and lay on top of him.

Mr. Humphrey survived, although a bit bruised and battered. After it became clear nobody in the auditorium was trying to assassinate the vice president, things eventually calmed down. But it probably was an evening Hubert Humphrey never forgot.

Charleen has had her share of tragedies but seems always to triumph over them. Her second husband was a victim of lead poisoning, which got into his system while he was stripping old paint from their historic three-story house on Sullivan's Island, near Charleston, South Carolina. Later, in a moment of despondency and madness, he set fire to the house and remained inside, killing himself while it burned to the ground. Charleen was out of town at the time, but everything she owned, including all of her own papers and correspondence from Ezra Pound, Alec Wilder, and others, was destroyed.

Later she built a new house on Isle of Palms, adjacent to Sullivan's Island. During a hurricane warning she was on the mainland and wanted to get back to the island, to try to salvage some things in case her house was in the path of the storm. Fortunately she was not allowed to go back. The storm destroyed the house and probably would have destroyed her if she had been in it. Afterward she said, "I have nothing from my life. Not even family photographs."

But soon the smile was back on Charleen's face. She remarried and put her life back together. And as far as I'm concerned, she can become the new Raquel Welch if she wants to.

The Shearing Touch

George Shearing is not only one of the world's great pianists, he is also one of the funniest men around. "The Shearing Touch" on piano has made the sensitive, emotional, and unique style of the British-born pianist immediately recognizable. Most people know that George has been blind since birth, but since he talks about seeing friends, watching television, or looking at the world, one sometimes forgets that he is not sighted. George has a keen sense of humor, and he makes people comfortable about his handicap. When asked if he has been blind all of his life, George says, "Not yet."

His wife, Ellie, in mock anger, may say to him, "Shearing, if you don't shape up, I am going to move some of the chairs in the living room." This threat from Ellie is empty, because George moves easily around the large Shearing condo on Central Park East in New York. Even in a strange hallway or room, by snapping his fingers, George can hear the sound that bounces back from the wall, helping him to maneuver on his own.

The Shearings are master bridge players, and George's photographic memory lets him recall the dummy cards once they are called out to him at the beginning of each hand. Players during their first encounter with George and his bridge game are dumbstruck when he pulls a card from his hand and says, "Hope you don't mind that I am trumping that trick." That is, until they notice that all the playing cards are marked in Braille.

George's mind is lightning quick. He can hear a song for the first time and perform it a few moments later. The second time he plays the song, he will add his own improvisations.

Ellie has taught George to cook, and he is a gourmet chef. It is disconcerting, however, when we watch him slice carrots. No, he has never injured a finger.

I love a story he tells about meeting a fan of Charlie Coonce (a well-known British pianist) during a train trip in England. The fan recognized George and asked him if he had ever met Charlie Coonce. George admitted that he had, indeed, met Mr. Coonce and that they were friends. Now, beside himself with excitement, the fan asked for more information about his idol.

It appears that Charlie Coonce, a rather mediocre but highly successful pianist, had a style that involved his playing very loudly for a few bars, then suddenly diminishing the sound to a double pianissimo (very, very soft). Then after a few bars of the soft sound, the Coonce piano would, without warning, become double forte (very, very loud).

George's seatmate on the train then asked, "How on earth does Mr. Coonce get that range of dynamics in his piano playing, from very loud, down to a whisper, then back again to the loud sound?"

Shearing told the man, "It is a technique that is kept secret, known only to the recording team and a few friends. But since you are such a great fan, and I know I can trust you to keep this secret, I will explain how it is done. Charlie Coonce has a close friend, almost like a brother. They grew up together, and he travels everywhere with Charlie. Now, part of the secret technique is that Charlie Coonce plays his piano in a very large wooden box, which travels with Charlie everywhere. The box has a door on it, of course, and because Charlie's boyhood friend knows Charlie so well, the friend knows when to open and shut the door on the box."

We had been friends for many years before George patted my head one day and exclaimed, "My God, Loonis, I didn't know you were black."

There can be few pleasures in life as great as sitting just inches away from the piano keyboard while George Shearing performs. Recently, after enjoying Ellie's incomparable popovers with bacon and eggs, I settled into a chair beside George and listened to him play Delius and Ravel. And finally Michel Legrand's "You Must Believe in Spring" and my own "Songbird." And for dessert Ellie sang a Shakespeare sonnet that George had set to music.

It was a perfect way to spend a late Saturday morning. Or any morning, anytime!

The Man Who Wrote My Favorite Song

People often ask me what is my favorite song. That's a tough question for someone who has heard as many songs as I have, who has played hundreds of songs, written hundreds of songs. But I do have a favorite, and it's "Have Yourself a Merry Little Christmas."

The man who wrote it, Hugh Martin, was born in Birmingham, Alabama, more than eighty years ago, and although he has lived most of his life in New York and California, Hugh Martin has not lost that soft musical sound of the South in his speech. He is like a Eudora Welty portrait of the Southern Gentleman. And besides that, he is one of America's most gifted composers.

Examine his songs, such as "Have Yourself a Merry Little Christmas," "The Boy Next Door," or "Every Time," and you know Hugh Martin is a kind soul with a big heart. One recent example:

Sally Dunn, a young New York actress-singer-dancer, was auditioning for a role in the revival of Hugh's show *High Spirits*. He did not know Sally, but because someone told him a couple of nice things about the girl, Hugh called her at her apartment in New York to wish her good luck. He even gave her a few tips about how to approach the role Sally was hoping to get. Sally got the role. After the producers gave her the good news, she walked to the apron of the stage and with a great big smile told the producer and others backing the show, "By the way, Mr. Hugh Martin told me to say thank you and give you his best regards."

Hugh never passes up an opportunity to thank every artist, the accompanists, and the arrangers when they have performed one of his numbers. That is quite unusual for an important composer—to take time and thank everyone who had a part in a recording or a personal appearance.

Gene Puerling is perhaps the greatest vocal arranger in the world, but Gene's modesty was shaken when Hugh called him one day to say, "Mr. Puerling, your arrangement of 'Have Yourself a Merry Little Christmas' is the very finest I have ever heard. In fact, I would say that you made my song better than it really is."

Hugh is a deeply religious man who plays for a church choir every Sunday. He has written some lovely hymns, and he has asked his publisher to retitle his best-known Christmas song to make it "Have Yourself a Blessed Christmas."

The song was written for Judy Garland to perform in the movie *Meet Me in St. Louis,* along with "The Boy Next Door" and "The Trolley Song." Hugh was Judy's pianist, arranger, and musical adviser for many years, and he still has respect and love for Judy, even though they had some tense moments because of her volatile temper.

He has remained a kind of mentor for Mickey Rooney, too, and Hugh has written a new show, *Maggie and Jiggs,* with Mickey in mind for the lead.

So, for all those who have asked, "Have Yourself a Merry Little Christmas" is my favorite of all popular songs, and I feel very privileged that I can call the man who wrote it my friend.

The Guv

Robert Farnon is known among many musicians and singers as the greatest orchestral arranger in the world. He is affectionately called "Governor" or "the Guv," but I have heard him called another name, too. One night singer Julius LaRosa noticed a note lying on my desk, and the letterhead read Robert Farnon, La Falaise, Guernsey, U.K. Julius exclaimed, "You've heard from God!" That's what Margaret Whiting calls Farnon, too.

Robert Farnon was born in Canada around 1921, and when he grew up he became conductor and orchestrator for the CBC. He is a gifted composer, and among his best works is a suite called "Canadian Impressions."

After World War II, in which he served as a captain, he moved to England. He has been in residence on Guernsey Island off the coast of England ever since.

Besides conducting the London Philharmonic Orchestra, Robert's fame as perhaps the most gifted arranger spread around the world, and for many years it has been the dream of every performer to record with Farnon. He has conducted recording sessions with Frank Sinatra, Tony Bennett, Vera Lynn, George Shearing, Eileen Farrell, Lena Horne, and any others who could afford him. He continues to compose, and many of his pieces are now standards—"How Beautiful Is Night," "Cascades to the Sea," and "Country Boy" are a few—and his film scores such as *Captain Horatio Hornblower* are widely admired.

Robert is a gentle Santa Claus of a man, now white-haired and a bit over-weight. A nervous performer is immediately put at ease when he walks into the room. If nothing else, his sense of humor wins them over. A lot of famous conductors make the pilgrimage to London just to see the master at work. Peter Matz (Barbra Streisand's conductor), ballet conductor Milton Rosenstock, Broadway conductor Rodney Bennett, and a long list of admirers have watched him conduct recording sessions.

Some of the artists who can afford to have Farnon conduct a hundred-piece orchestra and write the arrangements are not always among the most talented of performers. Pia Zadora, for instance, is a sexy young actress who wanted very much to have Farnon conduct record albums for her. Since her husband at the time owned "much of the world," he could afford to grant her wish, and Pia Zadora sang on two CDs directed by Bob Farnon. Most critics lambasted her for wasting the talent of one hundred musicians. On the other hand, there were many, like me, who enjoyed listening to Pia's recordings.

"She is capable, I think," Bob told me. "She is also a very sweet girl, and I enjoyed doing the projects with her." But he added, "She is not the greatest actress living, however, and I realized that when I was obliged to go to the opening of a show she did here in London."

The show was *The Diary of Anne Frank*. That role was unimaginable for the curvy blonde sexpot, and I said so. Bob agreed, and he said that it was a rather unfortunate bit of casting. Then he said, "If you know the story, you'll remember in the third act the Nazis break into the Amsterdam apartment where she has been hiding. At that moment, the London audience cried out, 'She's in the attic!'"

A well-known American singer who had always wanted to do an album with Robert Farnon is cursed with having no sense of rhythm, and he skips beats and has to be led through every song until at last he gets it. Or somewhat gets it. The orchestra finished recording the charts, but the singer was unable to record his part accurately. So Robert suggested to him, "Why don't you take the tracks and record them in California? They're on a different time there, anyway." To date, the CD has not surfaced.

Bob and his wife, Pat, live in a seventeenth-century house on Guernsey. "The house is even older than me," he told me last year. "I was walking across the floor on the second story, minding my business, when suddenly the floor gave way and tossed me and a lot of furniture down to the first floor. Oh, well, the termites had lived there longer than I had."

Lady Marian

She is one of the great jazz pianists in the world. Among the women who play jazz piano, she is the greatest. She is one of the very few women in the entertainment business who does not care who knows she is approaching her eighty-fifth birthday. Her name is Marian McPartland.

Marian was born in England, and although she has lived in America for more than forty years, she has never lost that cultured ladylike British speech. Oh, she has picked up a few American phrases that are still unspelled in the daily press, but for the most part she sounds like Queen Elizabeth opening a new museum.

A lot of women in music get very Hollywood, meaning they adopt facades and like to play "the star." Not Marian. She does not have time for phonies and folks full of themselves.

At her age, Marian may look fragile when she walks onstage (she has had her share of broken bones and hip replacements, etc.), but when she sits down and grabs a handful of keys on the piano, she is twenty-five, thirty, even twenty-one again. The energy that comes from her at the piano is stunning. Her arpeggios seem to flow from her fingers, and she moves lightning-quick through single-line improvisations. Her amazing harmonic sense has improved over the years. She is not one of those pianists who sticks to the song sheet. And she is as modern as tomorrow's technology. She is also one of the best composers around today.

Marian McPartland, with Loonis observing.

It was sometime in the 1970s when Nan and I were telling Marian that we were taking our children to London for their first visit. Marian said, "I'm sure you will take the kids to Windsor to see the castle, so while they are looking around, why don't you pay a visit to my aunt and uncle who have a shop on High Street. They are jewelers to Her Majesty, so you will recognize the shop."

Several weeks later we left the children to tour the castle and Nan and I took a walk along High Street. Suddenly we spotted the royal crest in a shop window, announcing that the establishment serves the royal family in England. It was Marian's aunt's jewelry shop. Once inside we explained that we were friends of her niece. Marian's aunt was not very impressed.

A British lady can be, if she so decides, very snobbish. This attractive gray-haired woman said something like, "Ooh yes, is Niece Marian still playing in those little bars in America?" When she said "bars" it sounded like she was smelling sheep dung. We realized the lady thought her niece was playing in sleazy joints, like maybe in the slums of Baltimore. I explained that Marian had played at Carnegie Hall and at the White House, and when she played a club, it was always the most prestigious room in town. As an example I mentioned the Carlyle, where most of the guests just got back from a yachting trip with the Duchess of Alba. The others hoped that they had been spotted while fishing with Prince Charles in Scotland. I laid it on thick for Marian's aunt, who began to smile a little and occasionally butt in with, "Oh, really?"

In a minute or so she called her daughter and son-in-law in to meet Nan and me. Before we left, the aunt insisted we have lunch with her, and the son-in-law walked down High Street to show us a children's shop that we wanted to visit. Before we said goodbye, Lady Marian's relatives had a nice, new picture of her.

The next time we saw Marian, I told her, "We met your aunt, your cousin, and her husband in Windsor. You didn't tell me that they did not realize you were one of the great pianists in America. I think you rose in stature after I got through telling them who you are."

Marian laughed. "I should have warned you that my relatives there always figured that, as a woman playing jazz piano, I was just one cut above being a hooker. No, they have never had much respect for me because of my work. Well, thank you for telling them I was a lady, after all."

She is a lady, of course, this indestructible woman who continues to amaze all of us. She can be "one of the boys," but invite her to tea and count on being charmed. I call her indestructible because she does not let obstacles keep her from playing piano. When she broke her arm a few years ago, she called a pianist in Canada, a woman who admired Marian to the point that she played like her, and the Canadian lady played one hand on piano, and Marian played the other. She canceled but one concert! She had a hip replacement not long ago, and she was back at the keyboard before we learned she was out of the hospital.

Once when Marian was visiting, I handed her a lyric. Within twenty minutes she had completed writing one of her loveliest melodies to accompany my words. Her tune, "Willow Creek," almost describes the lazy, pastoral place I had tried to describe in the lyric. When she read the line, "a perfect day to chase a dragonfly," she asked, "What in the world is a dragonfly? Let's change it to butterfly."

Isn't that the way a nice English lady would think? That butterfly can land in our garden anytime she wants to.

The Mountain Man

Stanly Hicks was a legend in the history of mountain music. Composer of Appalachian bluegrass songs, banjo and dulcimer maker and player, a well-known storyteller, Mr. Hicks was a man I looked forward to meeting.

The mountain man agreed to let me interview him, and we settled on a date. I asked him for directions to his home. In his soft Appalachian voice, Mr. Hicks asked if I knew how to get to Valle Crucis. I did.

"Well," he began, "you'uns come on through Valle Crucis and go on to Vilas. When you'uns get there, take yourself a left-handed turn and go awhile, about half a mile, and then take a right-handed turn. Go on awhile after that and take another left-handed turn. It's just a piece you go and then you take another right-handed turn."

At that point, I had serious doubts that the videographer, John Steed, and I could find Mr. Stanly Hicks. Why would every turn be half a mile? I let him finish his directions, and then I asked if he could give me some landmark I would be passing near his home. Finally he told me that just before I reached his place, I would pass a "waste house."

"Will there be a sign there to say it is the waste house?" I asked.

"Son, don't you know what a waste house is?" He assumed I did not, so he explained. "A waste house is a house that has gone to waste. Don't nobody live there."

Well, of course.

We found Mr. Hicks. His place was just down the road from the waste house. John and I thought we had driven smack into a movie set. There in a small clearing, with a green wooded hill behind it, was a log cabin. Sitting on the front steps of the cabin was an elderly man with the most gentle face you've ever seen. He was wearing bib overalls and a red-and-white checked shirt. He was playing a home-made banjo and singing. When we approached the steps, he rose and said, "Been expecting you'uns." He smiled, and there were a few teeth missing.

For the next hour, Mr. Hicks played and sang for us, and I kept thinking as this sunburned and leathery-faced icon performed for us, "Why did I wait so long to meet this man?" There was something about Stanly Hicks that made me know, as I looked into his watery blue eyes, that I was seeing someone very special.

He told us about the time he was invited to sing at the White House. "But I didn't go," he said. "We got up that mornin', and my mama wasn't feelin' too good. She was supposed to go, too, to show the president and his wife how to clog. Mama's ninety-two, and the trip was gonna be too hard for her, so we just didn't go. I reckon President Kennedy didn't miss us too much."

He showed me his favorite banjo. "I made it myself. See, it's got three bullet holes in the head. It's skin, you know. Well, it was my brother who got mad and while the skin was hanging up curing, he took his rifle and shot it. But it was such a nice skin I made this here banjo with it, anyway."

We spent a quiet afternoon with Mr. Hicks. He played and sang several mountain songs. He told us folktales, some of which had been handed down from his grandmother. Mostly they were stories about hard times that mountain folk didn't fret about, and there were ghost stories. He spoke of the Brown Mountain lights, an eerie phenomenon that appears over Brown Mountain on nights after there has been a rain. His version had to do with the death of someone and, according to Mr. Hicks, the yellowish round lights that dance above the mountaintop are lanterns, searching for the killer. I saw the lights once. They have never been really explained.

Mr. Hicks had no desire to move to or visit the city. "Too many people driving around there going nowhere," he declared. "Besides, we got all the people we need around here. Oh, if you'uns wants to come, you're welcome. But we ain't gonna make you come live here."

John Steed and I were silent for five minutes as we drove back down the mountain and headed home. Finally I said, "I have the feeling that as soon as we got out of sight, Mr. Hicks got in his Cadillac, drove up the hill to his big white-columned house, went inside and told his wife, 'Well, I fooled two more of 'em.'"

John shook his head. "No, no," he said, "Mr. Hicks wouldn't do that. He's too nice to do a trick like that."

And I knew John was right.

The Name of My Hero Is Joe

He must have moments when depression consumes him and when terror bites him like a mad animal. I have to think there must be moments of black despair, but I have never seen anything but life in Joe Martin.

As I write this, Joe Martin, trapped in unrelenting ALS, can use only his eyes to connect with the world and the people around him. But those eyes smile and laugh and say, "I love you." Joe's eyes now are unforgettable, and they express more excitement, more love, than a child's on Christmas morning.

Joe is still young. Too young to be wheeled from place to place. Too young not to have been able to dance with his daughter at her wedding recently. He is too young to have to depend on someone to wipe and bathe and dress him. He is old enough, however, to know he is a role model, a hero to everyone who knows him, even if only casually. But there is no way you could know Joe casually. When you are in his presence, you realize he is extraordinary. There is an aura of greatness about him. It is all there in his eyes—incredibly blue eyes.

He can speak only through a mechanical voice, but through that voice he pours the thoughts of a brilliant mind, the wisdom of a great heart, the inspiration of an undiminished spirit. Through that voice he spoke to the officials of county government, eloquently and passionately, on behalf of the arts and against the bigotry that would restrict creative expression and compassion in his community. Through that voice, and using his brother Jim, the former governor, as straight man, he entertained and challenged an audience with hilarious satirical commentary on the current political scene.

In the prison of his disease this bank executive with a PhD forged a new career as a writer, publishing a moving memoir and a fine novel.

Joan Martin is also in my prayers every night. She is Joe's wife, and she is pretty incredible, too. She let Joe plan all the details for their recent trip to Norway, and like all of us, she was amazed that he was able to book all the travel plans, the hotels, transportation, making sure the vehicles would accommodate his wheelchair and that restaurants had access for the disabled.

And I am sure there were instances, many of them, when Joe had to call on his absolutely wonderful sense of humor in solving problems. He is a very funny man with an Ogden Nash command of words.

It's exciting to see Joan's love for Joe in her eyes. Damn it, if only everyone in the world could see Joe and Joan Martin handle their lives with dignity, compassion, humor, and most of all, love.

I learned that Joe and Joan would be attending a concert I played a year or so ago. So as a valentine to him, with a little help from Jerry Shinn, I wrote something called "The Name of This Song Is Joe," which was performed that night on stage. A part of the lyric reads:

> We all have heroes
> With class and style,
> But they're all zeroes
> Once you've seen Joe Martin smile.

Elegy and Ode to Joy : V

It's a nice trip . . . maybe much too short a trip, this life.

—Loonis McGlohon, in a 1996 interview

The Real Blues : 24

The tenth annual Friends of Alec Wilder Concert was held on the afternoon of Saturday, February 19, 1994, at St. Peter's Church in New York City. Loonis Mc-Glohon was scheduled to be the master of ceremonies that year and, as always, to be part of the musical program.

Memorial concerts to honor dead composers are not particularly rare, but surely there is nothing else quite like this one. Once each year, musicians and singers, some of their spouses, children, and special friends, and assorted other people who either knew and loved Alec Wilder or his music, or both, gather at the church. They play and sing and listen to some of his songs and some of his "serious" music, and as a finale the entire audience sings something by Wilder, as a sort of hymn of benediction. Before and after the concert, and during the intermission, they mingle and exchange Alec Wilder stories.

The church, at Lexington Avenue and Fifty-fourth Street, is affiliated with the Evangelical Lutheran Church in America but is perhaps known and attended more for its music than because of its denomination. It hosts jazz concerts and uses jazz music in some of its services. The interior of its sunken sanctuary is blond wood and stone, with high ceilings, steep angles, tall windows, and skylights. A schedule posted that February outside the church announced weekly midday concerts, and "jazz vespers" at 5 P.M. every Sunday. Over the years Loonis had produced a number of concerts and programs demonstrating the linkage between jazz and religious music, particularly spirituals, and he had long contended that jazz really began with church music. Whatever the truth of that, jazz had certainly found a home at St. Peter's.

That Saturday morning Nan and Loonis McGlohon got up early to pack and get to Charlotte/Douglas International Airport for the flight to New York. They descended at midmorning out of a gray winter sky. On the streets of Manhattan there were piles of dirty snow along the curbs. They arrived at the church in time for the scheduled rehearsals, but a lot of the other participants weren't there yet. A number of flights had been delayed because of fog. Rehearsals would be late starting. That was a blessing for Loonis, because it gave him time to lie down for a bit and recover from the trip.

He had recently gone to the doctor to complain of stomach pains. The doctor had ordered tests, and when the results came back, he telephoned Loonis and asked him to come to his office, and to bring Nan. The tests showed that Loonis had lymphoma, a malignancy in the lymph nodes. He was seventy-two years old, and now he knew there was a good chance he would never be seventy-three.

To friends who learned of his illness, Loonis said, "I've had a wonderful life. If this is it, so be it. I have no complaints. But I'm not giving up." The words were heartfelt and sincere. But the disease and the diagnosis nevertheless had weakened him, physically and emotionally. Some friends had suggested that he not try to make the New York trip in late February. But the Wilder concert was a very special occasion for him, and he had agreed to host that year's event, and to play.

The abbreviated rehearsals were finished by lunchtime. Someone went out for sandwiches while Loonis found a place along one of the tiers leading down to the sanctuary where there was room for him to stretch out and rest again. That and the food revived him. When the program began, Loonis was on his feet, smiling, introducing the opening music as though nothing bad had ever happened to him. He would learn and demonstrate in the months and years ahead that something about performing could lift him temporarily out of his misery. He could be feeling half dead, and then when he got in front of an audience he would feel alive again.

The sky had cleared and sunlight slanted through the skylights into the sanctuary and sparkled on the clean snow in the small courtyard just beyond the windows. Despite the limited rehearsal time, the program went smoothly. Musicians from the Eastman School of Music in Rochester, where Wilder had been a sort of unofficial student as a young man, played his Sonata for Bassoon and Piano and a suite, and the Eastman Trombone Choir played a medley of Wilder songs: "It's So Peaceful in the Country," "Lady Sings the Blues," and "While We're Young." After an intermission, Loonis and his trio played a few of the lesser-known songs by Wilder and then accompanied one of Wilder's favorite singers, Barbara Lea. The concert concluded with Loonis and the trio and the trombone choir playing, and the audience singing, "I'll Be Around." That hadn't been rehearsed, of course, and it sounded rather mournful.

Afterward, everyone gathered for punch and cookies in a large room just outside the sanctuary. Nan knew a few of the other wives there, and on such occasions they always groaned and laughed as they swapped stories about Wilder's slovenly habits and his sometimes rude eccentricities. A few minutes of socializing was all Loonis could handle. He found a quiet corner to rest for a while, and then he and Nan went to Fran Miller's apartment on Central Park, where they were staying for the night.

But he was revived again for dinner at a restaurant, at a table long enough to accommodate a few friends who had come with them from Charlotte, Wade St. Clair, who had come up from Washington for the concert, some of the musicians who had performed that afternoon, and a few New York friends, including Marlene and Billy VerPlanck. Loonis was usually the life of such parties, but his fatigue was beginning to show that evening. As everyone left the restaurant there was perhaps more hugging and kissing than usual.

On Sunday he and Nan flew back to Charlotte, and that week he began chemotherapy.

Loonis was well aware that he had been showered with blessings all of his life. His gratitude for that was constant and very real and undiminished by occasional disappointments. He also knew that every life, at least as we know it, has to end. Intellectually he had no problem with that. His father and mother had died, and for at least a decade he had been at that time of life when parents, aunts, uncles, and other loved ones and friends were dying. Spiritually he was confident that life as he knew it was *not* the end. But nothing prepares anyone for what he was about to endure: physical misery, helplessness, fear, inevitable depression.

Debilitating nausea was a common consequence of the chemotherapy Loonis was receiving. For weeks he was sick, weak, discouraged, depressed. At one point he swore he would never go through it again, even if it meant the difference between life and death—a vow he would later retract. It was an experience that defied even the power of music to comfort and lift and elate, even for someone who loved music as much as Loonis did.

A musician who has played the kind of music Loonis played, and then has to confront the grim reality Loonis was facing, recognizes that life eventually is beyond the emotional reach of melodies and harmonies. Much of jazz music is based on the blues, so Loonis knew about the blues. In the folklore of the African American experience, the blues is a way of dealing with your misery by expressing it, by juxtaposing the flat and the natural of the same note to create a mournful, even morbid kind of dissonance, by coaxing sounds out of a guitar that are barely more tolerable than fingernails on a blackboard, by moaning, screaming, howling about sexual obsession and sexual betrayal. But beneath all that, the blues is really about saying "To hell with it" and getting back to living. That's the difference between the blues you can sing or play or enjoy hearing and the blues you feel when you face the prospect of never being able to get back to living. The blues is an expression of a self-pitying but sensual kind of depression, in which pleasure and pain intermingle into something even more intense. That's the difference between the depression that comes with a bad day or a temporary setback or a romantic disappointment, and the depression that douses the spark of life even as life goes on, that numbs the body and the spirit until there is no intensity about anything, and the things you cared about most have lost all appeal. That's why the blues is ultimately a cheap thrill, fraudulent, dancing around the edges of the abyss for the amusement of people who have never had to look into the abyss—but eventually will. Loonis had the blues, but not the kind you can play or sing for anyone's commiseration, much less anyone's entertainment.

The great, perhaps greatest, American writer, F. Scott Fitzgerald, wrote that in the real dark night of the soul it was always three o'clock in the morning. That was Fitzgerald's literary version of the blues, and maybe as good a blues lyric as anyone ever wrote, but it was fraudulent, too—the romantic self-pity of a drunk. The real dark night of the soul is when you're enduring treatment that makes you want to die, in order to keep you alive, with no guarantee that you won't die just as soon anyway.

Loonis is that rarest of human beings,
a genuinely good person. I don't think
he can help himself. . . . He goes through life
doing wonderful things.
—Charles Kuralt

Bonus Tracks : 25

For a while cancer and chemotherapy destroyed his desire to work, to create, drained the joy from his life—took the Loonis out of Loonis. But the treatment worked. The tumor shrank. He began to feel better. Calls and letters helped, including one that was signed simply Francis Albert. Soon he was back on the telephone, calling friends. As word of his illness had spread, invitations to play had all but stopped, and at first he couldn't have cared less. But now he was complaining that he wasn't getting any gigs because everyone thought he was dead. He called a friend at the *Observer* and asked him to please write something saying that contrary to what everyone might believe, Loonis McGlohon was alive and available to play for all occasions.

The National Collegiate Athletic Association's Final Four basketball championship tournament was scheduled for the Charlotte Coliseum that spring, and Loonis had been asked to produce a musical program for the entertainment of coaches, NCAA and tournament officials, and guests at the North Carolina Blumenthal Performing Arts Center. Charles Kuralt would also be on hand to interview the four coaches onstage. Although he was still weak and occasionally feeling sick, Loonis was determined to meet his commitment and be part of the city's big week in the national sports spotlight. He put together a band, wrote some original music, brought in Marlene VerPlanck to sing it, and that night he was on stage, conducting from the piano, wearing a wool cap to cover a scalp left hairless by chemotherapy.

Soon he was playing regularly again, hatching new projects. There would be recurrences of the cancer and more chemotherapy, but nothing as devastating as the first schedule of treatments. He knew he was on borrowed time (as everyone is), and he was determined to squeeze the last drop out of every bit of time he had left. It was an up-and-down life. Treatments were still downers, but between periods of treatment, he worked and rejoiced, visited friends in person and by phone, scheduled gigs near home and far away. Annual jazz festivals at Pinehurst and at the Grove Park Inn in Asheville were automatically on his agenda.

He resumed some of his volunteer activities, such as the annual visit to Western North Carolina Center, a residential facility for children with special needs, in Morganton, seventy-five miles northwest of Charlotte. He would play for the children there, talk to them about music, and admire and encourage their own artistic efforts.

One of his more innovative projects involved, again, Charles Kuralt. In time for Valentine's Day 1997, Loonis and Charles went into a studio and taped something called *Our Funny Valentine: A Salute to America's Greatest Love Lyrics.* Kuralt had always dreamed of being a singer. This was the closest he would ever come. Loonis played, and Charles spoke, reciting the lyrics to the great love songs while Loonis played the melodies. Only Kuralt could have carried it off. His voice had the depth and richness of Billy Eckstine's or Johnny Hartman's. His inflection, timing, phrasing, with only occasional exceptions, were perfect. The show aired on public radio stations that year and deserves to air every Valentine's Day, forever.

It was the last time Loonis and Charles would work together. In the early summer of that year, Kuralt became ill and was hospitalized in New York. He was diag-

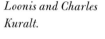

Loonis and Charles Kuralt.

nosed with lupus, and he died on July 4. When Loonis got the news, he and Nan were at their house on Beech Mountain. Kuralt was to be buried in Chapel Hill, the home of his beloved alma mater, in a historic cemetery among the graves of some of the other distinguished sons and daughters of the University of North Carolina. Planners of the event wanted Loonis to be part of the services, and of course he agreed, even though he was not feeling well.

The morning before he got the call about Kuralt's death, he had asked some Charlotte friends who were also at Beech Mountain to drive him to Valle Crucis, which was eight up and down, twisting and turning mountain miles away. He wanted to show them an old church up on the side of a mountain there. It was a lovely day and the church, a tiny, narrow, classic wooden structure, was worth the trip. A small graveyard of old, bleached headstones was staggered down the hill-side. There was an old story about one of them, about the young man who was buried there and the young woman who had loved him and lost him because one was from North Carolina and one was from Tennessee, just a few miles away. Loonis pointed out the grave and told the story. As always, he loved to tell stories. But he was obviously weak and running out of energy. On the drive back to Beech Mountain he was uncharacteristically quiet. Back at his house he spent most of the rest of the day in bed. Then came the bad news about his friend Charles.

Complicating his schedule was the fact that the Kuralt services were the same date as the night he was booked for a performance at Lees-McRae College in Banner Elk, about five miles from his Beech Mountain house. A friend suggested that he cancel the Lees-McRae concert. Everyone would understand. Otherwise, he and Nan would have to drive the four- or five-hour trip to Chapel Hill, spend one night, pay tribute to Charles and bury him, and then drive back to Beech Mountain and hope to get there in time for the performance. But the old show-biz cliché that the show must go on was a reality for Loonis. The people at Lees-McRae were counting on him, and he would be there. And he was.

When he was introduced, he walked out on the stage smiling, sat down at the piano, counted off a beat for Terry Peoples and Bill Stowe and started playing a bright, up-tempo number to the delight of a full house, an auditorium packed with people who had no idea what he had been through to be there. He introduced his trio and then brought on Jim Stack, who played vibes and also sat in for Loonis at the piano on a couple of numbers, which Loonis surely appreciated.

After the concert there was a reception. Friends who knew something about Loonis's condition thought he surely would skip it, but he didn't. He was there, thanking people for coming, shaking hands, greeting old friends and making new ones, being Loonis. Then for the next few days he collapsed.

His hair had grown back, and life was almost back to normal, except for the periods of treatment, and the periods when he had no commitments and nobody was looking and he simply crashed. But he added something else to his schedule. He donated his time and talent to programs for cancer victims and cancer survivors in Charlotte and in neighboring communities. If they needed music, he would play. If they needed a speaker, he would talk. And he sought out cancer patients to befriend and encourage, particularly one Charlotte woman, a few years younger than he was. He introduced himself and over a period of months he visited her, and when he couldn't visit he telephoned. And when she died, he attended her funeral.

The Mecklenburg County Bar Association usually gives its annual Liberty Bell Award to someone who has made some significant contribution to the practice of law or the administration of justice. But on Law Day 1997, the lawyers put the usual qualifications aside and gave the Liberty Bell Award to Loonis McGlohon. They decided he had meant so much to their community for so long and in so many ways that they simply wanted to honor him.

Meanwhile, NCNB Performance Place at Spirit Square had become NationsBank Performance Place, as the bank had continued to acquire other banks in its climb to the top of the banking world and had changed names. In December of 1997, Hugh L. McColl Jr., chief executive officer of NationsBank, once again demonstrated the sensitivity, sensibility, vision, and good sense that had made and would continue to make him and his bank the most valuable corporate citizens in Charlotte's history. He announced that the bank was relinquishing its title rights to the theater at Spirit Square. NationsBank Performance Place would be renamed the Loonis McGlohon Theater, in honor of the person who more than anyone else had made it a magical place. In a letter to Loonis, McColl wrote, "My company and I would like to honor you and the contribution you have made to Charlotte and the arts world. It is a special privilege to honor your accomplishments."

In announcing the name change, McColl said, "Loonis could have lived anywhere in the world, but he chose to stay in Charlotte and share his talent and gifts with us throughout his career. And to him we are thankful."

On April 8, 1998, a full house was in attendance for the dedication of the renamed theater. Of all the wonderful nights of music and entertainment the old sanctuary had hosted, none could match this one. Loonis, of course, didn't just sit back and accept tributes and accolades. He was there with a trio—Terry Peoples on bass and James Baker on drums—and he played. That was, after all, what Loonis did. He was joined on stage by Gene Bertoncini, one of the world's great guitarists, the venerable trumpeter Joe Wilder, who had played with almost every band worth hearing over the past half century, Phil Thompson on saxophones, Jim

Stack on piano and vibes, and a few singers: Daryle Rice, Mike Campbell, Maddy Winer, Marlene VerPlanck, Marlena Shaw. And the Charlotte Children's Choir.

Ty Boyd, who had been a good friend of Loonis's since their days at WBT in the early 1960s, and had gone on to a highly successful career as a motivational speaker and coach, was the master of ceremonies. He had the pleasure of reading congratulatory notes from people who couldn't be there: Tony Bennett, Eileen Farrell, Margaret Whiting, who wrote that if she could have been there she "would have been a tearful puddle on the middle of the floor," and Frank Sinatra, who wrote, "Barbara and I send our blessings."

The final number on the program brought Loonis and everyone else on stage for a sort of closing jam session. You would have thought nothing could top that, but then, when the audience demanded an encore, everyone returned to the stage and invited the audience to join them as they sang "North Carolina Is My Home."

At the dedication of the McGlohon Theater in Spirit Square, April 8, 1998: from left, Lisa Whitman (Max's fiancée), Loonis's grandson Max McGlohon, Reeves McGlohon, Brooke Shepherd (Peggy's daughter), and Peggy McGlohon.

In the spring of 1999 Loonis returned to London for a series of performances. In early April he appeared with the British singer Robert Habermann at a restaurant and jazz venue called Pizza on the Park, in Knightsbridge, where he was billed as "the world-famous American pianist Loonis McGlohon." On April 18 he performed at a meeting of the Robert Farnum Society, where he was described in the program as "a very special guest . . . the great songwriter, pianist, arranger, composer Loonis McGlohon." He rushed back home in time to play at the Cabarrus Vocal Ensemble Spring Concert April 30 at A. L. Brown High School auditorium in Kannapolis, North Carolina.

In June, Loonis went to Hickory, North Carolina, to give the keynote address at a Cancer Survivors Day sponsored by a Hickory hospital.

Later that year, Mayor Rudolph Giuliani proclaimed August 26 "Loonis McGlohon Day" in New York City. As part of a summer festival, Loonis was honored on that date with an outdoor concert at Lincoln Center. A number of Loonis's friends from Charlotte and elsewhere traveled to the big city for the occasion. It turned out to be another example of Loonis's ability to rise, magnificently, to an occasion, despite the debilitating effects of his disease and its treatment. The concert was scheduled for the late afternoon of August 26. Early that morning, Loonis telephoned a friend who was staying in the same hotel. He said he was feeling very sick and needed to take some medicine, but he couldn't take it on an empty stomach. He didn't want to wake Nan. "Could you meet me downstairs and get something to eat so I can take my medicine?" he asked.

Both of them had learned the day before that breakfast at the hotel dining room cost about the same as dinner with wine at an upscale Charlotte restaurant, so they walked a few doors up the street to Mickey Mantle's. Loonis was weak and unsteady on the way. His friend held his arm and wondered how Loonis was going to get through the day and the evening.

A few hours later there were rehearsals, and then the concert, on the plaza outside Lincoln Center. Heat and humidity were high enough to make people sitting quietly in their seats sweat profusely. As the afternoon faded into twilight under threatening skies, a parade of great musical talents paid tribute to Loonis by playing his music. Gene Bertoncini on guitar, Joe Wilder on trumpet, Jay Leonhart, the most in-demand jazz bassist in New York, Bill Kirchner on sax, Bernard "Pretty" Purdie on drums, the magnificent Marian McPartland, singers Mike Campbell, Maddy Winer, Marlene VerPlanck, Barbara Lea—all played and sang the great McGlohon songs and the great McGlohon-Wilder songs. There were also a number of musicians and music publishing and recording executives in the audience, along with Loonis's friends and family from Charlotte and elsewhere, and New York music lovers who had heard of Loonis McGlohon and read about the event in the

New York Times and the *New Yorker* and wandered in to find out for themselves what all the excitement was about.

And there was a strong feeling as the sky darkened and the air cooled a bit and an occasional breeze stirred that there were kindred spirits looking on, too: surely Alec Wilder, Teddi King, Mabel Mercer, Johnny Hartman, Charles Kuralt. Maybe even Max and Bertha McGlohon.

As a finale, Loonis joined Marian McPartland at the piano for a romping blues.

After the concert, the delegation of friends of Loonis from Charlotte boarded a charter bus that took them to an Italian restaurant where Loonis had booked a room large enough to hold them and the musicians from the concert and assorted other friends—maybe forty or fifty in all. Everyone there knew someone else there, but no one there knew everyone else there—except Loonis. As they were finishing their dinners, Loonis stood and got everyone's attention. Those who knew how sick he was marveled that he could stand at all, late in the evening of such a long day. But he welcomed everyone, and then he stood behind someone's chair and in-

On Loonis McGlohon Day in New York City, August 26, 1999, on the plaza at Lincoln Center: Marian McPartland at the piano, Marlene VerPlanck in the background.

troduced him to the rest of the room, calling his name, telling everyone where he was from. Then he moved to the next chair and did the same thing. It made Reeves McGlohon nervous. Had his father started something he couldn't finish? Did he have the stamina? Could he remember everyone's name?

But Loonis was on a roll—perhaps "in the zone," as sports psychologists call it. He continued to move from person to person, calling each name, adding brief biographies, maybe a funny story or two, praising their accomplishments with his usual hyperbole. One by one, he introduced them, every person in the room, smiling, laughing, teasing, embellishing, without stumbling over a single name or a single fact. It was the most amazing virtuoso performance of the art of friendship anyone there had ever seen or could ever have imagined.

In October, Marian McPartland came to Charlotte to play for a celebration of Loonis's seventy-eighth birthday at the McGlohon Theater at Spirit Square.

Cancer continued to be an unexpected and unwelcome intruder in what was otherwise a happy and satisfying part of his life. Age was also taking its toll. He was losing his hearing, which did not seem to bother him when he was playing piano with his trio or accompanying a singer but was noticeable in conversation. One summer night in the mountains he and Nan had dinner with several friends at a crowded restaurant. Conversation around the table was lively. On the way out of the restaurant Loonis remarked that he was sure a lot of interesting things had been said, but he hadn't heard any of them.

He had reached the point in his life where age and illness and suffering had largely removed any inhibitions about speaking his mind. He had tried over the years to make his peace with what was happening in popular music, had tried with some success to understand and appreciate what younger people liked about it. But his objections to the monotony and vulgarity of some of the rock music of the 1960s had turned out to be prophetic, and inadequately so. He was particularly offended now by the style of rock called rap, and by the behavior its practitioners mimicked and influenced, and on occasion he was not particularly careful about choosing his words when he expressed his feelings about it.

One acquaintance, too young to remember when racism was a way of life in the South—when it was not only politically correct but politically mandatory— remarked that Loonis sounded like a racist. Perhaps there were others who wondered if Loonis, as he grew older, was reverting to the racism of his young adult and childhood environment. In truth Loonis had never been a racist. His boyhood

playmates were black. His boyhood heroes were black musicians. His favorite music, the music that shaped his career and his art, was rooted in black culture. What some might have interpreted as racism was his increasingly outspoken outrage at the way so many black musicians and black music executives had abandoned or corrupted the great heritage of black blues and jazz music, America's greatest indigenous musical tradition. In the process, they were creating entertainment that confirmed and promoted the worst stereotypes of racial inferiority—ignorant, violent, socially irresponsible, sexually abusive, and ultimately suicidal. As Loonis saw it, some of the wealthiest and most successful young black men were setting the worst possible examples for the poorest of their young brothers.

When he thought of Billie Holiday, Jimmie Lunceford, Joe Williams, Thelma Carpenter, and so many others, and realized that so many young black performers had never heard of any of them and had no knowledge of, or respect for, their legacy, it broke his heart, and it made him angry—and at some point he stopped making any effort to repress or hide his anger.

Three of North Carolina's most distinguished and valuable citizens, Charles Kuralt, William Friday, and Loonis McGlohon, at a celebration of the twenty-fifth anniversary of Friday's statewide public television program, North Carolina People. *(Photo by and courtesy of Hugh Morton.)*

Still a great-looking couple: Loonis and Nan dressed for yet another special occasion.

The Charlotte World Affairs Council presented Loonis with its annual World Citizen Award in September of 2001. That same month, Reeves, Fan, and Laurie and spouses hosted a birthday party at the Tower Club in Charlotte to celebrate Nan's eightieth birthday, August 24, and Loonis's, which was September 30. Along with dozens of friends, there were grandchildren Allan McGlohon, Brooke Shepherd, Graham Smith, Laurie Smith, Edward Shouse, and Hilary Shouse. The only missing grandchild was Max McGlohon, whose wife, Lisa, within a few days would present Nan and Loonis with their only great-grandchild, Brady Daniel McGlohon.

It had been almost eight years since Loonis was diagnosed with lymphoma—more years than he had dared hope for. They had included some of the worst times of his life, but they had been mostly good years. He considered them a gift, a bonus, for which he was grateful. At the party that night he told friends that the latest scans showed him free of cancer. He was looking forward to some more good years. He had more projects in mind. It was a very happy occasion.

Within a few weeks he was down for the count.

Late that year Dr. Billy Wireman, the president of Queens University at Charlotte, wrote Loonis to tell him Queens was awarding him an honorary doctorate at its winter commencement. Wireman is a frequent traveler to the Far East, and on several occasions Loonis had told him he would love to go with him on a trip to China. When he received Wireman's letter, he telephoned in response. By then he was too sick to go anywhere. He said, "Billy, I appreciate the doctorate, but I'd really rather you'd take me to China."

On Thanksgiving Day of 2001, the entire McGlohon family got together for the last time with Loonis. They met at Reeves and Peggy's home in Mount Holly. Peggy, with her irrepressible sense of humor and one of the world's quickest smiles, always seemed to be able to cheer Loonis even during his worst times. But that Thanksgiving Day was a physical and emotional struggle for Loonis. The brightest moment was seeing his two-month-old great-grandson, Brady, for the first time. He mustered enough strength to prepare his oyster casserole, which, along with Nan's turkey, was an important Thanksgiving tradition for the family. But he and Brady

The McGlohon family at the home of Reeves and Peggy McGlohon in Mount Holly, North Carolina, Thanksgiving Day 2001.

spent much of the day napping peacefully together. They woke up just long enough to be part of a family photograph on the front steps of the house.

Joining the list of very close friends over the past eight years was his oncologist, Dr. Jim Boyd. Dr. Boyd's treatments had kept Loonis alive and functioning long after he and all his friends had feared the end was near. Now the end truly *was* near, but when the North Carolina Society of New York City wanted to honor Loonis in New York and induct him as a member in December, Dr. Boyd wanted him to be there. Other New York friends, when they learned Loonis was coming, arranged for a party in his honor the following night at the Firebird Russian Restaurant. Dr. Boyd went with Loonis and Nan to New York to help him get through the two events. They made it there and back. It was his last trip.

There's a lot that you can't put into words.

—Gene Bertoncini

Obbligatos : 26

In 1995, Charlotte public television station WTVI produced a program in tribute to Loonis McGlohon. In preparation for the program, Stuart Grasberg interviewed a number of Loonis's friends and musical colleagues, asking them to talk about Loonis, about what made him and his music so special. Here are some excerpts from transcripts of those interviews.

Gene Bertoncini: He's not at all an egotist in any way. When you play with an egotist who wants to show off, it just becomes a battle. When you feel comfortable playing with someone, you kinda feel like anything you play is gonna be right. That's a wonderful sense that he gives off as a leader and as a fellow player.

There are interesting turns in his music . . . you don't expect it, but they're comfortable interesting turns. It's not done for the sake of a turn, it feels right to be there.

Jim Stack: He lays down either beautiful or swing, whatever you need behind you, and it's just very comfortable. Inspiring, too. It's comfortable because Loonis knows what he's doing and is always thoughtful.

Marlene VerPlanck: Listen to any lyric that he's written, any song. . . . You will find such a wholesome, beautiful, warm, lovely quality about his writing . . . and a wonderful way of putting those words and music together.

He's just the most sincere and the warmest person I know. He's one of our best friends. I guess he's a lot of people's best friend, because he has that quality . . . he makes you feel like you are the most special person in the world.

Choir Director Loonis McGlohon in the sanctuary of Carmel Presbyterian Church in Charlotte. (Photo from and courtesy of The Charlotte Observer.*)*

Joe Wilder: Loonis has a great understanding of musicians, instrumentalists as well as vocalists. And he treats you as an artist, and he becomes the canvas on which you show your wares, you know, and he gives you every opportunity to do what you can do to the best of your ability.

Alice Crosgrove: Loonis is just such a special person, and he has made choir so much fun. . . . I think it's a God-given gift that Loonis has, of just making everybody comfortable. He can, if you only met him one time, remember your name, and he'll be able to talk to you and remember things about you. And this has to be a God-given gift. There's a depth about him. Maybe a lot of people don't know. He is sensitive to everything. How you feel, how the congregation feels, he can just pick up on all those things in a heartbeat.

Charles Kuralt: Loonis and I went to hear Joe Williams one night. And the next thing you know, Joe was sitting at our table, and he and Loonis were discussing how some Duke Ellington riff went. Joe said it went, "Doo, doo doo doo doo." And Loonis said, "No, it didn't, it went doo, doo doo doo doo doo doo doo." I'm a musical ignoramus, but I loved sitting at that table hearing those two consummate musicians, one of them rich and famous, Joe Williams, and one of them my pal Loonis, talking about music.

He is capable of the kind of friendship that just goes very deep and is very loyal. The kind of friendship that you never forget.

Coda: Sacred Music : 27

He died on Saturday, January 26, 2002. On the following Tuesday a "Service of Memorial and Thanksgiving to God for Loonis Reeves McGlohon" was held at Carmel Presbyterian Church. The sanctuary was filled, and dozens of other mourners stood outside or went into the room where a reception with the family would follow the service. Noting the attendance, the Reverend Wendell Ligon said, "Loonis is tickled to death that his service is the hottest ticket in town."

There were a lot of tears and a fair amount of laughter. Thinking about Loonis being gone made everyone sad, but thinking about Loonis made everyone happy.

There were wonderful eulogies. Someone like Loonis is a eulogist's dream.

But most important, there was music. As people filed in, pianist Rick Bean played several of Loonis's better-known popular songs. Later there was a medley of three of the many sacred songs he wrote: Joyce Cariaga sang "Light One Candle," Maddy Winer sang "In a Quiet Place," and the choir he had directed for all those years sang "Teach Me, Lord."

The closing hymn was "Joyful, Joyful, We Adore Thee," based on the glorious "Ode to Joy" theme from the last movement of Beethoven's Ninth Symphony. After the congregation had sung the last line of the hymn—"Joyful music leads us sunward in the triumph song of life"—the benediction was pronounced and the congregation, smiling and crying, began to file out.

As they left they could hear the postlude. It was the song Loonis had written for Wade St. Clair, and no doubt a lot of other people, titled "Good Old Friends" —another sacred song.

One unspoken lesson of the service that day, and of Loonis McGlohon's life, is that all good music is sacred.

Thanks

I like to think this book would have been written eventually, no matter what. But it would have been much more difficult to find the time and sustain the effort without the encouragement and generous support of dozens of friends and fans of Loonis McGlohon.

Jim Babb, a person of significant business and civic accomplishments, was an executive at WBT and WBTV during much of Loonis's time there, and a beloved and valued friend to Loonis and the McGlohon family. At my request, and with the assistance of Michael Marsicano, president of the Foundation for the Carolinas, Jim put together a committee—Sally Van Allen, Susan Kuralt Bowers, Dr. Jim Boyd, Ty Boyd, Parks Helms, Hugh Morton, Jack Tate, Van Weatherspoon, Pat Williamson —to raise money to support this project. The substantial response was evidence of the broad and deep admiration and affection Loonis's life and work had inspired in his community and far beyond. Thanks to those donors, the committee was able to pay a grant to the author and put enough money in the bank to help, if necessary, with the cost of publishing the book.

Loonis McGlohon was one of the most distinguished alumni of East Carolina University, and when the manuscript was finished, Jim Babb contacted officials at that campus to ask if ECU would like to be involved in the publication of the book. Their response was positive and enthusiastic. Jim Lanier, president of the ECU Foundation, and Carroll Varner, director of academic library services at the Joyner Library at ECU, arranged to have the book published by the ECU Foundation. The remaining money raised by the Babb committee was contributed to help pay production costs, and any net proceeds will go to the library at ECU, which already houses many of Loonis's papers and manuscripts.

I am deeply grateful to all the above for their efforts, and to the contributors, listed below.

I'm also grateful to Nan McGlohon for enduring more than one long interview at a time when remembering and talking about Loonis and their life together probably still involved some pain along with the obvious joy; and to Reeves McGlohon, Fan McGlohon Smith, and Laurie McGlohon Shouse for sharing their memories of life with their father; and to spouses Peggy McGlohon, Skipper Smith, and Larry Shouse for talking about their experiences as part of the McGlohon family. Reeves was unfailingly resourceful and helpful in numerous other ways as well, including planning and hosting, along with Peggy and Nan, a memorable trip to Ayden and Greenville and Crisp, to give me a better sense of the places where Loonis grew up, went to college, first played and wrote music, fell in love, got married.

Joanna Virkler was our volunteer photo editor, and she chose most of the photographs in this book.

Stuart Grasberg of public television station WTVI provided transcripts of interviews done in the production of that station's tributes to Loonis.

David Perlmutt, one of the finer of the many fine writers who have worked at *The Charlotte Observer* in my time, wrote moving and sensitive stories about the final weeks of Loonis' struggle against disease. His stories, including the obituary and an account of the funeral, were valuable resources, as were the personal recollections and thoughts he shared with me.

A number of other people offered valuable information and encouragement. They know who they are, and I hope they know how much I appreciate their help.

Jerry Shinn

List of Patrons

On behalf of East Carolina University Foundation and Foundation For The Carolinas, thank you to the following patrons whose generosity helped make this book a reality.

Mary Lou and Jim Babb
Carol and Irwin Belk
Janet and Rick Bean
Mary and Walt Beaver
Lee and Alan Blumenthal
Jimi and Henry Boggan
Deborah and Harold Bouton
Eleanor C. Boyd
Judy and Jim Boyd
Pat and Ty Boyd
Daisy and Henry Bridges
Me Me and Charlie Briley
Broadcast Music, Inc., Nashville, TN
Broadcast Music, Inc., New York, NY
Sarah Bryant
Mark Cabaniss
Sara and Cliff Cameron
Molly and George Carver
Barbara and Steady Cash
John H. Clark
Derick S. Close
Catherine and Quincy Collins

Judy and John Crosland
Barbara and Edward Crutchfield
Peggy and Bob Culbertson
Gwin and Bob Dalton
Mr. and Mrs. Rufus Dalton
Linda and Mark De Castrique
Mary Anne and Alan T. Dickson
Sis and Tom Dillon
Joe Epley
Frances and Donald Evans
Mary Elizabeth Francis
Ida and Bill Friday
Sarah Belk Gambrell
Polly and Bill Gilliam
Jane and Rusty Goode
Patty and Bill Gorelick
Mary Ann and Chuck Grace
Mary and Stuart Grasberg
Gail and Harry Grim
Dale F. Halton
Gordon Hamrick
Eleanor and Parks Helms

Sis and Robin Hinson
Ursula and Jim Hlavacek
Susan and Lew Hooper
Anne Howe
Lynda G. Jamison
Camille N. Johnston
Lou and Edwin Jones
Alex Josephs
Dr. and Mrs. Don Joyce
Jan Karon
Sue and Bill Keenan
"Knowing The Word Class," Carmel
    Presbyterian Church
Sandra and Leon Levine
Margaret Lewith
Zaydee and Antonio Lopez-Ibanez
Rose and Abraham Luski
Sonia and Isaac Luski
Dorothy and Powell Majors
Leslie and Michael Marsicano
Genie and Calvin Martin
Annette and Robert Mason
Esten and Bob Mason
Beth & Tom Matthews
Elenor and John Maxheim
Ruby and Doug Mayes
Loonis Reeves McGlohon Family Trust,
    Peggy and Reeves McGlohon, Laurie
    and Larry Shouse, Fan and Skipper
    Smith
Nan McGlohon
Dee Dee and Peter McKay
Betty and Joe Millsaps
Ann and Rolfe Neill
Eleanor and Bill Nichols
Betty and Jim Nisbet
Leslie and Paul Paliyenko
Rose and Bailey Patrick
Cyndee and Robert Patterson
Mary Carson and Norman Pease, Jr.

Ruth and Jack Pentes
Marilyn and George Persons
Kathryn and Norris Preyer
Mary and David Rhew
Sarah and Paul Richardson
Anita B. & Howard S. Richmond
    Foundation
Martha Robbins
Sally and Russell Robinson
Rotary Club of Charlotte
Sara and Richard M. Salisbury
Susan and Bob Salvin
Dr. and Mrs. Nasi Samily
Helen S. (Vernon) Scarborough
Rebecca and Gordon Schenck
Laurie and Russell Schwartz
Elly (Elinor) and Marc Smilow
Jane and Gibson Smith
Southwood Corporation
Claudia and Wesley Sturges
Sylvia and Cullie Tarleton
Claire and John Tate
Marji and Jack Tate
Ann and Ed Thomas
Betty and McNeill Upchurch
Sally and Bill Van Allen
Marlene and Billy VerPlanck
Judy and Richard Vinroot
Joanna and Howard Virkler
WBTV3/Jefferson Pilot Communications
Eva May and Bill Walker
Kay and Van Weatherspoon
Lisa and Randy White
Jacque and Bob Williams
Pat and Bill Williamson
Gloria and Donald Wood
Velva and Tom Woollen
Joan and Robert Zimmerman
2 Anonymous Patrons

Index

Notes: The abbreviation "LM" refers to
  Loonis McGlohon in this index.
Page numbers of photographs are in
  italics.

Acoustic Barn, xvii
Adderly, Cannonball, 96
Agresta, Phil, 84
"Air for Alto" (Wilder & McGlohon),
  130–31
"Air for Flute" (Wilder), 143
"Air for Oboe" (Wilder), 143
Albam, Manny, 157
Albritton, Gladys, 43–44, 165–66
Aldren, Buzz, 217–19
Alexander, Frances, 148–49, 152, 153, 243
Algonquin Hotel, 123, 138, 149–51
Allen, Gracie, 15
All In Good Time (McConnell), 202
Allyn, David, 138, 156
American Federation of Musicians, 65
American music. *See* Great American
  Songbook
American Popular Singers project, 155–56,
  162, 201, 204–5
*American Popular Song: The Great Inno-
  vators, 1900–1950* (Wilder), 135, 139

American Popular Song project, 135–41,
  169–72
  singers, 155–56
  Whitney Balliett review, 139, 198, 200
Amos and Andy, 15
Andrews, Julie, 217
Anselmo, Andrew, 161
Apollo 14, 216–17
Apollo 13 astronauts, 217–19
April Green (musical production), 81
Ardrey, Robert, 146
Arlen, Harold, xii, 135
  covers of, 162, 179, 180, 192
  influence on LM, 38, 145
Armstrong, Louis, 16, 162
Armstrong, Neil, 217–19
Artie (clarinet player), 59–60
As Time Goes By (Haymes), 171–72
Atwell, Father Henry, 141
Audiophile record label, 140, 157, 170–72
Auld, George, 39
Austin, Fletcher, 84
Austin, Gene, 18
Avakian, George, 40
Ayden, NC, 2–13
Ayden Christian Church, 8
Ayden Dispatch, 49

Babb, Jim, 96, 263
Bach Oratorio Singers, 161
Bailey, Mildred, 26, 38, 143
Bailey, Pearl, 184–85, 190
Bake, William, 211
Baker, Chet, 78
Baker, James, 248–49
Ballad Records, 171–72
Balliett, Whitney, 139, 198, 200
Bankhead, Tallulah, 152
Bank of America, 118
Banks, Dick, 81
Barber, Frederick, Jr., 201
Barber, Samuel, 93
Barefoot in the Park (TV series), 185
Battinger (trumpet player), 57–59
Beach Boys, 98
"Be a Child at Christmas" (McGlohon), 109
"Be a Child" (Wilder & McGlohon), 128
beach music, 79
Bean, Bob, 84
Bean, Janet, 159
Bean, Rick, 159, 261
Beatles, 98, 100, 108
bebop, 63–67, 77
Beech Mountain, x, 131–32, 134–35, 205, 247
Beiderbecke, Bix, 16
Belk, Joe, 80
Belk, John, 96
Belk, William Henry, 75
Belk department store, 75, 81, 117
Beneke, Tex, 37, 169
Bennett, Rodney, 232
Bennett, Tony, 137, 138, 141, 231
    covers of Wilder tunes, 144
    Loonis McGlohon Theater dedication, 248–49
Benny, Jack, 15
Bergen, Edgar, 15
Berlin, Irving, xii, 17, 135

Bernstein, Leonard, 162
Bertoncini, Gene, 173, 248–49, 250, 257
Betts, Doris, 103
Bicentennial Jazz Festival, 96
Big Brothers of America, 116–17, 118
"Billie's Bounce," 91
"Birthday Candles" (McGlohon), 107
"Birth of the Cool" band, 78
"Blackberry Winter" (McGlohon & Wilder), xviii, 130, 172, 202
Blankenship, Earl, 80, 85, *86*
Blood, Sweat, and Tears (rock band), 101
bluegrass music, 71, 235–36
the Blue Note, 189
blues, xii, 19, 63, 125, 243–44
Blythe, Legette, 96
Bodner, Mr. and Mrs. (Algonquin Hotel owners), 151
Boone, Daniel, 210
Bordnicks club gig, 26
Both Sides of the Coin (television show), 93
Bowers, Susan Kuralt, 263
Boyd, Jim, xi, 256, 263
Boyd, Ty, 91, *94,* 215, 249, 263
"The Boy Next Door" (Martin), 230, 231
Breach, Joyce, 128
Brendle, Ron, 172
Briarhoppers, 90
The Bridges of Madison County (film), 192
Brinkley, David, 210
broadcasting career of LM
    awards, 92–93
    country music, 95–96
    interviews, 91
    Nocturne set, *86, 87*
    public broadcasting, 95
    television productions, 93
    themes, 86–87
    See also American Popular Song project; WBT-WBTV
Broadway, 16–17

Brookmeyer, Bob, 157

Broughton, Margaret, 44

Brown, Lois Green, 44, 47

Brown, Mrs. (landlady), 74

Brubeck, Dave, xvii, 23, 78, 96, 204

Buck, George, 140

"Bull Fiddles in a China Shop" (Wilder), 143

Burnett, Carol, 165

Burns, Doug, 157

Burns, George, 15

Burns, Skip, 227–28

Burroughs, Edgar Rice, 11–12

Burton, Gary, 96

Butterfield, Billy, 22, 39

cabaret music, 139–40

Café Carlisle, 139–40

Cain, Jackie, 138, 157

Calloway, Cab, 37

Campbell, Jim, 210

Campbell, Mike, 172, 205, 249, 250

"Canadian Impressions" (Farnon), 231

cancer volunteer work, 248, 250

Capitol Theater, NYC, 26

Captain Horatio Hornblower (film), 232

Cariaga, Joyce, 261

Carmel Presbyterian Church, 105, 159, 199, 211–12, *258*, 261

    See also church activities of LM

Carmichael, Hoagy, xii

Carol Burnett Show, 165

Carolina Beach big band gig, 25–26

Carolina Caribbean Corporation, 132, 134–35

Carowinds theme park, 134

Carpenter, Thelma, 135, *136*, 182–87, *183*, 190, 253

Carradine, John, 150

"Cascades to the Sea" (Farnon), 232

Catlett, Sidney, 39

CBS network, 83, 90, 209, 224–25

CBS *Sunday Morning* show appearance, 201

champagne story, 31–34

Charles, Sonny, 27–28

Charlie McCarthy (radio character), 15

Charlotte, NC, 71–72

    appearances by Eileen Farrell, 159, 205

    appearances by Margaret Whiting, 204, 249

    appearances by Marlene VerPlanck, 201, 204–5, 248–49

    Freedom Park band shell benefit, 80, 115

    jazz scene, 79–82

    LM's move to, 69–70, 72–73

    local charity work, 80–82, 115–20, 246, 248

    local musical productions, 81–82, 96

    NCAA Final Four tournament, 245

    NPR affiliates, 137

    Open Kitchen restaurant, 79

    racial segregation, 110

    school desegregation, 117

    Singing Christmas Tree concert, 201

    Spirit Square project, 172, 202–5, 248–49

    Westover Hills neighborhood, 75

    See also WBT-WBTV

Charlotte Children's Choir, 249

Charlotte Choral Society, 201

Charlotte Junior Women's Club, 118, 199

Charlotte-Mecklenburg County Bicentennial celebration, 96

Charlotte Symphony, 80, 115, 212

Charlotte World Affairs Council, 254

Chicago (rock band), 101

"Chicken Scratch" (McGlohon), 91

childhood of LM, 2–13

    church, 8

    family farm, 8–11

    Great Depression, 10–11

    playmates, 5, 10

(childhood of LM, *continued*)
    reading, 11–12
    travel, 12
    See also education of LM; musical roots
      of LM
children. *See* family of LM
"The Children Met the Train" (Wilder),
    143
A Child's Christmas, 115–16
"Child's Introduction to the Orchestra"
    (Wilder), 144
choir. *See* church activities of LM
Christian, Charlie, 39
"Christmas Back Home" (McGlohon),
    109
"Christmas Child" (McGlohon), 109
"Christmas Is Just About Here" (McGlo-
    hon), 109
"Christmas Is Love" (McGlohon &
    Lamont), 109
"A Christmas Jubilee Concert: A Tribute
    to Loonis McGlohon," 212
"A Christmas Memory" (McGlohon), 109
Christy, June, 78, 84
church activities of LM, 5–6
    Bible study, 12
    black church music, 110, 118–20
    childhood, 2, 8
    choir and music director, 12–13, 15, 75,
      105, 199, 211–12, *258*
    dinner on the grounds, 8
    jazz interests, 241
    Mountain Boy, 141
    sacred songs, 261
    senior high fellowship, 93
    Sunday School accompanist, 20
Clark, Septima Poinsett, 118–20, *119*
Clooney, Rosemary, 77, 144, 200
Coastal Carolina Community College, 201
Coates. Carroll, 109
Colby, Douglas, 151
Cole, Cozy, 37

Cole, Grady, 84, 90–91
Cole, Nat "King," 78, 84
Coleman, Cy, 141
Collins, Mike, 217–19
Collins, Pat, 217, 219
Coltrane, John, 192
Colvard, Dean, 96
Come Blow Your Horn (television show),
    93
Composer of the Year award, 107
composing of LM, 61, 82, 197
    arrangements by Farnon, 157–58
    children's influence, 107
    Christmas songs, 109
    collaborations with Alec Wilder, xviii,
      125–35, 141–42, 144, 147–48, 197–98
    Grammy nominations, 202
    Jaycee Jollies productions, 81
    Land of Oz, 131–35, 144
    Mountain Boy, 141–42
    musical structure, 40
    sacred music, 5, 261
    "Songbird" (McGlohon), 140–41
Concert by the Sea album (Garner), 78
Connor, Chris, 78, 84
Cook, Barbara, 156
Coonce, Charlie, 229–30
Cooper, Virginia Belle, 8, 19–20
Cosby Show, 186
Cosgrove, Alice, 259
Cotton Club (film), 185
Count Basie Orchestra, xvii, 18, 178,
    182–83, 189
"Country Boy" (Farnon), 232
country music, 71, 90, 125
Cousin Ralph, 31–34
Crawford, Jimmy, 37
Crisp, NC, 43
Cronkite, Walter, 226
Crosby, Bing, 15
Crutchfield, Charles, 72, 73, 89–91, 100
Cutshall, Bob, 39

dancing
    R&B, 97
    shag, 78–79
    swing, 18–19, 64–65
Dankworth, Johnny, 128
Dardanelle (singer), 212
Davidson College, 118
Davis, Miles, 78, 79
Davis, Patty, 211
Day, Doris, 77
"The Day After Christmas" (McGlohon), 109
day jobs of LM, 69, 74, 89, 202
    See also WBT-WBTV
Debussy, Claude, 81
Dee (playmate), 10
Delius, Frederick, 81, 230
DeSalle, Peter, 184
Desmond, Paul, 78
The Diary of Anne Frank (play), 232
"Dinner on the Grounds" (McGlohon), 8, 82, 91, 210
Dior, Rick, xvii–xviii
Disney World, 134
"Don't Mail the Letter" (McGlohon), 82
Doodletown Pipers, 172
Dooley, Jim, 80
Dorsey, Tommy, 18, 45
Dorsey brothers, 18, 65
Dorsey Brothers band, 169
Down Beat, 64
Downtown United Presbyterian Church, Rochester, NC, 141
Driggers, Leo, 55–56
Duke, Washington, 210
Dunn, Sally, 230

Eagles Baptist Church, 49
Earle, Edna (cousin), 11
East Carolina Teachers College (now University), 20–21, *21*, 44–47, 212, 263

East Carolina University Chancellor's Forum, 13
Eastman School of Music, 39, 148, 242
East Trade Street park, 117–18
Eastwood, Clint, 192
East Woods Press, 211
Eberle, Ray, 37
ECU Foundation, 263
Ed Sullivan Show, 162
education of LM, 2, 8, 11
    college, 20–23, 36–37
    music, 8, 18–20, 22–23
    segregation, 10
    See also musical roots of LM
Eldridge, Roy, 27
Elizabeth (British cabaret singer), 190
Ella award, 176
Ellington, Duke, 18, 190
Ellis, Anita, 138
El Morocco club, 79
Engvick, William, 51
Erskine College, 200
Ervin, Sam, 210
Etters, Clarence, 91
Eure, May, 19–20
Evans, Gil, 40, 78
"Every Day I Have the Blues," 178
"Everything I Love" (McGlohon), 158
"Every Time" (Martin), 230

Faille, Tommy, 95–96
family of LM, 6
    champagne story, 31–34
    children, 103–14, 197
    experiences with Alec Wilder, 126–28, 144
    farming, 8–11
    gatherings and celebrations, 213–14, 254, 255, *255*
    grandchildren, 108, 205, 211, 254–55
    home in Charlotte, 105–6
    parents, 2, 6, 7–8, 11

(family of LM, *continued*)
  piano inheritance, 113–14
  vacations, 109–11
Famous Door club, 26
"The Farmer" (Kuralt), 210
farming, 8–11
Farnon, Pat, 232
Farnon, Robert, 157–58, 231–32
Farrell, Eileen, ix, xvi, 155–67, *156, 159,*
    226, 231
  American Popular Singers project,
    155–56, 201
  American Popular Song project,
    138–39, 155–56
  Carnegie Hall tribute to Wilder, 156–57
  covers of Wilder–McGlohon tunes,
    128, 130
  influence of Mabel Mercer, 180
  Living Legend Award, 161
  LM's recollections of, 161–67
  Loonis McGlohon Theater dedication,
    249
  performance with Mabel Mercer, 163
  personal traits, 163–67
  recordings with LM, 157–58, 162,
    212–13
  singing career, 155, 161–62
  singing style, 166–67
  visits to Charlotte, 158–59, 165, 175,
    205
  work with LM, 156–58, 162–64, 212–13
Ferguson, Jim, 163, 201
Ferrer, Jose, *92*
Fields, Dorothy, xii
First United Methodist Church, 201–2
Fitzgerald, Ella, 26, 37, 108, 176
Fitzgerald, F. Scott, 244
"Fools Rush In," 191
Forrest, Helen, 38, 39, 41
"Forty-Eight Hours in the Vatican"
    (Kuralt), 224–25
Forty-Niners UNCC basketball team, 96

For You, For Me, Forevermore (Haymes),
    171–72
Foster, Stephen, 93
Foundation for the Carolinas, 263
Four Freshmen, 78, 84, 91
Fredette, Carol, 205
Freedom Park band shell, 80, 115
Fricks, Luther, 57
Friday, Bill, 226, *253*
Friends of Alec Wilder Concert, 241

Gabriel Award, 93
Gardner, Ava, 36, 210
Garland, Judy, 162, 166, 231
Garner, Erroll, 23, 78, 90
Gary, Kays, 92, 115, 171, 199
Gavin, James, 172
Gaylor, Melba, 12
Gehrig, Lou, 226
Gene Krupa band, 27
General Phonographic Corporation, 16
Genghis Khan, 225
Genovese, Dan, 35
George Foster Peabody Award, 141
Gershwin, George, xii, 17, 93, 135, 179, 192
Gershwin, Ira, xii
Getz, Stan, 157, 204
Gilder, Rusty, 91
Gillespie, Dizzy, xvii, 64, 65, 91, 204
Gitler, Ira, 65
Giuliani, Rudolph, 250
"Go Away, Little Boy," 189
Godfrey, Arthur, 183–84
Gone with the Wind (Mitchell), 12
Goodman, Benny, 18, 38, 41, 113, 143,
    177–78
Goodman (Benny) orchestra, 38–41, 65
"Good Old Friends" (McGlohon), 261
Gould, Jack, 84
Grable, Betty, 171
Grace, Bishop "Daddy," 110
Graham, Frank Porter, 210

Graham, Ronnie, 56–59, 61

Grammy nominations, 202

Grandfather Mountain, 205, 220, 222

Grandma Moses, 144, 145

Grasberg, Stuart, 259, 264

Great American Songbook, xii, 16–17, 63, 66, 140
    See also *American Popular Song* project

Great Depression, 10–11, 46–48, 83–84

Green, Lois, 44, 47

Greenacre, 43

Grey, Joel, 204

Grey, Zane, 12

Griffith, Andy, 31, 70, 210

Grove Park Inn, Asheville, NC, 173

"Grow Tall, My Son" (McGlohon), 107, 180

Habermann, Robert, 111, 250

Haig, Al, 64

Hammerstein, Oscar, xii

Hampson, Thomas, 142, 153

Hampson, Zena, 153

Hardy Boys mysteries, 12

Harlem, 16, 63–64, 67

Hart, Lorenz, xii, 180

Hartman, Johnny, 192–94, *193,* 200, 205

Hartman, Tedi, 193–94

Hatley, Spence, 22–23, 36
    big band summer, 25
    military service, 55–56
    Pensacola gig, 28–29

"Have Yourself a Merry Little Christmas" (Martin), 109, 230–31

Hawkins, Coleman, 27

Haymes, Dick, ix, 137, 138, 171–72, 198

"Heartaches," 84

"Heebie Jeebies" (Armstrong recording), 16

Helms, Parks, 263

Henderson, Fletcher, 18, 40

Henry, Doug, xvii–xviii, 157

Hickory House, 26

Hicks, Stanly, xvi, 235–36

High Spirits (Martin), 230

Hildreth, Tom, xvii–xviii

Hilley, Steve, 35–36

Hilliard, Harriet, 26

Hi-Los, 78

Hines, Earl "Father," 37

hip-hop, 252

"His First Long Pants" (Wilder), 143

Hodges, Bill, 80

Hodges, Luther, 221

Hodges, Luther, Jr., 96

Holiday, Billie, 27–28, *28,* 38, 91, 192, 253

Holiday, Judy, 180

Hope, Bob, 221

Horne, Lena, 180, 231

The Hornet's Nest (musical production), 81, 96

Horowitz, Vladimir, 226

Hot Five band, 16

Houlik, James, 130–31

Howard, Bart, 180

"How Beautiful Is Night" (Farnon), 232

Hughes, Lois, 35

Hugo, Victor, 12

Humphrey, Hubert, 227–28

"A Hundred Years from Today," 191

Hungry I, 180

Hunt, Jim, 201, 207–9

Hyslop, Greg, 157

"I'd Like to Go Back Home for Christmas" (McGlohon), 109

"I Know It's Christmas" (McGlohon), 109

"I'll Be Around" (Wilder), 143, 242

"I'll Let You Go" (McGlohon), 82

"I'm Coming, Virginia," 91

improvisation, 63–64

"In a Quiet Place" (McGlohon), 261

interview process, x

Iris Award, 93

"I Thought about You," 191

It Might as Well Be Spring (Whiting), 176

"It's Christmas Time" (McGlohon), 109

"It's So Peaceful in the Country"
    (Wilder), 142, 143, 242

"I've Grown Accustomed to Her Face," 91

Jackie and Roy duo, 199

Jackson, Andrew, 210

Jackson, Dot, 112

Jamal, Ahmad, 79, 204

James, Harry, 38

Japanese trip, 199–200

Jarrett, Keith, 130

jazz, xii, 16–17
    bebop, 63–67, 77
    big bands, 25, 77
    dancing, 18–19, 64–65, 78–79
    Harlem Renaissance, 16
    modern jazz, 66, 77–78, 79, 99
    New Orleans style, 16, 18
    swing, 18–19, 64–65, 77, 98

The Jazz Singer (movie), 17

Jefferson Standard Life Insurance Com-
    pany, 83, 90, 92

Jimmie Lunceford band, 18, 36–37

jitterbug, 78

Johnson, Andrew, 210

Johnson, Betty, 186–87

Johnson, Max, 32

Jolson, Al, 17

Justice, Charles, 226

"Just One of Those Things" (Porter), 180

Kahn, Madeline, 180

KDKA radio, 15

Kelly's Stables, 26, 27

Kennedy, John F., 236

Kenton, Stan, 91

Kern, Jerome, xii, 16–17, 135, 162, 179

Kid Ory's jazz band, 16

Kimball, C. M., 89

King, Martin Luther, Jr., 118

King, Teddi, 128, 130, 138–40, 198

King, Wayne, 90

Kinsey, Gene, 39

Kirby, Lee, 84

Kirchner, Bill, 250

Kirk, Andy, 37, 38

Klincewicz, Watson, 57–58

Knauff, Billy, 35, 49, 69, 72–74, 81

Knauff, Marguerite, 49, 69, 72, 74

Knauff band, 35, 36, 46, 73
    with Jim Stack on vibraphone, 80–81
    LM's return to Charlotte, 61

Kral, Roy, 157

Kuralt, Charles, 9, 201, 207–11, 221–26
    collaborations with LM, 224
    illness and death, 246–47
    NCAA Final Four tournament, 245
    "On the Road" series, 209, 224–25
    Our Funny Valentine project, 246
    pictures, *208, 223, 246, 253*
    radio career, 224
    WTVI tribute to LM, 257, 259

Kuralt, Petie, 226

Kyser, Kay, 210

Lackey, Jim, xvii–xviii, 80, 91, *92*

"Lady Sings the Blues" concert, 28

"Lady Sings the Blues" (Wilder), 242

Laine, Cleo, 128

Lamar, Alice, 132–33

Lamont, John, 109

Land of Oz, 131–35, 144

Larkins, Ellis, 157

LaRosa, Julius, 156, 180, 198, 205, 231

"Laura," 92

Lawrence, Steve, 138, 180

Lawrence Welk band, 126–27

Laxton, F. M., 83

Lea, Barbara
    American Popular Song project, 138,
        139

covers of LM songs, 130

Loonis McGlohon Day in NYC, 250

performances with LM, 148, 242

recordings with LM, 198

LeCroy, George, 80

Lee, Pat, 118

Lee, Peggy, 144

Lees-McRae College, 247

Legrand, Michel, 230

Leonhart, Jay, 157, 163, 250

Les Miserables (Hugo), 12

Let's Get Away from It All (Campbell & McGlohon), 172

Levy, Robert, 130

Liberty Bell Award, 248

"Light One Candle" (McGlohon), 261

Ligon, Rev. Wendell, 261

Lincoln Center concert, 250–52

Listen to the Words concert, 157

"Little Girl Blue," 181

"Loch Lomond," 191

Lodge (club), 79

Loew's State Theater, NYC, 37

Lombardo, Guy, 90

Loonis in London (McGlohon), 202

Loonis McGlohon and the Trio Play, 91–92

Loonis McGlohon Day in NYC, 250–52

Loonis McGlohon Theater, 248–49, *249*

Loonis McGlohon Trio, 80, 202, *203*

appearances, 157, 200–202, 212–13, 247

Loonis McGlohon Theater dedication, 248–49

North Carolina Is My Home project, 210

recordings with Dick Haymes, 171

recordings with Eileen Farrell, 162, 212–13

"Sketches in Jazz," 200–201

Spirit Square opening celebration, 204

tribute concert for Alec Wilder, 157

Looss, Walter, 39

"Love among the Young" (Wilder), 123

Lovelace, Edward Young, 43

Lovelace, Francis Pitt Eagles, 43, 44, 45

Lovelace, Nan Flournoy. *See* McGlohon, Nan

Lovers and Losers (King & McGlohon), 198

Loving Friends (Campbell & McGlohon), 172

"Lullaby of Birdland," 92

Lunceford, Jimmie, 18, 36–37, 253

lymphoma, ix, xv, xvii, 242–45, 250–52, 254

Lynn, Vera, 231

Madison, Dolley, 210

Maggie and Jiggs (Martin), 231

Maher, James T., 135

Mancini, Henry, 79, 177

Mann, Herbie, 96

Mantes, Delores, *73*

Marianna, FL training field, 55–56

Marsicano, Michael, 263

Martin, Hugh, 109, 139, 170, 230–31

Martin, Jim, 212, 237

Martin, Joan, 238

Martin, Joe, 236–38, *237*

Martin, Skippy, 39

M*A*S*H* (television series), 61

Massey, Julian, 113

Matz, Peter, 232

Maxwell, Jimmy, 39

May, Jesse, 87–88

Mayes, Doug, 84

Mayo, Mary, 130, 134, 199–200, 210–11

McColl, Hugh L., Jr., 248

McConnell, Rob, 202

McElwee, Ross, 226

McGarity, Lou, 39

McGhee, Brownie, 204

McGlawhorn, Jeremiah, 6

McGlohon, Allan (grandson), 108, 211, 254, *255*

McGlohon, Benjamin Franklin and Lois, 6

McGlohon, Bertha Andrews (mother), 6, *6*, 31–34, 45

McGlohon, Brady Daniel (great-grandson), 254–55, *255*

McGlohon, Caleb Joseph and Winifred Eugenia (grandparents), 6, 8–9, 10–12

McGlohon, Frances Lovelace (daughter), 105, *107*, 264
  childhood, 106–14
  education, 197
  experiences with musicians, 126–27, 189
  family gatherings and celebrations, 213–14, 254–55, *255*
  marriage, 108

McGlohon, John, 6

McGlohon, Joseph Allen (brother), 6

McGlohon, Laurie Lee (daughter), 105, *107*, 264
  childhood, 106–14
  education, 197
  experiences with musicians, 126–27, 145, 189
  family gatherings and celebrations, 213–14, 254–55, *255*
  marriage, 108

McGlohon, Lisa, 254, *255*

McGlohon, Loonis Reeves, ix
  autograph collection, 37–38
  awards and honors, 2, 107, 118, 141, 199, 201, 202, 212, 248–49, 254–56
  birth, 6
  cancer volunteer work, 248, 250
  children, 103–14, 197
  computer use, 213
  cooking, 109, 255
  courtship and marriage, 45–51, *50*
  death, xii, 261
  80th birthday, 254
  50th anniversary, 213–14
  50th birthday, 197–98
  local charity work, 80–82, 115–20, 246, 248
  lymphoma, ix, xv, xvii, 242–45, 250–52, 254, 255–56
  memorial service, 261
  military service, 49, 55–63, 69
  nicknames, 35, 75
  personal traits, ix, 4–5, 6, 109, 112–13, 115, 125, 199
  retirement from WBTV, 202
  78th birthday, 252
  story-telling skills, xi
  Thanksgiving, 2001, 255, *255*
  views on race, 252–53

McGlohon, Loonis Reeves, Jr. (son), 104, *106*, 165, *249*, 264
  childhood, 106–14
  education, 197
  family gatherings and celebrations, 213–14, 254–55, *255*
  Loonis McGlohon Day in NYC, 252

McGlohon, Marvin (uncle), 10–11

McGlohon, Max Cromwell (father), 6

McGlohon, Max (grandson), 108, 211, *249*, 254–55, *255*

McGlohon, Nan, ix–x, 43–51, 263, 264
  birth and family background, 43–44
  children, 103–14
  cooking, 106, 125
  courtship and marriage, 45–51, *50*
  education, 44–47
  experiences with Alec Wilder, 126–28, 145
  fiftieth anniversary, 213–14
  grandchildren, 108, 254–55
  piano inheritance of LM, 113–14
  pictures, *50, 60,* 254
  relationship with Eileen Farrell, 158, 165
  Thanksgiving, 2001, 255, *255*
  80th birthday party, 254
  during WWII, 56

McGlohon, Ned (uncle), 11

McGlohon, Peggy, 108, *249*, 255, *255*, 264

McGlohon, Raymond Berkley, 6

McGlohon, Sol (uncle), 9, 10–11

McLean, Clyde, 80, 84, 100

McMillan, Alex, 204

McPartland, Marian, 26, 141, 204, *233*,
 233–35
 Carnegie Hall tribute to Wilder, 157
 LM's 78th birthday celebration, 252
 Loonis McGlohon Day in NYC,
  250–51, *251*

Mecklenburg County Bar Association
 award, 248

Meet Me in St. Louis (film), 231

Melody Fair, 89

Mercer, Johnny, xii, 177, 213

Mercer, Mabel, 135, 179–82, *181*, 226
 American Popular Singers project, 156
 American Popular Song project, 137–38
 Carnegie Hall tribute to Wilder, 157
 covers of Wilder-McGlohon songs,
  128, 130
 influence on other singers, 155, 162,
  180, 182
 performance with Eileen Farrell, 163
 Rockingham, NC performance, 200
 singing career, 179–82
 work with LM, 182, 201

Meredith College, 44

Metronome, 64

Michael's Pub, 140

Michelangelo, 225

Mildred (black bear), 222

Milhaud, Darius, 23

military bands, 55–63

Miller, Frances Alexander, 148–49, 152,
 153, 243

Miller, Glenn, 37, 45

Miller, Mitch, xvi, 143, 148

Mills Brothers, 143

Miss North Carolina Pageant, 81

"Misty" (Garner), 78

Mitchell, Margaret, 12

modern jazz, 66, 77–78, 79, 99

Mondello, Pete, 39

Monk, Thelonious, 64, 96

Montiero, Eddie, 199

Montoya, Carlos, 204

"Moon River" (Mercer & Mancini), 177

Moore, Dudley, 128

Moore, Misty, 82

Morath, Max, 204

"The More I See You," 171

Morton, Hugh, 216, 220–22, *221*, 226, 263
 Beech Mountain, 205
 North Carolina is My Home project, 211

Morton, Julia, 220–21

The 100 Most Beautiful Songs, 202

Mostel, Zero, 149–50

Mountain Boy (Wilder & McGlohon),
 141–42

Mounted Records, 170

Mulligan, Gerry, 157

"The Murder of Two Old Men . . .", 227

Murphy, Mark, 141

Murrow, Edward R., 210, 226

musical roots of LM, 15–23
 American optimism, 13
 black music, 5, 18–19, 20
 church, 12–13, 15
 dancing, 18–19
 Erroll Garner, 78, 90
 Goodman orchestra, 39–40
 impressionism, 81
 jazz, 16–19
 mentors, 22–23
 radio, 15, 17–18

"My Blue Heaven" (Austen), 18

My Romance (Campbell & McGlohon),
 172

"The Name of This Song Is Joe" (McGlohon), 238

National Association for the Advancement of Colored People (NAACP), 120
National Conference of Christians and Jews, 118
National Endowment for the Arts, 136–38
National Federation of Music Clubs, 93
National Public Radio
    American Popular Singers project, 155–56, 201
    American Popular Song project, 137–41, 147–48, 162, 169–72, 192
NationsBank Performance Place, 248
NCAA Final Four tournament, 245
NCNB. *See* North Carolina National Bank
NCNB Performance Place, 204, 248
Nelson, Ozzie, 26
Newcomb, Alan, 84
Newcomers program, 123–25
New Deal programs, 11, 47–48
Newport Jazz Festival, 79
New York City, 37–38, 65, 250
    LM's plans to move, 69–70
    summer jazz scene, 26–29
    1964 World's Fair, 110
"Ninety-eight Cents Worth of Trash" (radio script), 100
"Nobody's Heart" (Rodgers & Hart), 179
Nocturne (WBTV jazz show), 75–76, 80, 82, 85–88, *86–87*
North Carolina Association of Arts Councils, 212
North Carolina Award, 212
North Carolina Department of Travel and Tourism, 210
North Carolina Disciples of Christ, 8
North Carolina Is My Home (Kuralt), 207–11, 222, 224
"North Carolina Is My Home" (McGlohon), 249
North Carolina National Bank (NCNB), 118, 199, 204, 248

North Carolina Performing Arts Center, 117
North Carolina Society of New York City, xi, 256
Norvo, Red, 26

O. Henry, 210
Odetta, 93, 204
Okeh record label, 16
"The Old North State," 210
Oliver, King, 16
"Once Upon a Summertime," 92, 182
"On the Road with Charles Kuralt" series, 209, 224–25
On the Square (musical production), 81
Onyx Club, 26
Open Kitchen restaurant, 79
Oratorio Singers of Charlotte, 212
"Origins of Jazz in the Church" performance, 80
Osmond, Donny, 189
Our Funny Valentine project, 246
"Our Love Is Here to Stay," 188
Ouzer, Louis, 142, 153
"Over the Rainbow" (Arlen), 132, 166

Palitz, Mortimer, 51
Paramount Theater, NYC, 26, 37
parents. *See* family of LM
Parker, Charlie "Bird," 64, 65, 67
Parker, Dorothy, 149
Pat Lee Show, 90
Peabody Award, 93, 141
Pearl Street Park, 118
Pecan Grove club, 79
Penderlea initiative, 11
Pensacola gig, 28–29, 32
Pentes, Jack, 81, 92, 116, *131,* 131–33
Peoples, Terry
    Loonis McGlohon Theater dedication, 248

Loonis McGlohon Trio, 157, 201–2, *203*, 247
Perez, Linda, 80
Performance Place, 204, 248
Perlmutt, David, 264
Pete's Tavern, 190
Phantom of the Opera (play), 226
Phipps, Dick, 135–36, 155
phonographs, 17–18, *18–19*
pictures of LM
    with Alec Wilder, *124*
    at Carmel Presbyterian Church, *258*
    with Charles Kuralt, *208, 223, 246*
    with Charles Kuralt and William
       Friday, *253*
    childhood, *7*
    with Eileen Farrell, *156, 159*
    with Hugh Morton, *221*
    with Joe Martin, *237*
    Loonis McGlohon Trio, *203*
    with Marion McPartland, *233*
    with Nan, *50, 60, 254*
    with *Nocturne* trio, *92, 94*
    at the piano, 1950's, *80*
    Thanksgiving, 2001, *255*
    WBTV *Nocturne* set, *86*
    wedding day, *50*
Piedmont Airlines, 210
Pietà (Michelangelo), 110
Ploss, Bill, 152–53
Polk, H. P., 80
Polk, James K., 210
Pope John Paul, 225
popular music. *See* Great American
    Songbook
Porter, Cole, xii, 179, 180, 192
Porter, William Sidney, 210
Pot (playmate), 10
Poulain, Jacques, 112
Pound, Ezra, 146–47, 227, 228
Powell, David, 200, 204

Powell, Earl "Bud," 64
Powell, Mel, 39
Presbyterian Church U.S., 93
Preservation Hall Jazz Band, 204
Presley, Elvis, 5, 97–99, 117
Prevatte, Norman, 76, 81, 85
Previn, André, 157, 162
progressive jazz. *See* modern jazz
Project 60 radio program, 90, 91, 93
Puerling, Gene, 231
Purdie, Bernard "Pretty," 250
Pzazz Records label, 82

Queens University at Charlotte, 254–55

race music, 79
racial segregation, 5, 70, 120, 179, 252–53
    bands and music, 18–19, 36–38, 79
    bebop, 64–65
    black churches, 118–20
    in Charlotte, NC, 110, 117
    childhood experiences, 10
    school desegregation, 117
radio, 2, 15, 17–18
    American Popular Singers project,
       155–56, 201
    American Popular Song project, 137–41,
       147–48, 162, 169–72, 192
    automobile listening, 94–95
    CBS network, 83
    news, 83–84
    phonograph broadcasts, 83
    public broadcasting networks, 95
    See also WBT-WBTV
Radio Moscow, 90
Ragan, Sam, 226
Raiford, Bob, 84
    with *Nocturne* trio, *92*
    WBTV jazz shows, 85–87, *86–87*
Raleigh, NC, 12
Ralph Flanagan Orchestra, 73, 198

Ramsey, Lo, 28–29, 80

rap music, 252–53

Rascovich, Mark, 76, 86

Ravel, Maurice, 81, 145, 230

Reagan, Bob, 156, 162

recording industry, 100

recordings of LM, 197
    as accompanist, xix, 198
    American Popular Singers project,
        204–5
    American Popular Song project, 200,
        204–5
    on Audiophile, 140
    with Barbara Lea, 198
    with Eileen Farrell, 157–58, 162, 212–13
    last, December 2001, xvii–xix
    Loonis McGlohon and the Trio Play,
        91–92
    with Margaret Whiting, 212
    with Marlene VerPlanck, 170–71, 198,
        200
    with Maxine Sullivan, 192
    with Misty Moore, 82
    reviews, 198, 202
    solo album, 202
    with Teddi King, 198

recording technology, 78

record purchases, 38

Redman, Don, 18

Reed, Rex, 100

Reference Recordings, 157

Reflection Sound Studios, 157–58, 171

Reilly, Peter, 171

reviews of LM, 139, 198, 200, 202

rhythm and blues (R&B), 5, 19, 78–79, 97

Rice, Daryle, 173, 205, 249

Robbins, Grover, 131–32, 134

Robbins, Harry, 131–32

Robert Farnum Society, 250

Robinson, Les, 39

rock and roll, xii, 79, 95, 97–101, 108, 125,
    252

Rodgers, Richard, xii, 17, 135, 140, 180, 192

Rooney, Andy, 226

Rooney, Mickey, 231

Roosevelt, Eleanor, 45

Rose, Lee, 96

Rosenstock, Milton, 232

Round Table, 149

Rountree Christian Church, 8

*The Rowe String Quartet Plays on Your
    Imagination* (television show), 93

Salvation Army award, 118, 200

Sam (playmate), 10

Sauter, Eddie, 40, 65

Scheer, Julian, 217

Schuller, Gunther, 157

Schweitzer, Albert, 144, 145

Secret Fantasy (Campbell), 172

segregation. *See* racial segregation

Sellers, Ralph (uncle), 31–34

Serenade to Autumn (fashion show), 81,
    115, 199

shag (dance), 78–79

Shaw, Artie, 18, 65

Shaw, Marlena, 93, 115, *188*, 188–90, 205,
    249

Shearing, Ellie, 229–30

Shearing, George, xvii, 228–30, 231
    appearances in North Carolina, 173,
        199, 204
    covers of LM songs, 157
    influence on LM, 66
    Nocturne trio, *94*
    quintet instrumentation, 85

Shepherd, Brooke (granddaughter), 108,
    109, 211, 249, 254, 255

Sherman's March (film), 226

Shinn, Jerry, 238

"A Ship Without a Sail" (Rodgers), 198

Short, Bobby, 135, 137, 139–40, 156

Shouse, Edward (grandson), 108, 211, 254,
    255

Shouse, Hilary (granddaughter), 108, 254, *255*

Shouse, Lawrence Edward "Larry," 108, 111–12, 213, 264

Sills, Beverly, 162

Simmons, Norman, 178

Simone, Nina, 96

Sinatra, Frank, 77, 78, 84, 171, 231

    American Popular Song project, 138

    covers of McGlohon tunes, 201

    covers of Wilder–McGlohon tunes, 128

    covers of Wilder tunes, 143–44

    influence of Mabel Mercer, 180, 182

    Loonis McGlohon Theater dedication, 249

    recording of Wilder's concert pieces, 143

Singing Christmas Tree concert, 201

"Sketches in Jazz," 200–201

Skylight Inn, 3

Sloan, Peter, 105

"Slow Dance" (Wilder), 143

Smith, Carrie, *86*

Smith, Dean, 221, 226

Smith, Ervin Caldwell "Skipper," 108, 111–12, 264

Smith, Graham (grandson), 108, 211, 254–55, *255*

Smith, Kate, 15, 163, 166

Smith, Laurie (granddaughter), 108, 211, 254, *255*

Smith, Mamie, 16

Smith, Ray, 11

Smith, Stuff, 27

Smithsonian Institution concert, 141, 147–48

Snyder, John, xvii–xix

"Soft as Spring" (Wilder), 39–41, 123, 143

"Someone to Watch Over Me," 184

"Sonata for Bassoon and Piano" (Wilder), 242

Sonderman, Joe, 117–18

"Songbird" (McGlohon), xviii–xix, 66, 140–41, 156, 157, 166, 202, 230

Songs of the Soul (television program), 93

Sonny Charles Band, 28–29

Sonny Terry & Brownie McGhee duo, 204

The Sound of Music (musical), 217

South Carolina Educational Radio and Television Network, 135–37

Southern, Jeri, 84

Southern Railway job, 74, 89

"South to a Warmer Place" (Wilder & McGlohon), 128

Spectrum, 89

The Spirits of Rhythm, 27

Spirit Square, Charlotte, NC, 172, 202–5, 248–49

Spivak, Charlie, 169

Spivey, Creighton, 80, 85, *86,* 91, *92*

"Spring Has Sprung" (McGlohon), 91

St. Andrew's College, 80

St. Clair, Wade, 81, 215–20, *216,* 261

St. Peter's Church, NYC, 241

Stack, Jim, xi, xvii–xix

    lifelong association with LM, 80–81

    Loonis McGlohon Theater dedication, 248–49

    Loonis McGlohon Trio, 80, 157, 247

    Nocturne trio, 85, *86, 92*

    WTVI tribute to LM, 257

Steed, John, 235–36

Stone, Desmond, 39, 127, 135, 141–42

Stowe, Bill, 157, 163, 200–202, *203,* 204, 247

Strand Theater, NYC, 26

"Street Walkin' Woman," 189

Streisand, Barbara, 127, 175–76, 180

Studio Party, 89

Sullivan, Maxine, 155–56, 190–92, *191,* 205

"Summertime," 92

"Sunday Blues" (McGlohon), 91

Swale, Dr. (army veterinarian), 60
Swansea, Charleen, 146–47, 226–28
swing, 18–19, 64–65, 98
Swing to Bop (Gitler), 65

Tate, Jack, 263
Taylor, Billy, 226
"Teach Me, Lord" (McGlohon), 261
Teagarden, Jack, 37
Tempo in Jazz, 89
Terry, Sonny, 204
"That's What We Love about Christmas"
    (McGlohon & Coates), 109
"This Is the Day" (McGlohon), 96
This Time It's Love (Farrrell), 158
Thompson, Phil, 157, 248–49
Thornhill (Claude) band, 36, 40
Three Deuces club, 26, 65
345th Army Air Force, 55–63
Thurber, James, 149, 204
Timberlake, Bob, 200
Tokyo-American Club, 199–200
Tough, Dave, 36–37
travel of LM, 202
    abroad, xv, 110–12, 250
    childhood, 12
    gig destinations, 25–28, 109–10, 111
    Japanese trip, 199–200
    New York City, 26–29, 37–38, 65, 110,
    250, 256
"The Trolley Song" (Martin), 231
Truman, Harry, 145
Tuckahoe, NY gig, 26
Tyner, McCoy, 204

United House of Prayer for All People, 110
University of North Carolina at Charlotte,
    96

Valle Crucis, 247
Van Allen, Sally, 263
Varner, Carroll, 263

Vaughan, Sarah, 138, 167
VerPlanck, Billy, 169, 170, 171, 210
VerPlanck, Marlene, 169–71, *170*, 189
    American Popular Singers project, 156
    American Popular Song project, 138, 140,
        169–70
    appearances in Charlotte, 201, 204–5,
        249
    commercial singing, 169
    covers of Wilder-McGlohon songs, 128,
        130
    Loonis McGlohon Day in NYC, 250,
        251
    Loonis McGlohon Theater dedication,
        249
    NCAA Final Four tournament, 245
    North Carolina Is My Home project, 210
    recordings with LM, 170–71, 198, 200
    WTVI tribute to LM, 257
Virkler, Joanna, 264
Von Trapp, Maria, 217

"Wait Till You See Her," 181
Wallington, George, 91
"Waltz for a Toy Ballerina" (McGlohon),
    107
Ward, Butch, 91
Ward, Virgil, 44
Water for Africa project, 118
Waters, Ethel, 91
WBT-WBTV, 71, 72
    announcers, 84
    community service, 116–18
    first interview, 73
    Forty-Niners UNCC basketball team, 96
    founding of the radio station, 83
    fundraising, 186–87
    interviews, 91
    local charity work, 82
    musical programming, 90–96
    piano inheritance of LM, 113–14
    programming, 84–85, 90, 95, 123

record library, 91

retirement of LM, 202

staff positions of LM, xviii, 89–96, 116–18, 201

Water for Africa project, 118

WBT-FM, 137

weeknight jazz shows, 75–76, 80, 82, 85–86, *86–87*

"Wear the Sunshine in Your Hair" (McGlohon), 107

Weatherspoon, Van, 216, 263

Webb, Chick, 26

Webster, Ben, 27

Webster, Kurt, 84

Wein, George, 79, 96, 146, 156

Weissberg, Eric, 210

Welk, Lawrence, 126–27

West Coast "cool" jazz, 66, 77–78

Western North Carolina Center, 246

Westover Hills neighborhood of Charlotte, NC, 75, 105

Westover Hills Presbyterian Church, 75, 93, 105

"When Summer Dies" (McGlohon), 82

"When the Moon Comes Over the Mountain," 166

"When the Saints Go Marching In," 92

"When the World Was Young," 182

"Where's the Child I Used to Hold?" (Wilder & McGlohon), 129

"While We're Young" (Wilder), 51, 123, 153, 242

Whisnant, Charleen, 146–47, 226–28

Whisnant, Murray, xvii, 146–47

Whitfield, Weslia, 151

Whiting, Margaret, 5–6, 175–78, *176*

    American Popular Song project, 137

    appearances in Charlotte, 204, 249

    Loonis McGlohon Theater dedication, 249

    recordings with LM, 212

Whitman, Lisa, *249*

Wicker, Tom, 210

Wiest, Gil, 140

Wilder, Alec, ix, xii, xvi, 123–53, *124*

    Algonquin Hotel, 123, 149–51

    American Popular Song project, 135–41, *136*, 147–48, 155–56, 169–70

    Carnegie Hall tribute, 156–57

    collaborations with LM, xviii, 125–35, 141–42, 144, 147–48, 197–98

    concert pieces, 143–44

    daughter, 153

    death, 142, 152

    education, 39, 242

    fame and influence, 38–41, 162, 179, 180

    Friends of Alec Wilder Concert, 241

    influence on LM, 38–41

    Land of Oz, 131–35, 144

    letters, 146–47, 228

    LM's recollections of, 143–53

    medical care, 152–53

    Mountain Boy, 141–42

    Newcomers program at WBTV, 123–25

    octets, 143

    personal traits, 125, 128–29, 144–47, 149–51

    Project 60 radio program, 93

    songs, 40, 51, 143–44

Wilder, George, 149

Wilder, Joe, ix, 130, 248

    Carnegie Hall tribute to Alec Wilder, 157

    Loonis McGlohon Day in NYC, 250

    Loonis McGlohon Trio, 157

    WTVI tribute to LM, 259

Wilder, Margot, 153

Williams, Cootie, 39

Williams, Joe, 5, 156, 178–79, 253, 259

Williams, Mary Lou, 38

Williamson, Pat, 263

Williamson, William H., III, 204

"Willow Creek" (McPartland), 235

Windom, William, 204

"The Wine of May" (McGlohon), 66, 82, 91

Winer, Maddy, 172–73, 205, 249, 250, 261

Wingard, Matt, 80

Winterhalter, Hugo, 184

Wireman, Billy, 254–55

Wisehart, Bob, 93, 198

The Wiz (musical), 185

Wolfe, Thomas, 210

Wolverines band, 16

"Woman of the Ghetto," 188–89

women jazz pianists, 233

Woodard, Jimmy, 25

Woods, Carol, 205

World Citizen Award, 254

World War II, 48–49
bebop, 63
military service of LM, 49, 55–63, 69
radio, 83–84

WTVI tribute to LM, 257–59, 264

WWJ radio, 15

"You Must Believe in Spring" (Legrand), 230

"You Stayed Away Too Long" (McGlohon), 82

Zadora, Pia, 232

Zawinal, Joe, 96